Security
Fundamentals

Security
Fundamentals

Crystal Panek

SYBEX®
A Wiley Brand

This book is dedicated to my loving husband, William Panek, and to my two wonderful daughters, Alexandria and Paige. Thank you all for your love and support. I love you all more than anything!

Acknowledgments

I would like to thank my husband and best friend, Will, because without him I would not be where I am today—thank you! I would also like to express my love to my two daughters, Alexandria and Paige, who have always shown nothing but love and support. Thank you all!

I would like to thank everyone on the Sybex team, especially my associate acquisitions editor, Devon Lewis, who helped make this the best book possible. It's imperative to have the very best technical expert supporting you. I would like to thank Christine O'Connor, who was the production editor, and Kim Wimpsett for being the proofreader.

Finally, I also want to thank everyone behind the scenes who helped make this book possible. Thank you all for your hard work and dedication.

About the Author

 **Crystal Panek** holds the following certifications: MCP, MCP+I, MCSA, MCSA+ Security and Messaging, MCSE-NT (3.51 & 4.0), MCSE 2000, 2003, 2012/2012 R2, 2016, MCSE+Security and Messaging, MCDBA, MCTS, MCITP.

For many years she trained as a contract instructor teaching at such places as MicroC, Stellacon Corporation, and the University of New Hampshire. She then became the vice president for a large IT training company and for 15 years she developed training materials and courseware to help thousands of students get through their certification exams. She currently works on a contract basis creating courseware for several large IT training facilities.

She currently resides in New Hampshire with her husband and two daughters. In her spare time, she likes to camp, hike, shoot trap and skeet, golf, bowl, and snowmobile.

Contents at a Glance

Contents

Introduction

This book covers the following:

Chapter 1: Understanding Security Layers This chapter covers understanding the core security principles of confidentiality, integrity, and availability. It discusses the principles of threat and risk impact and the principle of least privilege and social engineering, attack surface analysis, and threat modeling. This chapter also discusses understanding physical security such as site security, computer security, removable devices and drives, access control, mobile device security, and keyloggers.

Chapter 2: Understanding Authentication, Authorization, and Accounting This chapter covers understanding user authentication, including multifactor authentication, physical and virtual smart cards, Remote Authentication Dial-In User Service (RADIUS), biometrics and using Run As to perform administrative tasks. This chapter also covers understanding permissions such as file system permissions and share permissions. It covers the Registry, using Active Directory, and enabling and disabling inheritance. It also discusses behavior when moving or copying files within the same disk or on another disk. It covers using multiple groups with different permissions, basic permissions and advanced permissions, as well as taking ownership, delegation, and inheritance. This chapter also discusses audit policies and using encryptions such as the Encrypting File System (EFS) and BitLocker (To Go) and discusses encryption algorithms and certificates, as well as using IPsec.

Chapter 3: Understanding Security Policies This chapter covers understanding password policies, such as password complexity, account lockout, password length, password history, time between password changes, and enforcing password policies by using Group Policies. This chapter also covers common attack methods, password reset procedures, and how to protect domain user account passwords.

Chapter 4: Understanding Network Security This chapter covers understanding dedicated firewalls, including the types of hardware firewalls and their characteristics, when to use a hardware firewall instead of a software firewall, using stateful versus stateless firewall inspection. This chapter also discusses using network isolation, including routing, using honeypots, perimeter networks, network address translation (NAT), Virtual Private Network (VPN) IPsec, and server/domain isolation. This chapter discusses understanding protocol security to include protocol spoofing, tunneling, DNSSEC, network sniffing, denial-of-service (DoS) attacks, and other common attack methods. We also discuss understanding wireless security. Finally, we discuss the advantages and disadvantages of specific security types, keys, service set identifiers (SSIDs), and using MAC filters.

Chapter 5: Protecting the Server and Client This chapter covers understanding Internet security, including browser security settings, and securing websites. We discuss encryption including MAIL encryption, signing, and other uses. This chapter discusses understanding malware, covering buffer overflow, viruses, polymorphic viruses, worms, Trojan horses, spyware, ransomware, adware, rootkits, backdoors, and zero-day attacks. This chapter discusses Security Compliance Manager and security baselines as well as understanding client protection including using antivirus, how to protect against unwanted software installations, User Account Control (UAC), how to keep client operating system and software updated, encrypting offline folders, and software restriction policies. This chapter also covers understanding email protection by using antispam, antivirus, spoofing, phishing, and pharming. It discusses client versus server protection, Sender Policy Framework (SPF) records, and PTR records. Finally, this chapter discusses understanding server protection to include the separation of services, hardening, ways to keep the server updated, using secure dynamic Domain Name System (DNS) updates, disabling unsecure authentication protocols, and Read-Only Domain Controllers (RODC).

Interactive Online Learning Tools

Studying the material in *Security Fundamentals* is an important part of self-learning, but we provide additional tools to help you prepare.

To start using these tools to jump-start your self-study, go to www.wiley.com/go/sybextestprep.

Lesson
1

Understanding Security Layers

Lesson Skill Matrix

Technology Skill	Objective Domain Description	Objective Domain Number
Introducing Core Security Principles	Understand core security principles	1.1
Understanding Physical Security as the First Line of Defense	Understand physical security	1.2
Performing Threat Modeling	Understand core security principles	1.1

Key Terms

access control

attack surface

attack surface analysis

availability

confidentiality

defense in depth

DREAD

egress traffic

flash drive

ingress traffic

integrity

keylogger

mobile devices

Principle of Least Privilege

removable device

residual risk

risk

risk acceptance

risk assessment

risk avoidance

risk mitigation

risk register

risk transfer

separation of duties

social engineering

STRIDE

threat

threat and risk management

threat modeling

 Real World Scenario

Lesson 1 Case

When thinking about security, most people start by thinking about their stuff. We all have stuff. We have stuff that we really care about, we have stuff that would be really difficult to replace, and we have stuff that has great sentimental value. We have stuff we really don't want other people to find out about. We even have stuff that we could probably live without. Now think about where you keep your stuff. It could be in your house, your car, your school, your office, in a locker, in a backpack or a suitcase, or a number of other places. Lastly, think about all of the dangers that could happen to your stuff. People could be robbed or experience a disaster such as a fire, earthquake, or flood. In any case, we all want to protect our possessions no matter where the threat comes from.

At a high level, security is about protecting stuff. In the case of personal stuff, it's about making sure to lock the door when leaving the house, or remembering to take your purse when leaving a restaurant, or even making sure to cover all the presents purchased for Christmas and putting them in the back of the car before heading back into the mall.

Many of the security topics we will discuss in this lesson boil down to the same common sense used every day to protect stuff. In the business environment, the stuff we protect is assets, information, systems, and networks, and we can protect these valuable assets with a variety of tools and techniques that we will discuss at length in this book.

In this lesson, we will start with the basics. We'll look at some of the underlying principles of a security program to set the foundation for understanding the more advanced topics covered later in the book. We'll also discuss the concepts of physical security, which is critical not only for securing physical assets but information assets as well. By the time we're done, you'll have a good idea how to protect stuff for a living.

Introducing Core Security Principles

A fundamental understanding of the standard concepts of security is essential before people can start securing their environment. It's easy to start buying firewalls, but until you understand what needs to be protected, why it needs to be protected, and what it's being protected from, you're just throwing money away.

Certification Ready

List and describe what CIA stands for as it relates to security. Objective 1.1

When working in the security field, one of the first acronyms to be encountered in the information security field is CIA. Not to be confused with the government agency with the same acronym, in information security, this acronym represents the core goals of an information security program. These goals are:

- Confidentiality
- Integrity
- Availability

Understanding Confidentiality

Confidentiality is a concept we deal with frequently in real life. We expect our doctor to keep our medical records confidential. We trust our friends to keep our secrets confidential. In the business world, we define confidentiality as the characteristic of a resource—ensuring access is restricted to only permitted users, applications, or computer systems. What does this mean in reality? Confidentiality deals with keeping information, networks, and systems secure from unauthorized access.

An area where this issue is particularly critical in today's environment is with the high-profile leaking of people's personal information by several large companies. These breaches in confidentiality made the news largely because the information could be used to perpetrate identity theft against the people whose information was breached.

There are several technologies that support confidentiality in an enterprise security implementation. These include the following:

- Strong encryption
- Strong authentication
- Stringent access controls

More Info

Lesson 2 contains more details on these security technologies.

Another key component to consider when discussing confidentiality is how to determine what information is considered confidential. Some common classifications of data are Public, Internal Use Only, Confidential, and Strictly Confidential. The Privileged classification is also used frequently in the legal profession. The military often uses Unclassified, Restricted, Confidential, Secret, and Top Secret. These classifications are then used to determine the appropriate measures needed to protect the information. If information is not classified, there are two options available—protecting all information as if it were confidential (an expensive and daunting task) or treating all information as if it were Public or Internal Use Only and not taking stringent protection measures.

 Classify all data and assets—it's the only way to effectively protect them.

Understanding Integrity

We define *integrity* in the information security context as the consistency, accuracy, and validity of data or information. One of the goals of a successful information security program is to ensure that the information is protected against any unauthorized or accidental changes. The program should include processes and procedures to manage intentional changes, as well as the ability to detect changes.

Some of the processes that can be used to effectively ensure the integrity of information include authentication, authorization, and accounting. For example, rights and permissions could be used to control who can access the information or resource. Also, a hashing function (a mathematical function) can be calculated before and after to show if information has been modified. In addition, an auditing or accounting system can be used that records when changes have been made.

Understanding Availability

Availability is the third core security principle, and it is defined as a characteristic of a resource being accessible to a user, application, or computer system when required. In other words, when a user needs to get to information, it's available to them. Typically, threats to availability come in two types—accidental and deliberate. Accidental threats would include natural disasters like storms, floods, fire, power outages, earthquakes, and so on. This category would also include outages due to equipment failure, software issues, and other unplanned system, network, or user issues. The second category is related to outages that result from the exploitation of a system vulnerability. Some examples of this type of threat would include a denial-of-service attack or a network worm that impacts vulnerable systems and their availability. In some cases, one of the first actions a user needs to take following an outage is to determine into which category an outage fits. Companies handle accidental outages very differently than deliberate ones.

Defining Threat and Risk Management

Threat and risk management is the process of identifying, assessing, and prioritizing threats and risks. A *risk* is generally defined as the probability that an event will occur. In reality, businesses are only concerned about risks that would negatively impact a computing environment. There is a risk that you'll win the lottery on Friday—that's not a risk to actively address, because it would be a positive. A *threat* is a very specific type of risk, and it is defined as an action or occurrence that could result in a breach in the security, outage, or corruption of a system by exploiting known or unknown vulnerabilities. The goal of any risk management plan is to remove risks when possible and to minimize the consequences of risks that cannot be eliminated.

The first step in creating a risk management plan is to conduct a *risk assessment*. Risk assessments are used to identify the risks that might impact an environment.

 In a mature risk assessment environment, it is common to record risks in a *risk register*, which provides a formal mechanism for documenting the risks, impacts, controls, and other information required by the risk management program.

After completing an assessment and identifying risks, the next step is to evaluate each risk for two factors. First, determine the likelihood that a risk will occur in the environment. For example, a tornado is much more likely in Oklahoma than in Vermont. A meteor strike is probably not very likely anywhere, although it's the example commonly used to represent the complete loss of a facility when discussing risk. After determining the likelihood of a risk, a user needs to determine the impact of that risk on their environment. A virus on a user's workstation generally has a relatively low impact on the company, although it can have a high impact on the user. A virus on a user's financial system has a much higher impact, although hopefully a lower likelihood.

After evaluating risks, it's time to prioritize them. One of the best mechanisms to assist with the prioritization is to create a risk matrix, which can be used to determine an overall risk ranking. A risk matrix should include the following:

- The risk

- The likelihood that the risk will actually occur

- The impact of the risk

- A total risk score

- The relevant business owner for the risk

- The core security principles that the risk impacts (confidentiality, integrity, and/or availability)

- The appropriate strategy or strategies to deal with the risk

Some additional fields that may prove useful in a risk register include:

- A deliverable date for the risk to be addressed.

- Documentation about the residual risk, which is the risk of an event that remains after measures have been taken to reduce the likelihood or minimize the effect of the event.

- A status on the strategy or strategies to address the risk. These can include status indicators like Planning, Awaiting Approval, Implementation, and Complete.

One easy way to calculate a total risk score is to assign numeric values to the likelihood and impact. For example, rank likelihood and impact on a scale from 1 to 5, where 1 equals low likelihood or low probability, and 5 equals high likelihood or high impact. Then, multiply the likelihood and impact together to generate a total risk score. Sorting from high to low provides an easy method to initially prioritize the risks. Next, review the specific risks to determine the final order in which to address them. At this point, external factors, such as cost or available resources, might affect the priorities.

After prioritizing all risks, there are four generally accepted responses to these risks. These responses include the following:

- Avoid

- Accept

- Mitigate

- Transfer

Risk avoidance is the process of eliminating a risk by choosing to not engage in an action or activity. An example of risk avoidance would be a person who identifies that there is a risk that the value of a stock might drop, so they avoid this risk by not purchasing the stock. A problem with risk avoidance is that there is frequently a reward associated with a risk—avoid the risk and you avoid the reward. If the stock in the example were to triple in price, the risk averse investor would lose out on the reward because he or she wanted to avoid the risk.

Risk acceptance is the act of identifying and then making an informed decision to accept the likelihood and impact of a specific risk. In the stock example, risk acceptance would be the process where a buyer would thoroughly research a company whose stock they are interested in, and after ensuring they are informed, make the decision to accept the risk that the price might drop.

Risk mitigation consists of taking steps to reduce the likelihood or impact of a risk. A common example of risk mitigation is the use of redundant hard drives in a server. There is a risk of hard drive failure in any system. By using redundant drive architecture, users can mitigate the risk of a drive failure by having the redundant drive. The risk still exists, but it has been reduced by a user's actions.

Risk transfer is the act of taking steps to move responsibility for a risk to a third party through insurance or outsourcing. For example, there is a risk that a person may have an accident while driving a car. Purchasing insurance transfers this risk, so that in the event of an accident, the insurance company is responsible to pay the majority of the associated costs.

One other concept in risk management that needs to be covered is *residual risk*. Residual risk is the risk of an event that remains after measures have been taken to reduce the likelihood or minimize the effect of the event. To continue with the car insurance example, the residual risk in the event of an accident would be the deductible a driver has to pay in the event of an accident.

 There are many different ways to identify, assess, and prioritize risks. There is no one right way. Use the techniques that best fit the environment and requirements.

While we are discussing risks, we need to look at two final concepts that will help you understand the foundations of security principles and risk management.

Understanding the Principle of Least Privilege

The *Principle of Least Privilege* is a security discipline that requires that a user, system, or application be given no more privilege than necessary to perform its function or job. On its face, this sounds like a very commonsense approach to assigning permissions, and when seen on paper, it is. However, when attempting to try to apply this principle in a complex production environment, it becomes significantly more challenging.

The Principle of Least Privilege has been a staple in the security arena for a number of years, but many organizations struggle to implement it successfully. However, with an increased focus on security from both a business as well as a regulatory perspective, organizations are working harder to build their models around this principle. The regulatory requirements of Sarbanes-Oxley, HIPAA, HITECH, and the large number of state data/ privacy breach regulations, coupled with an increased focus by businesses into the security practices of the business partners, vendors, and consultants, are driving organizations to invest in tools, processes, and other resources in order to ensure this principle is followed.

But why is a principle that sounds so simple on paper so difficult to implement in reality? The challenge is largely related to the complexity of a typical environment. It is very easy to visualize how to handle this for a single employee. On a physical basis, they would need access to the building they work in, common areas, and their office.

Logically, the employee needs to be able to log on to their computer, have user access to some centralized applications, access to a file server, a printer, and an internal website. Now, imagine that user multiplied by a thousand. The thousand employees work in six different office locations. Some employees need access to all the locations, while others only need access to their own location. Still others need access to subsets of the six locations; they might need access to the two offices in their region, for example. Some will need access to the data center so they can provide IT support.

Logically, instead of a single set of access requirements, there are multiple departments with varying application requirements. The different user types vary from a user to a power user to an administrator, and you need to determine not only which employee is which type of user, but also manage their access across all the internal applications. Add to this mix new hires, employees being transferred or promoted, and employees who leave the company, and you can start to see how making sure that each employee has the minimum amount of access required to do their job can be a time-intensive activity.

But wait, we're not done. In addition to the physical and user permissions, in many IT environments, applications also have a need to access data and other applications. In order to follow the Principle of Least Privilege, it is important to ensure the applications have the minimum access in order to function properly. This can be extremely difficult when working in a Microsoft Active Directory environment, due to the extremely detailed permissions included in Active Directory. Determining which permissions an application requires to function properly with Active Directory can be challenging in the extreme.

To further complicate matters, in industries where there is heavy regulation, like Finance or Medical, or when regulations like Sarbanes-Oxley are in effect, there are additional requirements that are audited regularly to ensure the successful implementation and validation of privileges across the enterprise.

Getting into a detailed discussion of how to implement and maintain the Principle of Least Privilege is beyond the scope of this book, but there are some high level tools and strategies to be aware of:

Groups   Groups can be used to logically group users and applications so that permissions are not applied on a user-by-user basis or application-by-application basis.

Multiple User Accounts for Administrators   One of the largest challenges when implementing the Principle of Least Privilege relates to administrators. Administrators are typically also users, and it is seldom a good idea for administrators to perform their daily user tasks as an administrator. To address this issue, many companies will issue their administrators two accounts—one for their role as a user of the company's applications and systems, and the other for their role as an administrator.

Account Standardization   The best way to simplify a complex environment is to standardize on a limited number of account types. Each different account type permitted in an environment adds an order of magnitude to the permissions management strategy. Standardizing on a limited set of account types makes managing the environment much easier.

Third-Party Applications   There are a variety of third-party tools designed to make managing permissions easier. These can range from account lifecycle management applications to auditing applications and application firewalls.

Processes and Procedures   One of the easiest ways to manage permissions in an environment is to have a solid framework of processes and procedures for managing accounts. With this framework to rely on, the support organization doesn't have to address each account as a unique circumstance. They can rely on the defined process to determine how an account is created, classified, permissioned, and maintained.

 A perfect implementation of the Principle of Least Privilege is very rare. A best effort is typically what is expected and is achievable.

Understanding Separation of Duties

Separation of duties is a principle that prevents any single person or entity from being able to have full access or complete all the functions of a critical or sensitive process. It is designed to prevent fraud, theft, and errors.

When dealing with orders and payments, it is common to divide those processes into two or more sub-processes. For example, in accounting, the Accounts Receivable employees review and validate bills, and the Accounts Payable employees pay the bills. In any case, those users involved with the critical processes do not have access to the logs. A third set of employees would review and validate what has been occurring and validate that there are no suspicious activities.

When working with IT, while there may be administrators with full access to an application or service, such as a database, the administrators should not be given access to the security logs. Instead, the security administrators regularly review the logs, but these security administrators will not have access to data within the databases. To maintain separation of duties, perform user rights and permissions on a regular basis to ensure that separation of duties is maintained.

Understanding an Attack Surface

One final concept to tackle when discussing core security principles is the idea of an attack surface when evaluating an environment. The concept of an *attack surface* with respect to systems, networks, or applications is another idea that has been around for some time. An attack surface consists of the set of methods and avenues an attacker can use to enter a system and potentially cause damage. The larger the attack surface of an environment, the greater the risk of a successful attack.

In order to determine the attack surface of an environment, it's frequently easiest to divide the evaluation into three components:

- Application
- Network
- Employee

When evaluating the application attack surface, look at things like the following:

- Amount of code in an application
- Number of data inputs to an application
- Number of running services
- Ports on which the application is listening

When evaluating the network attack surface, consider the following:

- Overall network design
- Placement of critical systems
- Placement and rule sets on firewalls
- Other security-related network devices like IDS, VPN, and so on

When evaluating the employee attack surface, consider the following:

- Risk of social engineering
- Potential for human errors
- Risk of malicious behavior

After evaluating these three types of attack surface, you will have a solid understanding of the total attack surface presented by the environment and a good idea of how an attacker might try to compromise the environment.

Performing an Attack Surface Analysis

An attack surface analysis helps to identify the attack surface that an organization may be susceptible to. Because the network infrastructure and necessary services and applications are usually complicated, particularly for medium and large organizations, performing an *attack surface analysis* can also be just as complicated. When completed, the attack surface analysis can be used to determine how to reduce the attack surface.

Certification Ready

What is an attack surface analysis? Objective 1.1

When analyzing a network, the first priority is to determine the security boundaries within an organization. As a minimum, an organization should have an internal network, a DMZ, and the Internet. However, when an organization has multiple sites, or multiple data centers, the organization will also have individual sites, multiple DMZs, and multiple Internet connections. A good place to determine security boundaries is to look at the organization's network documents. Ensure that the organization has proper documentation, which includes network diagrams.

After determining the security boundaries, the next step is to determine everything that connects at those security boundaries. Typically, this includes routers and firewalls, but it might also include some level-3 switches. Next, look at the security mechanisms used for the routers, firewalls, and switches and any security rules associated with those security mechanisms.

With an understanding of the network infrastructure, the next step is to analyze the logs to see which traffic is allowed and which traffic is blocked. *Ingress traffic* is traffic that originates from outside the network's routers and proceeds toward a destination inside the network. *Egress traffic* is network traffic that begins inside a network and proceeds through its routers to its destination somewhere outside of the network.

While network ingress filtering makes Internet traffic traceable to its source, egress filtering helps ensure that unauthorized or malicious traffic never leaves the internal network. Egress traffic might reveal incidents in which an attacker has already gained access to the internal network, or perhaps has gained access to internal users who might be releasing confidential information to the attacker with or without their knowledge. Inter-workload communications should remain internal; they should not transverse the perimeter.

It is important to review egress and ingress traffic on a regular basis. When examining egress and ingress traffic, look at the source and target addresses as well as the ports used. The ports help identify the applications and services to which the traffic packets are related. When creating rules that allow traffic in and out, use descriptive names and consider using templates that can help standardize the setup of multiple firewalls and routers.

In addition to examining egress and ingress traffic, analyze traffic to and from critical systems or systems that contain confidential information. This might help identify problems internally and externally. There might be things that aren't noticed when analyzing egress and ingress traffic.

Testing can also be performed to identify open ports, services, and/or applications that are running on a system and what can be accessed from the outside. There are applications that can test all ports and test for known vulnerabilities. It is also important to configure intrusion detection/prevention systems, including setting alerts that indicate potential threats as they happen.

While analyzing traffic patterns, look at which traffic is encrypted and which traffic is not encrypted. This can help determine which traffic is essential and which traffic could be easily captured. In addition, this helps determine whether encryption should be established for unencrypted data and whether encryption policies need to be established.

To identify application attack services, assess all running network services and applications that communicate with other computers. Then, access best practice guides or hardening guides to learn how to disable any unnecessary program and service so that they cannot be used against you.

When a decision has been made to deploy or adopt a software solution or to build a software solution, it is important to build security into the solution from the beginning. If the organization developed the software solution, make sure the developers and designers are following best practices; their work should be audited from time to time to minimize the risk posed by security vulnerabilities. For third-party applications, choose companies that follow best practices. Ensure they have an update mechanism and process in place for security updates.

Because users often provide the biggest attack surface, remember to review current security policies to make sure that they are being followed. Also, determine whether any policies need to be created or modified. Ensure that all administrators and users are aware of the appropriate policies; if they aren't, ensure that they receive any necessary training.

When evaluating servers, review administrative accounts from time to time to ensure that proper access is provided to the right people. Also, review open sessions. Create and deploy a password policy to make sure that passwords are being changed periodically and that those passwords are strong enough.

Reviewing and reducing attack surfaces should be done periodically to ensure systems are as secure as possible. Also, update the list of attack surfaces as new vulnerabilities are discovered, as new systems are added, and as systems change.

Understanding Social Engineering

One of the key factors to consider when evaluating the employee attack surface is the risk of a social engineering attack. *Social engineering* is a method used to gain access to data, systems, or networks, primarily through misrepresentation. This technique typically relies on the trusting nature of the person being attacked.

In a typical social engineering attack, the attacker will typically try to appear as harmless or respectful as possible. These attacks can be perpetrated in person, through email, or via phone. Attackers will try techniques including pretending to be from a Help Desk or Support Department, claiming to be a new employee, or in some cases even offering credentials that identify them as an employee of the company.

Generally, this attacker will ask a number of questions in an attempt to identify possible avenues to exploit during an attack. If they do not receive sufficient information from one employee, they may reach out to several others until they have sufficient information for the next phase of an attack.

Some techniques for avoiding social engineering attacks include the following:

Be Suspicious   Phone calls, emails, or visitors who ask questions about the company, its employees, or other internal information, should be treated with extreme suspicion, and if appropriate, reported to the security organization.

Verify Identity   When receiving inquiries that you are unsure of, verify the identity of the requestor. If a caller is asking questions that seem odd, try to get their number so you can call them back. Then, check to ensure that the number is from a legitimate source. If someone approaches with a business card as identification, ask to see a picture ID. Business cards are easy to print, and even easier to take from the "Win a Free Lunch" bowl at a local restaurant.

Be Cautious   Do not provide sensitive information unless certain not only of the person's identity but also of the person's right to have the information.

Don't Use Email   Email is inherently insecure and prone to a variety of address spoofing techniques. Don't reveal personal or financial information in email. Never respond to email requests for sensitive information and be especially cautious of providing this information after following web links embedded in an email. A common trick is to embed a survey link in an email, possibly offering a prize, or prize drawing, and then asking questions about the computing environment like "How many firewalls do you have deployed?" or "What firewall vendor do you use?" Employees are so accustomed to seeing these types of survey requests in their inbox that they seldom think twice about responding to them.

 The key to thwarting a social engineering attack is through employee awareness—if employees know what to look out for, an attacker will find little success.

Linking Cost with Security

When dealing with security, there are some points to keep in mind when developing a security plan. First, security costs money. Typically, the more money is spent, the more secure the information or resources will be (up to a point). So, when examining risk and threats, look at how much the confidential data or resource is worth to the organization if it is compromised or lost and how much money the organization is willing to spend to protect the confidential data or resource.

In addition to cost, strive to make the security seamless to the users who are using or accessing the confidential information or resource. If the security becomes a heavy burden, users will often look for methods to circumvent the security that has been established. Of course, training goes a long way in protecting confidential information and resources, because it will show users what to look for regarding security issues.

Understanding Physical Security as the First Line of Defense

There are a number of factors that need to be considered when designing, implementing, or reviewing physical security measures taken to protect assets, systems, networks, and information. They include understanding site security and computer security, securing removable devices and drives, access control, mobile device security, and identifying and removing keyloggers.

Certification Ready

Why is physical security so important to a server when access to usernames and passwords is needed? Objective 1.2

Most businesses keep some level of control over who accesses their physical environment. There is a tendency when securing computer-related asset and data to only look at the virtual world. Large companies in a location with a data center often use badge readers and/or keypads to provide access to the building and any secure areas. Guards and logbooks are also used to control and track who is in the building. Final layers of security include keys for offices and desk drawers. Similar measures are taken in smaller offices, albeit usually on a smaller scale.

Remember that if someone can get physical access to a server where confidential data is stored, they can, with the right tools and enough time, bypass any security that the server may use to protect the data.

This multi-layered approach to physical security is known as defense-in-depth or a layered security approach. Securing a physical site is more than just putting a lock on the front door and making sure the door is locked. Physical security is a complex challenge for any security professional.

Security does not end with physical security. It is also important to look at protecting confidential information with technology based on authentication, authorization, and accounting including using rights, permissions, and encryption.

Understanding Site Security

Site security is a specialized area of the security discipline. This section introduces some of the more common concepts and technologies that are typically encountered when working in the security field.

Understanding Access Control

Before we jump into site security details, it's important to understand what is meant by access control. *Access control* is a key concept when thinking about physical security. It is also a little confusing, because the phrase is frequently used when discussing information security. In the context of physical security, access control can be defined as the process of restricting access to a resource to only permitted users, applications, or computer systems.

Certification Ready

How does access control relate to site security? Objective 1.1

There are many examples of access control that people encounter every day. These include closing and locking a door, installing a baby gate to keep a toddler from falling down a staircase, and putting a fence around a yard to keep a dog out of the neighbor's flowers.

The difference between the access control practiced in everyday life and the access control encountered in the business world is the nature of what is being protected, and the technologies available to secure them. We will cover these topics in more detail through the rest of this lesson.

FIGURE 1.1   Example of a layered site security model

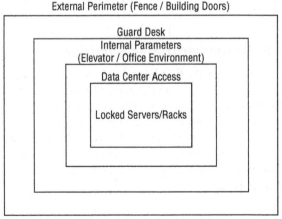

Site security deals with securing the physical premises. One of the fundamental concepts used when designing a security environment is the concept of defense in depth. *Defense in depth* is a concept in which multiple layers of security are used to defend assets. This ensures that if an attacker breaches one layer of defenses, there are additional layers of defense to keep them out of the critical areas of an environment.

A simple example of defense in depth in the "real world" is a hotel room with a locked suitcase. To get into a locked hotel room, a person needs to get the key lock to work. Once they are past the key, there is a deadbolt that must be bypassed. And once they are past the deadbolt, there is still the lock on the suitcase that must be breached.

There are several goals to keep in mind when designing a physical security plan.

Authentication   Site security addresses the need to identify and authenticate people permitted access to an area.

Access Control   Once a person's identity has been proven and they have been authenticated, site security determines what areas they can access.

Auditing   Site security also provides the ability to audit activities within the facility. This can be done through reviewing camera footage, badge reader logs, visitor registration logs, or other mechanisms.

For the purposes of this lesson, we will break the physical premises into three logical areas:

- The external perimeter, which makes up the outermost portion of the location. This typically includes the driveways, parking lots, and any green space the location may support. This does not include things like public roads.

- The internal perimeter, which consists of any buildings on the premises. If the location supports multiple tenants, the internal perimeter is restricted to only the buildings that an employee can occupy.

- Secure areas, which are locations within the building that have additional access restrictions and/or security measures in place. These can include data centers, network rooms, wiring closets, or departments like Research and Development or Human Resources.

Understanding External Perimeter Security

The external security perimeter is the first line of defense surrounding an office. However, security measures in this area probably vary the most of any that we will discuss. When trying to protect a Top Secret government installation, the external perimeter security will consist of multiple fences, roving guard patrols, land mines, and all sorts of other measures that aren't typically used in the corporate world. On the other hand, if an office is in a multi-tenant office park, the external perimeter security may consist of street lights. Most companies fall somewhere in between. Common security measures used for external perimeter security include the following:

- Security cameras
- Parking lot lights
- Perimeter fence
- Gate with guard
- Gate with access badge reader
- Guard patrols

One of the challenges associated with security cameras is that the security camera is only as good as the person monitoring it. Because monitoring cameras is a very expensive, resource-intensive undertaking, in most office environments there will not be anyone actively watching the cameras. Instead, cameras are used after the fact to determine what happened, or who was responsible.

 Test an organization's camera playback capabilities regularly. Because cameras are almost always used to review events after the fact, ensure that the system is successfully recording the data.

Understanding the Internal Perimeter

The internal security perimeter starts with the building walls and exterior doors and includes any internal security measures with the exception of any secure areas within the building. Security features that can be used to secure the internal perimeter include the following:

- Locks (exterior doors, internal doors, office doors, desks, filing cabinets, and so on)
- Keypads
- Security cameras
- Badge readers (on doors and elevators)
- Guard desk
- Guard patrols
- Smoke detectors
- Turnstiles
- Mantraps (devices that control access, such as double-doors)

The key security measures implemented in the internal perimeter are utilized to divide the internal space into discrete segments. This is a physical implementation of the Principle of Least Privilege. For example, if the office includes a Finance Department, Human Resources Department, and a Sales Department, it would not be unusual to restrict access to the Finance Department to only people who work in Finance. In general, Human Resources people don't need to be wandering around the Finance area. These segregations may be based on floors, areas, or even a series of offices, depending on the office layout.

Defining Secure Areas

Secure areas would include things like a data center, Research and Development Department, a lab, a telephone closet, a network room, or any other area that requires additional security controls not only from external attackers but also to restrict internal employee access. Secure area security technologies include the following:

- Badge readers
- Keypads

- Biometric technology (fingerprint scanner, retinal scanner, voice recognition, and so on)
- Security doors
- X-ray scanners
- Metal detectors
- Cameras
- Intrusion detection systems (light beam, infrared, microwave, and ultrasonic)

 Smaller offices that are not occupied at night may take advantage of remote monitoring, and intrusion detection systems in their internal perimeter. Larger locations typically have some activities going on during nights and weekends, which makes use of these technologies more of a challenge.

Understanding Site Security Processes

While technology forms a significant component when discussing physical security, the processes put in place to support the site security are just as critical. There should be processes at different levels of the site.

In the external perimeter, there might be processes to manage entry to the parking lot through a gate or a process for how often the guards will do a tour of the parking lots. Included in those processes should be how to document findings, how to track entry and exits, and how to respond to incidents. For example, the guard tour process should include instructions on how to handle an unlocked car or a suspicious person or, with the heightened awareness of possible terrorist attacks, how to handle an abandoned package.

In the internal perimeter, processes might include guest sign-in procedures, equipment removal procedures, guard rotation procedures, or details on when the front door is to be left unlocked. In addition, there should probably be processes to handle deliveries, how/when to escort visitors in the facility, and even what types of equipment may be brought into the building. For example, many companies prohibit bringing personal equipment into the office due to the risk that the employee could use their personal laptop to steal valuable company information.

In the secure area layer, there will generally be procedures for controlling who is permitted to enter the data center and how they will access the data center. In addition, you will have multiple mechanisms to ensure that only authorized people are granted access, including locked doors, biometric devices, cameras, and security guards.

 Cameras are available on virtually every cell phone on the market today. To ensure that cameras are not used in a facility, plan on taking phones at the door or disabling the camera function.

Understanding Computer Security

Computer security consists of the processes, procedures, policies, and technologies used to protect computer systems. For the purposes of this lesson, computer security will refer to physically securing computers. We will discuss other facets of computer security throughout the rest of the book.

In addition to all the measures we have discussed regarding physical security, there are some additional tools that can be used to secure the actual computers. Before we start discussing the tools, we need to differentiate between the three types of computers we will discuss:

Servers   These are computers used to run centralized applications and deliver the applications across a network. This can be an internal network for large businesses or across the Internet for public access. The computer hosting a favorite website is an example of a server. Servers are typically configured with redundant capabilities, ranging from redundant hard drives to fully clustered servers.

Desktop Computers   These computers are usually found in office environments, schools, and homes. These computers are meant to be used in a single location and run applications like word processing, spreadsheets, games, and other local applications. They can also be used to interact with centralized applications or browse websites.

Mobile Computers   This category includes laptop, notebook, tablet, netbook computers, and smartphones. These are used for the same types of functions as the desktop computer but are meant to be used in multiple locations (for example, home and office). Due to their size, mobile computers are considered to be less powerful than desktop computers, but with the advances in microprocessor technologies and storage technologies, this gap is rapidly narrowing.

When securing a server, the first thing to consider is where the server will be located. Servers are typically significantly more expensive than a desktop or mobile computer and are used to run critical applications, so the types of security typically used with servers are largely location-based. Servers should be secured in data centers or computer rooms, which typically have locked doors, cameras, and other security features we have discussed earlier in the lesson.

If a data center or computer room is not available, other options for securing server computers include the following technologies:

Computer Security Cable   A cable that is attached to the computer and to a piece of furniture or wall.

Computer Security Cabinet/Rack   A storage container that is secured with a locking door.

Desktop computers are typically secured by the same types of computer security cables that can be used with server computers. Desktop computers are frequently used in secure office environments, or in people's homes, and are not particularly expensive relative to other technologies. Most companies do not take extraordinary measures to protect desktop computers in their offices.

Mobile computers, due to their highly portable nature, have a number of technologies and best practices that can be leveraged to ensure they are not damaged or stolen.

Understanding Mobile Device Security

Mobile devices are one of the largest challenges facing many security professionals today. Mobile devices like laptops, PDAs (Personal Digital Assistants), and smartphones are used to process information, send and receive mail, store enormous amounts of data, surf the Internet, and interact remotely with internal networks and systems. When placing a 32 GB MicroSD memory card in a smartphone that a Senior Vice President can then use to store all the company's Research and Development information, the impact to the company when someone grabs his phone can be staggering. As a result, the security industry makes available a number of technologies for physically securing mobile devices, including the following:

Docking Station   Virtually all laptop docking stations are equipped with security features to secure a laptop. This can be with a key, a padlock, or both depending on the vendor and model.

NOTE   Docking station security only works when the docking station is enabled and secured to an immovable object. It's frequently just as easy to steal a laptop and docking station as it is to just take the laptop.

Laptop Security Cables   Used in conjunction with the USS (Universal Security Slot), these cables attach to the laptop and can be wrapped around a secure object like a piece of furniture.

Laptop Safe   A steel safe specifically designed to hold a laptop and be secured to a wall or piece of furniture.

Theft Recovery Software   An application run on the computer that enables the tracking of a stolen computer so it can be recovered.

Laptop Alarm   A motion-sensitive alarm that sounds in the event a laptop is moved. Some are also designed in conjunction with a security cable system so the alarm sounds when the cable is cut. PDAs and smartphones are typically more difficult to secure because they are a newer technology that has exploded in popularity. There are somewhat limited tools available for securing them. For now, configure a password to protect a PDA and phone, enable encryption, and remotely wipe a phone that is managed by an organization. Some of the devices include GPS components that allow users to track a phone or PDA.

Of course, there are some best practices (and, yes, these are based on common sense) that can be followed when securing laptops as well as PDAs or smartphones, including:

Keep your equipment with you.   Mobile devices should be kept with you whenever possible. This means keeping mobile devices on your person or in your hand luggage when traveling. Keep mobile devices in sight when going through airport checkpoints.

Use the trunk.   When traveling by car, lock the mobile device in the trunk after parking, if you are unable to take the mobile device with you. Do not leave a mobile device in view in an unattended vehicle, even for a short period of time, or left in a vehicle overnight.

Use the safe.   When staying in a hotel, lock the mobile device in a safe, if available.

Using Removable Devices and Drives

In addition to mobile devices, another technology that presents unique challenges to security professionals is removable devices and drives. See Figure 1.2 for some examples of common removable devices.

FIGURE 1.2   Some examples of common removable devices

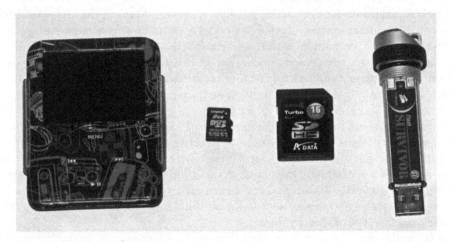

A *removable device* or drive is a storage device that is designed to be removed from the computer without turning the computer off. These devices range from the MicroSD memory card, which is the size of a fingernail and can store 32 GB (or more) of information, to an external hard drive, which can store up to 4 TB of data. CDs, DVDs, and USB drives are also considered removable drives, because they can be used to store critical data and are easily transportable.

These devices typically connect to a computer via a drive or by external communications ports like USB, Firewire, or, in the case of memory cards, through built-in or USB-based readers. These devices are used for a variety of purposes, including backing up critical data, providing supplemental storage, and transferring data between computers. In addition, applications can be run from USB drives. This storage is also used in music players like iPods and Zunes, as well as personal media players like the Archos and Creative's Zen devices.

There are three basic categories of security issues associated with removable storage:

- Loss
- Theft
- Espionage

The loss of the storage device is one of the most common issues people will encounter. USB drives are especially problematic in this regard. Typically the size of a pack of gum or smaller, these drives are often left in conference rooms, hotel rooms, or seat pockets on airplanes. The challenge is how to secure the gigabytes of data that is lost along with these drives. These devices can be protected with authentication and encryption. With Windows 7 and Windows Server 2008 R2, Microsoft released BitLocker To Go, which is used to protect data on mobile storage devices. Some companies may offer their own protection mechanism, such as IronKey. Of course, it is important to impress on users the value of these types of storage. Many users do not give a second thought to throwing a confidential presentation on a *flash drive* (a small drive based on flash memory) for a meeting. As part of the awareness efforts, educate users about the value of data and how easy it is to misplace these portable storage devices.

Theft is a problem with any portable piece of equipment. Many of the same measures discussed with respect to protecting mobile devices apply to these removable storage devices as well. For example, keep drives with you whenever possible. When this is not possible, secure drives in a hotel safe, locked desk drawer, or other secure location. Do not leave portable storage out where it can be easily removed from an accessible area. While the devices themselves are relatively inexpensive, the data on them can be irreplaceable or, worse, confidential.

The final area where these types of devices present a security issue is in conjunction with espionage. Many of these storage devices come in very small form factors, which make them particularly well suited to espionage. Flash drives can be disguised as pens, watches, or even as part of a pocketknife. Even more challenging, a music player or smartphone can include multiple gigabytes of storage. Even if external drives and music players are banned, removing employee's smartphones is virtually impossible. So how do you protect an environment from this type of security threat?

The key to this threat is not to try to defend the environment from the portable devices but instead to protect the data from any unauthorized access. This is where the Principle of Least Privilege is critical—ensure that employees can only access the data, systems, and networks they need to do their jobs so that keeping critical data off portable drives is much easier.

 Some environments address the issues associated with removable storage by using hardware or software configurations to prohibit their use. While this can be an effective strategy, it is also an expensive, resource-intensive activity. There are a limited number of businesses where this can be effectively implemented.

More Info

Encryption is frequently used to secure the data on removable drives. This will be discussed in detail in Lesson 2.

Understanding Keyloggers

A *keylogger* is a physical or logical device used to capture keystrokes. An attacker will either place a device between the keyboard and the computer or install a software program to record each keystroke taken and then use software to replay the data to capture critical information like user IDs and passwords, credit card numbers, Social Security numbers, or even confidential emails or other data. There are also wireless keyboard sniffers that can intercept the broadcast keystrokes sent between a wireless keyboard and the computer.

To protect against a physical keylogger, the best tool is visual inspection. Take a look at the connection between the keyboard and the computer. If there is an extra device in between, someone may be trying to capture keystrokes. This is especially important when working with shared or public computers, where attackers will utilize keyloggers to cast a wide net and grab whatever critical data someone might enter.

The best defense against a software keylogger is the use of up-to-date anti-malware software. Many software keyloggers are identified as malware by these applications. User Access Control and host-based firewalls can also be used to prevent a software keylogger from being installed.

To defend against a wireless keyboard sniffer, the best bet is to ensure that a wireless keyboard supports encrypted connections. Most of the current wireless keyboards will either operate in an encrypted mode by default, or at least permit users to configure encryption during installation.

More Info

Lesson 5 contains a more in-depth discussion of anti-malware and workstation firewall technologies.

Performing Threat Modeling

Threat modeling is a procedure for optimizing network security by identifying vulnerabilities, identifying their risks, and defining countermeasures to prevent or mitigate the effects of the threats to the system. It addresses the top threats that have the greatest potential impact to an organization.

Certification Ready

Explain the process of threat modeling. Objective 1.1

Threat modeling is an iterative process; it should be started when designing a system or solution and should be performed throughout the system or solution lifecycle. The reason for multiple passes is that it is impossible to identify all of the possible threats in a single pass. In addition, the infrastructure, system, or solution is always changing, and new threats are found.

The steps to perform threat modeling are:

Identify assets.   Identify the valuable assets that the systems must protect.

Create an architecture overview.   Gather simple diagrams and related information that show how the systems are connected, both physically and logically. Documentation should include a system, trust boundaries, and data flow.

Decompose the security components and applications.   Break down the architecture of the systems and application, including the underlying network and host infrastructure design, security profiles, implementation, as well as the deployment configuration of the systems and applications.

Identify the threats.   By examining the current architecture, system, applications, and potential vulnerabilities, identify the threats that could affect the systems and applications.

Document the threats.   Document each threat using a common threat template that shows the attributes of each threat.

Rate the threats.   Prioritize and address the most significant threats first. The rating process weighs the probability of the threat against the damage that could result should an attack occur. Certain threats might not warrant any action when comparing the risk posed by the threat with the resulting mitigation costs.

One easy way to calculate a total risk score is to assign numeric values to the likelihood and impact. For example, rank likelihood and impact on a scale from 1 to 5, where 1 equals low likelihood or low probability, and 5 equals high likelihood or high impact. Then, multiply the likelihood and impact together to generate a total risk score. Sorting from high to low provides an easy method to initially prioritize the risks. Next, review the specific risks to determine the final order in which to address them. At this point, external factors, such as cost or available resources, might affect the priorities.

STRIDE is an acronym for a threat modeling system that originated at Microsoft. STRIDE is also a mnemonic tool for security threats; it consists of six different categories, as shown in Table 1.1.

TABLE 1.1   STRIDE acronym

Element of STRIDE	Description	Security Properties That Can Reduce STRIDE Risk
Spoofing	Something or someone that pretends to be something that they are not. For example, an attacker could masquerade as a legitimate user or an email can be sent under another domain name or email address.	Authentication

Element of STRIDE	Description	Security Properties That Can Reduce STRIDE Risk
Tampering	Attackers modify or interfere with legitimate data.	Integrity
Repudiation	The user denies performing a certain action, which could be illegal and harmful.	Confirmation
Information Disclosure	A data breach and access to private information occurs, and too much information about a system and its data is accessed by unauthorized individuals.	Confidentiality
Denial-of-service	A service is brought down intentionally or unintentionally resulting in disruptions of applications or services.	Availability
Elevation of Privilege	A user gains privilege access greater than that for which he was approved, potentially accessing restricted data or performing restricted tasks.	Authorization

Use *DREAD* to measure and rank the threats risk level:

Damage Potential   How much damage can be inflicted on our system?

Reproducibility   Can the attack be reproduced easily?

Exploitability   How much effort and experience are necessary?

Affected users   If the attack occurs, how many users will be affected?

Discoverability   Can the threat be easily discovered?

Rank the threat level on a scale of 0 through 3 or 0 through 10, where the larger the number indicates the greater the threat.

Skill Summary

In this lesson, you learned:

- Before starting to secure an environment, a fundamental understanding of the standard concepts of security is needed.
- CIA (an acronym for Confidentiality, Integrity, and Availability) refers to the core goals of an information security program.
- Confidentiality deals with keeping information, networks, and systems secure from unauthorized access.
- One of the goals of a successful information security program is to ensure integrity or that the information is protected against any unauthorized or accidental changes.

- Availability is defined as a characteristic of a resource being accessible to a user, application, or computer system when required.
- Threat and risk management is the process of identifying, assessing, and prioritizing threats and risks.
- A risk is generally defined as the probability that an event will occur.
- After prioritizing risks, there are four generally accepted responses to these risks: Avoidance, Acceptance, Mitigation, and Transfer.
- The Principle of Least Privilege is a security discipline that requires that a user, system, or application be given no more privilege than necessary to perform its function or job.
- An attack surface consists of the set of methods and avenues an attacker can use to enter a system and potentially cause damage. The larger the attack surface of an environment, the greater the risk of a successful attack.
- The key to thwarting a social engineering attack is through employee awareness. If employees know what to look out for, an attacker will find little success.
- Physical security uses a defense-in-depth or a layered security approach that controls who can physically access resources of an organization.
- Physical premises can be divided into three logical areas: the external perimeter, the internal perimeter, and secure areas.
- Computer security consists of the processes, procedures, policies, and technologies used to protect computer systems.
- Mobile devices and mobile storage devices are one of the largest challenges facing many security professionals today, because of their size and portability.
- A keylogger is a physical or logical device used to capture keystrokes.
- Threat modeling is a procedure for optimizing network security by identifying vulnerabilities, identifying their risks, and defining countermeasures to prevent or mitigate the effects of the threats to the system.

Knowledge Assessment

You can find the answers in the Appendix.

Multiple Choice

1. Which of the following are valid risk responses? (Choose all that apply.)
    A. Mitigation
    B. Transfer
    C. Investment
    D. Avoidance

2. Which of the following are considered removable devices or drives? (Choose all that apply.)
    A. iPod
    B. Netbook
    C. USB flash drive
    D. Burnable DVD drive

3. Which of the following would be considered appropriate security measures for a building's external security perimeter? (Choose all that apply.)
    A. Motion detector
    B. Parking lot lights
    C. Turnstile
    D. Guard patrols

4. When traveling on business and headed out to dinner with a client, which of the following should be done to secure a laptop? (Choose the best answer.)
    A. Lock it in the car trunk.
    B. Store it out of sight in a dresser drawer.
    C. Secure it to a piece of furniture with a laptop security cable.
    D. Check it at the Front Desk.

5. Which of the following refers to the process of eliminating a risk by choosing to not engage in an action or activity?
    A. Mitigation
    B. Residual risk
    C. Avoidance
    D. Acceptance

6. Which of the following technologies could be used to help ensure the confidentiality of proprietary manufacturing techniques for an auto parts manufacturing business? (Choose all that apply.)

    A. Strong encryption

    B. Guard patrols

    C. A laptop safe

    D. Strong authentication

7. The information security acronym CIA stands for which of the following?

    A. Confidentiality, Identity, Access Control

    B. Confidentiality, Integrity, Access Control

    C. Confidentiality, Integrity, Availability

    D. Control, Identity, Access Control

8. Which of the following statements best describes the concept of core security principles?

    A. Core security principles refer to the internal security perimeter when setting up a layered physical security environment.

    B. Core security principles refer to the principles of confidentiality, availability, and integrity.

    C. Core security principles refer to leveraging security best practices.

    D. Core security principles refer to the four methods of addressing risk.

9. As the Chief Security Officer for a small medical records processing company, you have just finished setting up the physical security for your new office. You have made sure that the parking lot is illuminated, that you have guards at the door as well as doing periodic patrols, and you have badge readers throughout the building at key locations. You also have put biometric access technology on the data center door. And of course, you have cameras in the parking lot, building entrances, and the data center entrances.

    This type of implementation is known as: (Choose the best answer)

    A. Access Control

    B. Core Security Principles

    C. Security best practices

    D. Defense in depth

10. Which of the following refers to the process of disabling unneeded services and ports to make the system more secure?

    A. Reducing the attack surface area

    B. Mitigating a Trojan horse

    C. Security avoidance

    D. Defense in depth

11. Which type of network traffic originates from outside the network routers and proceeds toward a destination inside the network?

A. Ingress

B. Egress

C. Traverse

D. Encrypted

Fill in the Blank

1. _____ is characteristic of a business resource—ensuring access is restricted to only permitted users, applications, or computer systems.

2. If a user is deploying technologies to restrict access to a resource, they are practicing the _____ security principle.

3. Deploying multiple layers of security technology to defend assets is called _____.

4. An action or occurrence that could result in a breach in the security, outage, or corruption of a system by exploiting known or unknown vulnerabilities is a(n) _____.

5. A Risk Manager for a medium-sized pharmaceutical company who is asked to perform a formal risk analysis would most likely record the results of the risk assessment in a(n) risk _____.

6. _____ is a method used to gain access to data, systems, or networks, primarily through misrepresentation.

7. The consistency, accuracy, and validity of data or information is called _____.

8. A business traveler notices that there is an extra connector between the keyboard and the computer in a business center. She has most likely encountered a(n) _____.

9. _____ refers to the risk of an event that remains after measures have been taken to reduce the likelihood or minimize the effect of the event.

10. Implementing security measures must always be balanced with _____.

Matching and Identification

What is STRIDE short for?

S _____

T _____

R _____

I _____

D _____

E _____

Build List

Specify the correct order of steps necessary for performing threat modeling.

_____ Create an architecture overview.

_____ Identify assets.

_____ Rate the threats.

_____ Decompose the security components and applications.

_____ Identify the threats.

_____ Document the threats.

Business Case Scenarios

Scenario 1-1: Designing a Physical Security Solution

As the Security Manager for a medium-sized bank, you have been asked to design a security solution to keep a bank robber out of the bank after hours. The three areas of the bank that need to be secured are the parking lot, the building perimeter, and the vault. List what technologies should be used in each area of the bank.

Scenario 1-2: Securing a Mobile Device

An IT Manager for a Legal Services company with 5,000 employees is in the process of rolling out new mobile devices to the Sales Department. Which technologies and best practices should be used to keep these systems physically secure?

Scenario 1-3: Understanding Confidentiality, Integrity, and Availability

A server called Server1 is running Windows Server 2016. On Server1, a folder called Data is created and shared on the C drive. Within the Data folder, subfolders are created with each user's name within the organization. Each person's electronic paycheck is placed in each user's folder. Later, you find out that John was able to go in and change some of the electronic paycheck amounts, while also deleting some of the electronic paychecks. Explain which one (or more) of the CIA components was not followed.

Scenario 1-4: Managing Social Engineering

Your manager at the Contoso Corporation wants to put a training class together for end user security. He wants you to research the Internet for three cases or instances where someone used social engineering to break into a system and describe how they attempted to get access.

Real World Scenario

Workplace Ready: Understanding the Basics

Understanding security concepts is only the first step in learning about security. As a network administrator or security officer, you will be amazed how much going back to the basics will help you plan, implement, and update security procedures.

Lesson 2

Understanding Authentication, Authorization, and Accounting

Lesson Skill Matrix

Technology Skill	Objective Domain Description	Objective Domain Number
Starting Security with Authentication	Understand user authentication	2.1
Introducing Directory Services with Active Directory	Understand user authentication	2.1
Comparing Rights and Permissions	Understand permissions	2.2
Understanding NTFS	Understand permissions	2.2
Sharing Drives and Folders	Understand permissions	2.2
Introducing the Registry	Understand permissions	2.2
Using Encryption to Protect Data	Understand encryption	2.5
Understanding IPsec	Understand protocol security	3.3
Introducing Smart Cards	Understand user authentication	2.1
Configuring Biometrics, Windows Hello, and Microsoft Passport	Understand user authentication	2.1
Using Auditing to Complete the Security Picture	Understand audit policies	2.4

Key Terms

access control list (ACL)	hash function
accounting	inherited permission
Active Directory	IP Security (IPsec)
administrative share	Kerberos
asymmetric encryption	key
auditing	local user account
authentication	member server
authorization	Microsoft Passport
biometrics	multifactor authentication
BitLocker To Go	nonrepudiation
brute force attacks	NTFS
built-in groups	NTFS permissions
certificate chain	NTLM
certificate revocation list (CRL)	organizational units
computer accounts	owner
decryption	password
dictionary attack	permission
digital certificate	personal identification number (PIN)
digital signature	public key infrastructureregistry
domain controller	right
domain user	Secure Sockets Layer (SSL)
effective permissions	Security Account Manager (SAM)
encryption	security token
explicit permission	share permissions
group	shared folder

single sign-on (SSO)

smart card

symmetric encryption

Syslog

Trusted Platform Module (TPM) chip

user account

virtual private network (VPN)

virtual smart cards (VSCs)

Windows Biometric Framework (WBF)

Windows Hello

 Real World Scenario

Lesson 2 Case

The CIO for your company wants to discuss security. He asks what system is in place to ensure that users can access only what they need to access and nothing else. You respond by saying that the security model was built using the three A's—authentication, authorization, and accounting. He wants to know more about this model.

Starting Security with Authentication

In the realm of IT security, the AAA (Authentication, Authorization, and Accounting) acronym is a model for access control. *Authentication* is the process of identifying an individual, usually based on a user name and password. After a user is authenticated, the user can access network resources based on the user's authorization. *Authorization* is the process of giving individuals access to system objects based on their identity. *Accounting*, also known as *auditing*, is the process of keeping track of a user's activity while accessing the network resources, including the amount of time spent in the network, the services accessed while there, and the amount of data transferred during the session.

Nonrepudiation prevents one party from denying actions they carry out. If proper authentication, authorization, and accounting have been established, a person cannot deny their own actions.

Certification Ready

List the different methods used for authentication. Objective 2.1

Before any user can access a computer or a network resource, the user will most likely log on to prove their identity and to see if they have the required rights and permissions to access the network resources.

A logon is the process whereby a user is recognized by a computer system or network so that they can begin a session. A user can authenticate using one or more of the following methods:

- What a user knows, such as a password or personal identification number (PIN)
- What a user owns or possesses, such as a passport, smart card, or ID card
- Who a user is, based on biometric factors such as fingerprints, retinal scans, voice input, or other forms

When two or more authentication methods are used to authenticate someone, a *multifactor authentication* system is being implemented. A system that uses two authentication methods such as smart cards and a password can be referred to as a two-factor authentication.

Configuring Multifactor Authentication

To configure multifactor authentication, follow these steps:

1. In the AD FS Management Console, navigate to trust relationships and relying party trusts.
2. Select the relying party trust that represents your application (myapp), and then either by using the Actions pane or by right-clicking this relying party trust, select Edit Claim Rules.
3. In the Edit Claim Rules For myapp window, select the Issuance Authorization Rules tab and click Add Rule.
4. In the Add Issuance Authorization Claim Rule Wizard, on the Select Rule Template screen, select Permit Or Deny Users Based On An Incoming Claim Rule Template and click Next.
5. On the Configure Rule screen, complete all of the following tasks and click Finish.
   a. Enter a name for the claim rule, for example ClaimRule.
   b. Select Group SID As Incoming Claim Type.
   c. Click Browse, type in a name for the group, and resolve it for the Incoming Claim Value field.
   d. Select the Deny Access To Users With This Incoming Claim option.
   e. In the Edit Claim Rules For myapp window, make sure to delete the Permit Access To All Users rule that was created by default when you created this relying party trust.

Authentication Based on What a User Knows

The most common method of authentication with computers and networks is the password. A *password* is a secret series of characters that enables a user to access a file, computer, or program.

Using Passwords

Hackers will try to crack passwords by first trying obvious passwords, including the name of spouse or children, birthdays, keywords used by the user, hobbies of the user, and common passwords. Then hackers will try *brute force attacks*, which consist of trying as many combinations of characters as time and money permit. A subset of the brute force attack is the *dictionary attack*, in which all words in one or more dictionaries are tested. Lists of common passwords are also typically tested.

To make a password more secure, choose a password that nobody can guess. It should be lengthy and should be considered a strong or complex password. For more information about creating strong passwords, visit the following website:

```
https://blogs.microsoft.com/microsoftsecure/2014/08/25/create-stronger-
passwords-and-protect-them/
```

Because today's computers are much more powerful, some people recommend that passwords should be at least 14 characters in length. However, for some people, remembering long passwords is cumbersome, so they may start writing their passwords on a piece of paper near their desk. In these situations, you should start looking for other forms of authentication, such as a smart card or biometrics.

Remember to change passwords regularly, so that if a password is revealed to someone else, it will have been changed before they can attempt to use it. In addition, this shortens the time that someone has to guess a password, because they will need to try all over again.

Microsoft includes password policy settings within group policies to enforce a minimum number of characters, specify if the password is a complex password, suggest how often a user must change his password, state how often a user can reuse a password, and so on.

While passwords are the easiest method of authentication to implement and are the most popular authentication method, passwords have significant disadvantages because they can be stolen, spoofed, forgotten, and so on. A hacker may use social engineering where he calls the IT department for support and pretends to be someone else so that the IT department will reset the password for the hacker. Therefore, establish a secure process to reset passwords for users.

One method of establishing a self-service password service is where a user's identity is verified by asking questions and comparing the answers to previously stored responses, such as the person's birthday, name of their favorite movie, name of a pet, and so on. However, these can be relatively easily guessed by an attacker, discovered through low-effort research or social engineering.

When resetting passwords, there must be a method to identify the user asking for a password to be changed. Don't send the password through email, because if the password is compromised, the new password may be read, and if the user does not know the password, she would still not be able to retrieve it. Meeting with the person and asking for identification is a possible solution. Unfortunately, with large networks and networks that contain multiple sites, this may not be plausible. Another solution would be to call back and leave the password on a person's voice mail so that a user will need to provide a PIN to access, or the password could be sent to a user's manager or administrative assistant. In either case, the user should reset the password immediately after they log on.

Using a Personal Identification Number (PIN)

A *personal identification number (PIN)* is a secret numeric password shared between a user and a system that can be used to authenticate the user to the system. Because it only consists of digits and is relatively short (usually four digits), it is used for relatively low security scenarios like gaining access to the system or in combination with another method of authentication.

Authentication Based on What a User Owns or Possesses

Another type of authentication is based on what a user owns or possesses. The most common examples are the digital certificate, smart card, and security token.

The *digital certificate* is an electronic document that contains an identity such as a user or organization and a corresponding public key. Because a digital certificate is used to prove a person's identity, it can be used for authentication. Think of a digital certificate as a driver's license or passport that contains a user's photograph and thumbprint so that there is no doubt about the user's identity.

A *smart card* is a pocket-sized card with embedded integrated circuits consisting of non-volatile memory storage components and, perhaps, dedicated security logic. Non-volatile memory is memory that does not forget its contents when power is discontinued. Smart cards can contain digital certificates to prove the identity of someone carrying the card and may also contain permissions and access information. Because a smart card can be stolen, some smart cards will not have any markings on them so that they cannot be easily identified as to what they can open. In addition, many organizations will use a password or PIN in combination with the smart card.

A *security token* (or sometimes a hardware token, hard token, authentication token, USB token, cryptographic token, or key fob) is a physical device that an authorized user of computer services is given to ease authentication. Hardware tokens are typically small enough to be carried in a pocket and are often designed to attach to a user's keychain. Some of these security tokens include a USB connector, RFID functions, or Bluetooth wireless interface to enable transfer of a generated key number sequence to a client system. Some security tokens may also include additional technology such as a static password or digital certificate built into the security token, much like a smart card. Other security tokens may automatically generate a second code that will have to be entered to get authenticated.

Authentication Based on a User's Physical Traits

Biometrics is an authentication method that identifies and recognizes people based on voice recognition or a physical trait such as a fingerprint, face recognition, iris recognition, or retina scan. Many mobile computers include a fingerprint scanner, and it is relatively easy to install biometric devices at doors and cabinets to ensure that only authorized people will enter a secure area.

Biometric devices (see Figure 2.1) require a biometric reader or scanning device, software that converts the scanned information into digital form and compares match points, and a database that stores the biometric data for comparison.

FIGURE 2.1   A fingerprint scanner

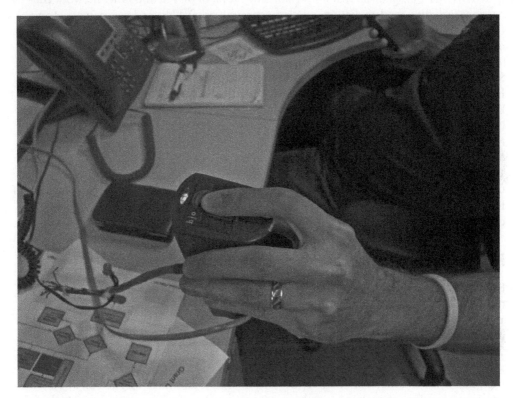

To initially use the biometric system, set up an enrollment station where an administrator enrolls each user, which includes scanning the biometric feature to be used for authentication. When selecting a biometric method, consider its performance, difficulty, reliability, acceptance, and cost. In addition, look at the following issues:

False Rejection Rate (False Negative)   Authorized users who are incorrectly denied access

False Acceptance Rate (False Positive)   Unauthorized users who are incorrectly granted access

Introducing RADIUS and TACACS+

Remote Authentication Dial-In User Service (RADIUS) and Terminal Access Controller Access-Control System Plus (TACACS+) are two protocols that provide centralized authentication, authorization, and accounting management for computers to connect to and use a network service.

The RADIUS or TACACS+ server resides on a remote system and responds to queries from clients such as VPN clients, wireless access points, routers, and switches. The server then authenticates a user name/password combination (authentication), determines if a user can connect to the client (authorization), and logs the connection (accounting).

RADIUS is a mechanism that allows authentication of dial-in and other network connections including modem dial-up, wireless access points, VPNs, and web servers. As an Internet Engineering Task Force (IETF) standard, RADIUS has been implemented by most of the major operating system manufacturers, including Microsoft Windows.

Network Policy Server (NPS) can be used as a Remote Authentication Dial-In User Service (RADIUS) server to perform authentication, authorization, and accounting for RADIUS clients. It can be configured to use a Microsoft Windows domain, an Active Directory Domain Services (AD DS) domain, or the local Security Accounts Manager (SAM) user accounts database to authenticate user credentials for connection attempts. NPS uses the dial-in properties of the user account and network policies to authorize a connection.

Another competing centralized AAA server is TACACS+, which was developed by Cisco. When designing TACACS+, Cisco incorporated much of the existing functionality of RADIUS and extended it to meet their needs. From a feature viewpoint, TACACS+ can be considered an extension of RADIUS.

Running Programs as an Administrator

Because administrators have full access to a computer or the network, it is recommended that a standard non-administrator user should perform most tasks, such as reading reports and sending email. Then, to perform administrative tasks, use the runas command or built-in options that are included with the Windows operating system.

Before Windows Vista, an administrator account was needed to do certain things, such as changing system settings or installing software. When logged on as a limited user, the runas command eliminated the need to log off and then log back on as an administrator. For example, to run the widget.exe as the admin account, execute the following command:

```
runas /user:admin /widget.exe
```

In newer versions of Windows, including Windows 10 and Windows Server 2016, the runas command has been changed to Run as administrator. With User Account Control (UAC), the Run as administrator command is rarely used, because Windows automatically prompts for an administrator password when needed.

More Info

Refer to Lesson 5 for a more detailed discussion of User Account Control (UAC).

Run a Program as an Administrator

To run a program as an administrator, perform the following steps:

1. Right-click the program icon or file that you want to open and choose Run As Administrator. If you want to right-click an item in the Start menu, right-click the program's icon, choose More, and then click Run As Administrator. See Figure 2.2.

2. Select the administrator account that you want to use, type the password, and then click Yes.

FIGURE 2.2   Using the Run as administrator option

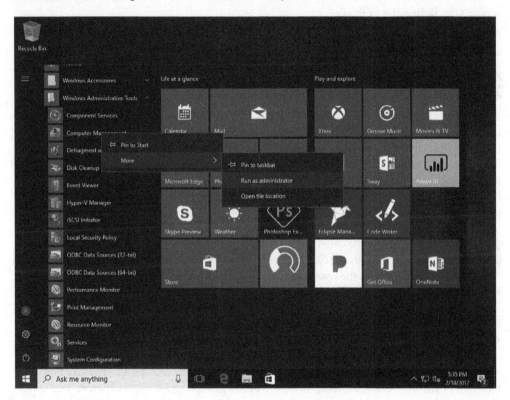

Introducing Directory Services with Active Directory

A directory service stores, organizes, and provides access to information in a directory. It is used for locating, managing, and administering common items and network resources, such as volumes, folders, files, printers, users, groups, devices, telephone numbers, and other objects. A popular directory service used by many organizations is Microsoft's Active Directory.

Certification Ready

What is the Active Directory primary method for authentication? Objective 2.1

Active Directory is a technology created by Microsoft that provides a variety of network services, including the following:

- Lightweight Directory Access Protocol (LDAP)
- Kerberos-based and single sign-on authentication
- Directory services, including DNS-based naming
- Central location for network administration and delegation of authority

The Lightweight Directory Access Protocol (LDAP) is an application protocol for querying and modifying data using directory services running over TCP/IP. Within the directory, the set of objects is organized in a logical hierarchical manner so that the objects can easily be located and managed. The structure can reflect geographical or organizational boundaries, although it tends to use DNS names for structuring the topmost levels of the hierarchy. Deeper inside the directory might appear entries representing people, organizational units, printers, documents, groups of people, or anything else that represents a given tree entry (or multiple entries). LDAP uses TCP port 389.

Kerberos is the default computer network authentication protocol, which allows hosts to prove their identity over a non-secure network in a secure manner. It can also provide mutual authentication so that both the user and server verify each other's identity. To make it secure, Kerberos protocol messages are protected against eavesdropping and replay attacks.

Single sign-on (SSO) allows a user to log on once and access multiple, related, but independent software systems without having to log on again. When a user logs on with Windows using Active Directory, the user is assigned a token, which can then be used to sign on to other systems automatically.

Lastly, Active Directory provides directory services that allow you to organize and name all of the network resources, including users, groups, printers, computers, and other objects, so that passwords, permissions, rights, and so on, can be assigned to the identity that needs them. A person who manages a group of objects can also be assigned. To help find resources, Active Directory is closely tied to DNS.

Understanding Domain Controllers

A *domain controller* is a Windows server that stores a replica of the account and security information of the domain and defines the domain boundaries. To make a computer running Windows Server 2016 a domain controller, it is necessary to first install the Active Directory Domain Services. Then, execute the dcpromo (short for dc promotion) command to make the server a domain controller.

After a computer has been promoted to a domain controller, there will be several MMC snap-in consoles available to manage Active Directory. These include:

Active Directory Users and Computers   Used to manage users, groups, computers, and organizational units.

Active Directory Domains and Trusts   Used to administer domain trusts, domain and forest functional levels, and user principal name (UPN) suffixes.

Active Directory Sites and Services   Used to administer the replication of directory data among all sites in an Active Directory Domain Services (AD DS) forest.

Active Directory Administrative Center   Used to administer and publish information in the directory, including managing users, groups, computers, domains, domain controllers, and organizational units. The Active Directory Administrative Center was introduced in Windows Server 2008 R2.

Group Policy Management Console (GPMC)   Provides a single administrative tool for managing Group Policy across the enterprise. GPMC is automatically installed in Windows Server 2008 and higher domain controllers and needs to be downloaded and installed on Windows Server 2003 domain controllers.

While these tools are installed on domain controllers, they can also be installed on client PCs so that Active Directory can be managed without logging on to a domain controller.

Active Directory uses multimaster replication, which means that there is no master domain controller, commonly referred to a primary domain controller, as was found on Windows NT domains. However, because there are certain functions that can only be handled by one domain controller at a time, domain controllers can take on separate roles.

One role is the PDC Emulator, which provides backwards compatibility for clients and is becoming very uncommon. However, it also acts as the primary domain controller for password changes and acts as the master time server within the domain.

A server that is not running as a domain controller is known as a *member server*. To demote a domain controller to a member server, run the dcpromo program again.

Understanding NTLM

While Kerberos is the default authentication protocol for today's domain computers, *NT LAN Manager (NTLM)* is the default authentication protocol for Windows stand-alone computers that are not part of a domain or when authenticating to a server using an IP address. It also acts a fallback authentication if it cannot complete Kerberos authentication, such as when blocked by a firewall.

NTLM uses a challenge-response mechanism for authentication, in which clients are able to prove their identities without sending a password to the server. After a random 8-byte challenge message is sent to the client from the server, the client uses the user's password as a key to generate a response to the server using an MD4/MD5 hashing algorithm and DES encryption.

Understanding Kerberos

With Kerberos, security and authentication are based on secret key technology, where every host on the network has its own secret key. The Key Distribution Center maintains a database of secret keys.

When a user logs on, the client transmits the user name to the authentication server, along with the identity of the service the user desires to connect to, such as a file server. The authentication server constructs a ticket, which randomly generates a key that is encrypted with a file server's secret key, and sends it to the client as part of its credentials, which includes the session key encrypted with the client's key. If the user enters the correct password, then the client can decrypt the session key, present the ticket to the file server, and use the shared secret session key to communicate between them. Tickets are time stamped and typically have an expiration time of only a few hours.

For all of this to work and to ensure security, the domain controllers and clients must have the same time. Windows operating systems include the Time Service tool (W32Time service). Kerberos authentication will work if the time interval between the relevant computers is within the maximum enabled time skew. The default setting is five minutes. Another option is to turn off the Time Service tool and then install a third-party time service. Of course, if there are problems with authentication, make sure that the time is correct for the domain controllers and the client having the problem.

Using Organizational Units

As mentioned previously, an organization could have thousands of users and thousands of computers. With Windows NT, the domain could only handle so many objects before some performance issues appeared. With later versions of Windows, the size of the domain was dramatically increased. While several domains can be used to define an organization, there could be one domain to represent a large organization. However, if there are thousands of such objects, a method is needed to organize and manage them.

To help organize objects within a domain and minimize the number of domains, use *organizational units*, commonly expressed as OUs. OUs can be used to hold users, groups, computers, and other organizational units. See Figure 2.3. An organizational unit can only contain objects that are located in a domain. While there are no restrictions on the number of nested OUs (an OU inside of another OU), a shallow hierarchy should be designed for better performance.

FIGURE 2.3 Active Directory organizational unit

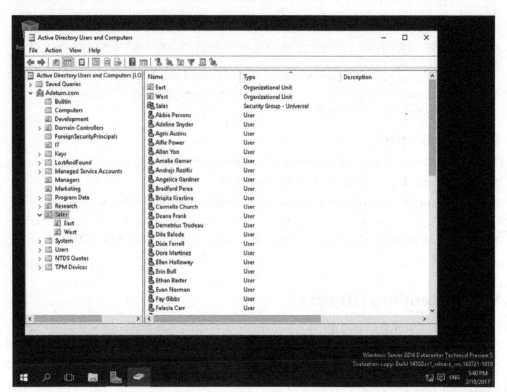

When Active Directory is first installed, there are several organizational units already created. These include computers, users, domain controllers, and built-in OUs. Different from OUs that you create, these OUs do not allow anyone to delegate permissions or assign group policies to them. Group policies will be explained later in this lesson. Containers are objects that can store or hold other objects. They include the forest, tree, domain, and organizational unit. To help manage objects, delegate authority to a container, particularly an organizational unit.

For example, let's say that a domain is divided by physical location. Assign a site administrator authoritative control to the OU that represents the physical location. The user will only have administrative control to the objects within the OU. Also, structure the OUs by function or areas of management. For example, create a Sales OU to hold all of the sales users. In addition, create a Printers OU to hold all of the printer objects and assign a printer administrator.

Similar to NTFS and the registry, permissions can be assigned to users and groups over an Active Directory object. However, control would normally be delegated to the user or group. Basic administrative tasks can be assigned to regular users or groups, and domain-wide and forest-wide administration can be assigned to members of the Domain Admins and Enterprise Admins groups. By delegating administration, groups within your organization can be allowed to take more control of their local network resources. Help secure the network from accidental or malicious damage by limiting the membership of administrator groups.

Delegate administrative control to any level of a domain tree by creating organizational units within a domain and delegating administrative control for specific organizational units to particular users or groups.

Delegate Control

To delegate control of an organizational unit, perform the following steps:

1. Open Active Directory Users And Computers.
2. In the console tree, right-click the organizational unit for which you want to delegate control.
3. Choose Delegate Control to start the Delegation Of Control Wizard and follow the instructions.

Understanding Objects

An object is a distinct, named set of attributes or characteristics that represent a network resource. Common objects used within Active Directory are computers, users, groups, and printers. Attributes have values that define the specific object. For example, a user could have the first name John, the last name Smith, and the logon name as jsmith, all of which identify the user.

When working with objects, administrators will use names of the object such as user names. However, Active Directory objects are assigned a 128-bit unique number called a security identifier (SID), sometimes referred to as globally unique identifier (GUID) to uniquely identify an object. If a user changes his name, you can change the name and he will still be able to access all objects and have all the same rights as before, because they are assigned to the GUID.

GUIDs also provide some security where, if a user is deleted, a new user account cannot be created with the same user name and expect to have access to all of the objects and all of the rights that the previous user had. If someone within the organization is let go and will be replaced, disable the account, hire the new person, rename the user account, change the password, and re-enable the account. The new hire will be able to access all resources and have the same rights that were assigned to the previous user.

The schema of Active Directory defines the format of each object and the attributes or fields within each object. The default schema contains definitions of commonly used objects such as user accounts, computers, printers, and groups. For example, the schema defines that the user account has the first name, last name, and telephone numbers.

To allow the Active Directory to be flexible so that it can support other applications, extend the schema to include additional attributes. For example, add badge numbers or employee identification to the user object. When installing some applications such as Microsoft Exchange, it will extend the schema, usually by adding additional attributes or fields so that it can support the application.

Users

A *user account* enables a user to log on to a computer and domain. As a result, it can be used to prove the identity of a user, which can then be used to determine what kind of access that user will have (authorization). It can be used for auditing so that if there is a security problem and something was accessed or deleted, the user account can indicate who accessed or deleted the object.

On today's Windows networks, there are two types of user accounts:

- The local user account
- The domain user account

A user account allows a user to log on and gain access to the computer where the account was created. The *local user account* is stored in the *Security Account Manager (SAM)* database on the local computer. The only Windows computer that does not have a SAM database is the domain controller. The administrator local user account is the only account that is created and enabled by default in Windows. While the administrator local user account cannot be deleted, it can be renamed.

The only other account created by default is the guest account. It was created for the occasional user who needs access to network resources on a low-security network. Using the guest account is not recommended and it is disabled by default.

A *domain user* is an account that is stored on the domain controller and allows the user to gain access to resources within the domain, assuming they have been granted permissions to access those objects. Like the computer local administrator account, the domain computer local administrator user account is the only account that is created and enabled by default in Windows when a domain is first created. While this domain administrator user account cannot be deleted, it can be renamed.

When creating a domain user account, supply a first name, a last name, and a user's logon name. The user's logon name must be unique within the domain. See Figure 2.4. After the user account is created, open the user account properties and configure a person's user name, logon hours, which computers a user can log on to, telephone numbers and addresses, what groups the person is a member of, and so on. You can also specify if a password expires, if the password can be changed, and if the account is disabled. Lastly, on the Profile tab, define the user's home directory, logon script, and profile path. See Figure 2.5.

FIGURE 2.4   A user account in Active Directory

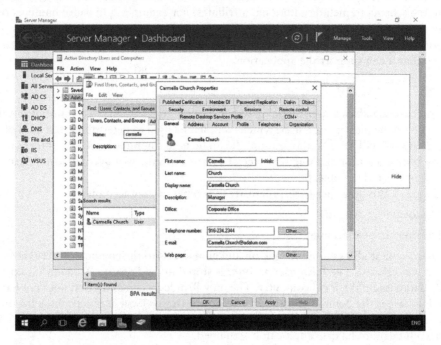

FIGURE 2.5   The Profile tab

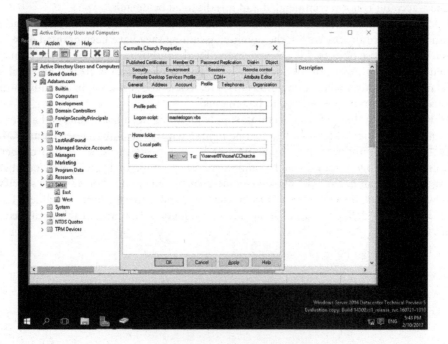

Computers

Like user accounts, Windows *computer accounts* provide a means for authenticating and auditing the computer's access to a Windows network and its access to domain resources. Each Windows computer to which you want to grant access to resources must have a unique computer account. It can also be used for auditing purposes, specifying what system was used when something was accessed. See Figure 2.6.

FIGURE 2.6   A computer account

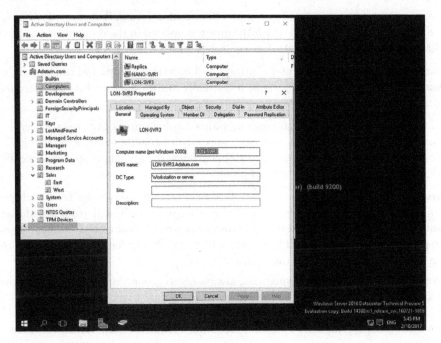

Using Groups

A *group* is a collection or list of user accounts or computer accounts. Different from a container, the group does not store the user or computer; it just lists them. The advantage of using groups is to simplify administration, especially when assigning rights and permissions.

A group is much like it sounds; it is used to group users and computers together so that when rights and permissions are assigned, they are assigned to the group rather than to each user individually. Users and computers can be members of multiple groups, and in some instances, a group can be assigned to another group.

Group Types

In Windows Active Directory, there are there are two types of groups—security and distribution. The security group is used to assign rights and permissions and gain access to a network resource. It can also be used as a distribution group. A distribution group is only for non-security functions such as email distribution and cannot be assigned rights and permissions to any resources.

Group Scopes

Any group, whether it is a security group or a distribution group, is characterized by a scope that identifies the extent to which the group is applied in the domain tree or forest. The three group scopes, also detailed in Table 2.1, are:

Domain Local Group   Contain global groups and universal groups and can contain user accounts and other domain local groups. It is usually in the domain where the intended resources are located.

Global Group   Designed to contain user accounts. Global groups can contain user accounts and other global groups. Global groups are designed to be "global" for the domain. After placing user accounts into global groups, the global groups are typically placed into domain local groups or local groups.

Universal Group   This group scope is designed to contain global groups from multiple domains. Universal groups can contain global groups, other universal groups, and user accounts. Because global catalogs replicate universal group membership, limit the membership to global groups. This way, if a member within a global group is changed, the global catalog will not have to replicate the change.

When assigning rights and permissions, always try to group the users and assign the rights and permissions to the group instead of the individual users. To effectively manage the use of groups when assigning access to a network resource using global groups and domain local groups, remember AGDLP (Accounts, Global, Domain Local, Permissions):

- Add the user account (A) into the global group (G) in its domain where the user exists.
- Add the global group (G) from the user domain into the domain local group (DL) in the resource domain.
- Assign permissions (P) on the resource to the domain local group (DL) in its domain.

If you are using a universal group, the mnemonic is expanded to AGUDLP:

- Add the user account (A) into the global group (G) in its domain where the user exists.
- Add global groups (G) from the user domain into the universal group (U).
- Add universal group (U) to the domain local group (DL).
- Assign permissions (P) on the resource to the domain local group (DL) in its domain.

TABLE 2.1   Group Scopes

Scope	Group can include as members...	Group can be assigned permissions in...	Group scope can be converted to...
Universal	Accounts from any domain within the forest in which this universal group resides Global groups from any domain within the forest in which this universal group resides Universal groups from any domain within the forest in which this universal group resides	Any domain or forest	Domain local Global (as long as no other universal groups exist as members)
Global	Accounts from the same domain as the parent global group Global groups from the same domain as the parent global group	Member permissions can be assigned in any domain	Universal (as long as it is not a member of any other global groups)
Domain Local	Accounts from any domain, global groups from any domain, universal groups from any domain, and domain local groups, but only from the same domain as the parent domain local group	Member permissions can be assigned only within the same domain as the parent domain local group	Universal (as long as no other domain local groups exist as members)

Built-in Groups

Like the administrator and guest accounts, Windows has default groups called *built-in groups*. These default groups have been granted the essential rights and permissions to get you started with groups. Some of the built-in groups include the following:

Domain Admins   Can perform administrative tasks on any computer within the domain. The default, the Administrator account, is a member.

Domain Users   Windows automatically adds each new domain user account to the Domain Users group.

Account Operators   Can create, delete, and modify user accounts and groups.

Backup Operators   Can backup and restore all domain controllers by using Windows Backup.

Authenticated Users   Includes all users with a valid user account on the computer or in Active Directory. Use the Authenticated Users group instead of the Everyone group to prevent anonymous access to a resource.

Everyone   All users who access the computer with a valid user account.

For more information on the available groups, visit the following website:

https://docs.microsoft.com/en-us/windows/security/identity-protection/
access-control/active-directory-security-groups

Understanding Web Server Authentication

When a person accesses a web server such as those running on Microsoft's Internet Information Server (IIS), several methods of authentication can be used.

When authenticating to a web server, IIS provides a variety of authentication schemes:

Anonymous (Enabled by Default)   Anonymous authentication gives users access to the website without prompting them for a user name or password. Instead, IIS uses a special Windows user account called IUSR_*machinename* for access. By default, IIS controls the password for this account.

Basic   Basic authentication prompts the user for a user name and password. However, while the user name and password is sent as Base64 encoding, it is basically sent in plain text. If it is necessary to encrypt the user name and password while using basic authentication, use digital certificates so that it is encrypted with https.

Digest   Digest authentication is a challenge/response mechanism, which sends a digest or hash using the password as the key instead of sending the password over the network.

Integrated Windows authentication   Integrated Windows authentication (formerly known as NTLM authentication and Windows NT Challenge/Response authentication) can use either NTLM or Kerberos V5 authentication.

Client Certificate Mapping   Uses a digital certificate that contains information about an entity and the entity's public key, which is used for authentication.

Comparing Rights and Permissions

Specifying what a user can do on a system, or to a resource, is determined by two things: rights and permissions.

Certification Ready
Describe how permissions are stored for an object. Objective 2.2

A *right* authorizes a user to perform certain actions on a computer, such as logging on to a system interactively or backing up files and directories on a system. User rights are assigned through local policies or Active Directory group policies. See Figure 2.7.

FIGURE 2.7   Group policy user rights assignment

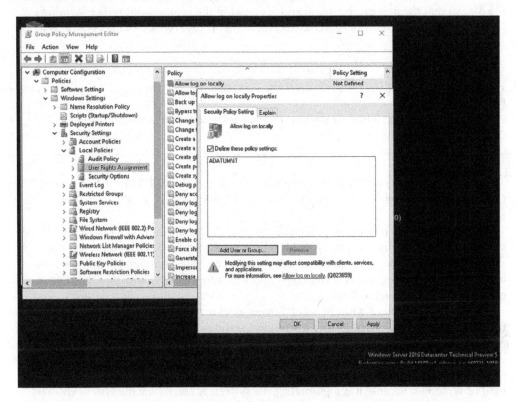

A *permission* defines the type of access that is granted to an object (an object can be identified with a security identifier) or object attribute. The most common objects assigned permissions are NTFS files and folders, printers, and Active Directory objects. To keep track of which user can access an object and what the user can do with that object, refer to the *access control list (ACL)*. The ACL lists all users and groups that have access to the object.

More Info
NTFS and printer permissions will be discussed in Lesson 3.

Understanding NTFS

The file system is a method of storing and organizing computer files and the data they contain to make it easy to find and access them. It also maintains the physical location of the files so that the files can be found and accessed in the future. Like earlier Windows operating systems, Windows Server 2016 supports FAT16, FAT32, and NTFS file systems on hard drives.

Certification Ready

What is used to protect files on a drive when they are accessed directly and remotely?
Objective 2.2

After partitioning a disk, the next step is to format the disk as FAT16, FAT32, or NTFS. Out of these three options, NTFS is the preferred file system to be used in today's operating systems.

FAT16, sometimes referred to generically as File Allocation Table (FAT), is a simple file system that uses minimum memory and has been used with DOS. Originally, it supported the 8.3 naming scheme, which allowed up to 8-character file names and 3-character file name extensions. Later, it was revised to support long file names. Unfortunately, FAT can only support volumes up to 2 GB.

FAT32 was introduced with the second major release of Windows 95. While the file system can support larger drives, today's Windows versions typically support volumes up to 32 GB. FAT32 also supports long file names.

NTFS is the preferred file system because it supports large volumes up to 16 exabytes (EB) and long file names. In addition, it is more fault tolerant than previous file systems used in Windows, because it is a journaling file system. A journaling file system ensures that a disk transaction is written to disk properly before being recognized. Lastly, NTFS offers better security through permissions and encryption.

Using NTFS Permissions

NTFS permissions allow you to control which users and groups can gain access to files and folders on an NTFS volume. The advantage with NTFS permissions is that they affect local users as well as network users.

Usually, when assigning NTFS permissions, an administrator would assign the following NTFS Standard permissions:

Full Control   Read, write, modify, and execute files in the folder; change attributes and permissions; and take ownership of the folder or files within.

Modify   Read, write, modify, and execute files in the folder; and change attributes of the folder or files within.

Read & Execute   Display the folder's contents; display the data, attributes, owner, and permissions for files within the folder; and run files within the folder.

List Folder Contents   Display the folder's contents; display the data, attributes, owner, and permissions for files within the folder.

Read   Display the file's data, attributes, owner, and permissions.

Write   Write to the file, append to the file, and read or change its attributes.

To manage NTFS permissions, right-click a drive, folder, or file; choose Properties; and then click the Security tab. As shown in Figure 2.8, the group and users who have been given NTFS permissions and their respective standard NTFS permissions appear. To change the permissions, click the Edit button.

FIGURE 2.8   NTFS permissions

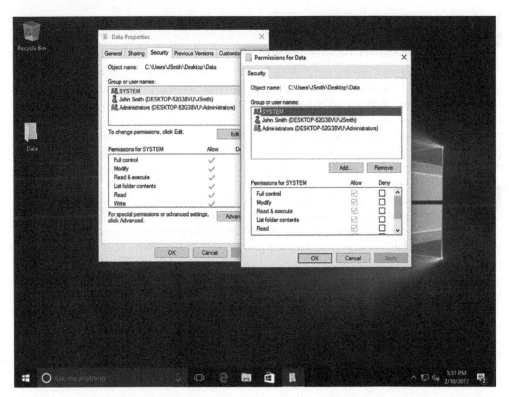

Groups or users granted Full Control permission on a folder can delete any files in that folder regardless of the permissions protecting the file. In addition, List Folder Contents is inherited by folders but not files, and it should only appear when viewing folder permissions. In Windows Server 2016, the Everyone group does not include the Anonymous Logon group by default, so permissions applied to the Everyone group do not affect the Anonymous Logon group.

To simplify administration, it is recommended to grant permissions using groups. By assigning NTFS permissions to a group, permissions are granted to one or more people, reducing the number of entries in each access list and reducing the amount of effort to configure when multiple people need access to the files or folders.

Understanding Effective NTFS Permissions

The folder/file structure on an NTFS drive can be very complicated with many folders and many nested folders. In addition, because it is recommended to assign permissions to groups, and permissions can be assigned at different levels on an NTFS volume, figuring out the effective permissions of a particular folder or file for a particular user can be tricky.

There are two types of permissions used in NTFS:

- *Explicit permission*: Permissions granted directly to the file or folder
- *Inherited permission*: Permissions granted to a folder (parent object or container) that flow into child objects (subfolders or files inside the parent folder)

When assigning permissions to a folder, by default the permissions apply to the folder being assigned and the subfolders and files of the folder. To stop permission from being inherited, select the "Replace all existing inheritable permissions on all descendants with inheritable permissions from this object" in the Advanced Security Settings dialog box and respond to the confirmation message. If the "Allow inheritable permissions from parent to propagate to this object" check box is cleared, the Security dialog box opens. When you click the Copy button, the explicit permission will be copied from the parent folder to the subfolder or file. Then, change the subfolder's or files explicit permissions. If you click the Remove button, it will remove the inherited permission altogether.

By default, objects within a folder inherit the permissions from that folder when the objects are created. However, explicit permissions take precedence over inherited permissions. So, if different permissions are granted at a lower level, the lower level permissions take precedence.

For example, there is a folder called Data. Under the Data folder, there is a folder named Folder1, and under Folder1, there is Folder2. If Allow Full Control is granted to a user account, the Allow Full Control Permission will flow down to the subfolders and files under the Data folder.

Object	NTFS Permissions
Data	Grant Allow Full Control (Explicit)
Folder1	Allowed Full Control (Inherited)
Folder2	Allowed Full Control (Inherited)
File1	Allowed Full Control (Inherited)

If Allow Full Control is granted on the Data folder to a user account, the Allow Full Control permission would normally flow down to Folder1. But if Allow Read permission is granted to Folder1 to the same user account, the Allow Read permission will overwrite the inherited permissions, and it will then inherit down to Folder2 and File1.

Object	NTFS Permissions
Data	Grant Allow Full Control (Explicit)
Folder1	Allowed Read (Explicit)
Folder2	Allowed Read (Inherited)
File1	Allowed Read (Inherited)

If a user has access to a file, the user will still be able to gain access to a file even if she does not have access to the folder containing the file. Of course, because the user doesn't have access to the folder, the user cannot navigate or browse through the folder to get to the file. Therefore, a user would have to use the universal naming convention (UNC) or local path to open the file.

When viewing the permissions, the status will be one of the following:

Checked   Permissions are explicitly assigned.

Cleared (Unchecked)   No permissions are assigned.

Shaded   Permissions are granted through inheritance from a parent folder.

Besides granting the Allow permissions, you can also grant the Deny permission. The Deny permission always overrides the permissions that have been granted, including when a user or group has been given Full Control. For example, if the group has been granted Read and Write permissions yet a person has been denied the Write permission, the user's effective rights would be the Read permission.

When you combine applying Deny versus Allowed with Explicit versus Inherited permissions, the hierarchy of precedence of permissions are:

1. Explicit Deny
2. Explicit Allow
3. Inherited Deny
4. Inherited Allow

Because users can be members of several groups, it is possible for them to have several sets of explicit permissions to a folder or file. When this occurs, the permissions are combined to form the *effective permissions*, which are the actual permissions when logging on and accessing a file or folder. They consist of explicit permissions plus any inherited permissions.

When calculating the effective permissions, first calculate the explicit and inherited permissions for an individual group and then combine them. When combining user and group permissions for NTFS security, the effective permission is the cumulative permission. The only exception is that deny permissions always apply.

For example, there is a folder called Data. Under the Data folder, there is a folder named Folder1, and under Folder1, there is Folder2. User 1 is a member of Group 1 and Group 2. If you assign Allow Write permission to the Data folder to User 1, the Allow Read permission to Folder1 to Group 1, and the Allow Modify Permission to Folder2 to Group 2, the user's effective permissions would be shown as:

Object	User 1 NTFS Permissions	Group 1 Permissions	Group 2 Permissions	Effective Permissions
Data	Allow Write Permission (Explicit)			Allow Write Permission
Folder1	Allow Write Permission (Inherited)	Allow Read Permission (Explicit)		Allow Read and Write Permission
Folder2	Allow Write Permission (Inherited)	Allow Read Permission (Inherited)	Allow Modify Permission* (Explicit)	Allow Modify Permission*
File1	Allow Write Permission (Inherited)	Allow Read Permission (Inherited)	Allow Modify Permission* (Inherited)	Allow Modify Permission*

* The Modify permission includes the Read and Write permissions.

As another example, there is a folder called Data. Under the Data folder, there is a folder named Folder1, and under Folder1, there is Folder2. User 1 is a member of Group 1 and Group 2. If you assign Allow Write permission to the Data folder to User 1, the Allow Read permission to Folder1 to Group 1, and the Deny Modified permission to Folder2 to Group 2, the user's effective permissions would be shown as:

Object	User 1 NTFS Permissions	Group 1 Permissions	Group 2 Permissions	Effective Permissions
Data	Allow Write Permission (Explicit)			Allow Write Permission
Folder1	Allow Write Permission (Inherited)	Allow Read Permission (Explicit)		Allow Read and Write Permission
Folder2	Allow Write Permission (Inherited)	Allow Read Permission (Inherited)	Deny Modify Permission (Explicit)	Deny Modify Permission
File1	Allow Write Permission (Inherited)	Allow Read Permission (Inherited)	Deny Modify Permission (Inherited)	Deny Modify Permission

View NTFS Effective Permissions

To view the NTFS effective permissions granted to a user for a file or folder, perform the following steps:

1. Right-click the file or folder and choose Properties.

2. Click the Security tab.

3. Click the Advanced button.

4. Click the Effective Access tab.

5. Click the Select A User option and type the name of the user or group you want to view.

6. Click the View Effective Access button, as shown in Figure 2.9.

7. Click OK.

FIGURE 2.9   Showing Effective Access NTFS permissions

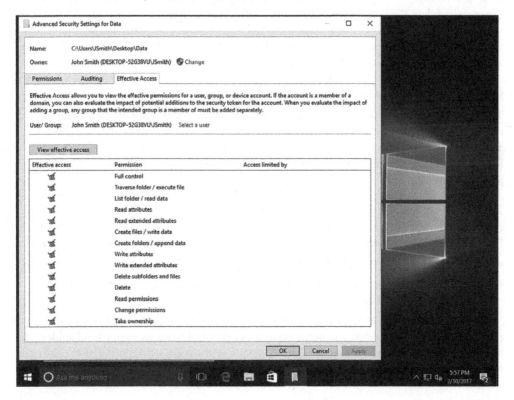

Understanding Inheritance

Inheritance is a key aspect to remember when setting up NTFS permissions. Keep in mind:

- Files and folders inherit the permissions of the destination folder when users copy the files and folders.

- Files and folder retain their permissions when users move files and folders within the same volume.

- Files and folders inherit the permissions of the destination folder when users move files and folders to a different volume.

Remember, that effective permissions are permissions granted to a user or group based upon the permissions granted through group membership and any permissions inherited from the parent object. Windows does not include share permissions as part of the effective permissions.

NTFS permissions are cumulative. For example, if a user in the finance group is given Read permissions to a folder and its contents and that user is also a member of the HR group, which has Write permission to the same folder, the user will have Read/Write permissions. In this situation, if you don't want the user to be able to write to the folder, then you can use the Deny permission and select the specific user account. The Deny permission always overrides the Allow permission.

Controlling Permission Inheritance

The directory structure is normally organized in a hierarchical manner, meaning that there are most likely subfolders within folders where the permissions will be applied. By default, in Windows 10, the parent folder's permissions are applied to any files or subfolders within that folder as well as any newly created objects. This is called *inherited permissions*.

You can see how permissions will be inherited by subfolders and files by clicking the Advanced button on the Security tab of a folder's Properties dialog box. This calls up the Permissions tab of the Advanced Security Settings dialog box. Clicking the Change Permissions button allows you to edit the options. You can edit the following:

- Include Inheritable Permissions From This Object's Parent

- Replace All Existing Inheritable Permissions On All Descendants With Inheritable Permissions From This Object

On the Security tab, if an Allow or Deny item in the Permissions list has a shaded check mark, this means that the permission was inherited from an upper-level folder. If a check mark is not shaded, this indicates that the permission was applied at the selected folder. This is known as an explicitly assigned permission. Knowing which permissions are inherited and which are explicitly assigned is useful when troubleshooting permissions.

Enable or Disable Inheritance

To enable inheritance, follow these steps:

1. Open File Explorer.
2. Locate the file or folder with disabled inherited NTFS permissions.
3. Right-click the file or folder, click Properties, and then click the Security tab.
4. Click the Advanced button. The Advanced Security Settings window will appear.
5. If you see the Change permissions button, click it.
6. Click the button that says Enable Inheritance.

   The inherited permissions will be added to the list of current permissions.

FIGURE 2.10   Advanced Security Settings – Enable Inheritance

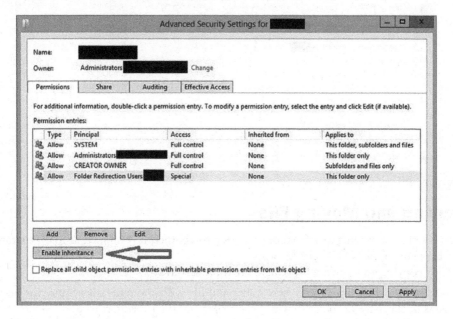

To disable inheritance, follow these steps:

1. Open File Explorer.
2. Locate the file or folder you want to take disable inherited permissions for.
3. Right-click the file or folder, click Properties, and then click the Security tab.
4. Click the Advanced button. The Advanced Security Settings window will appear.
5. Click the Disable inheritance button.

6. It will ask you to either convert inherited permissions into explicit permissions or remove all inherited permissions. If you are not sure, choose to convert them.

7. When done, click OK to close the dialog box.

FIGURE 2.11 Advanced Security Settings – Disable Inheritance

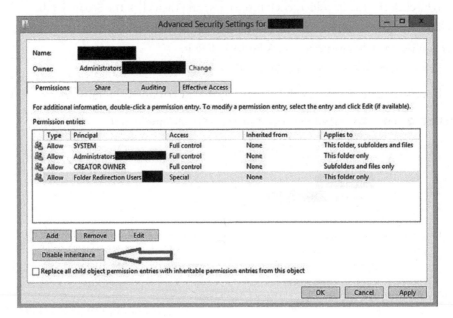

Copying and Moving Files

When copying or moving files from one location to another, it is important to understand what happens to the NTFS permissions.

When copying and moving files, there are three scenarios:

- If copying a file or folder, the new folder and file will automatically acquire the permissions of the drive or folder to which the folder and file is being copied.

- If the folder or file is moved within the same volume, the folder or file will retain the same permissions that were already assigned.

- If the folder or file is moved from one volume to another volume, the folder or file will automatically acquire the permissions of the drive or folder to which the folder and file is being copied.

Using Folder and File Owners

The *owner* of the object controls how permissions are set on the object and to whom permissions are granted. If, for some reason, access to a file or folder has been denied and the permissions need to be reset, take ownership of a file or folder and modify the permissions. All administrators automatically have the Take Ownership permission of all NTFS objects.

Take Ownership of a File or Folder

To take ownership of a file or folder, perform the following steps:

1. Open File Explorer and locate the file or folder for which you want to take ownership.

2. Right-click the file or folder, choose Properties, and then click the Security tab.

3. Click Advanced, as shown in Figure 2.12.

FIGURE 2.12   The Permissions tab

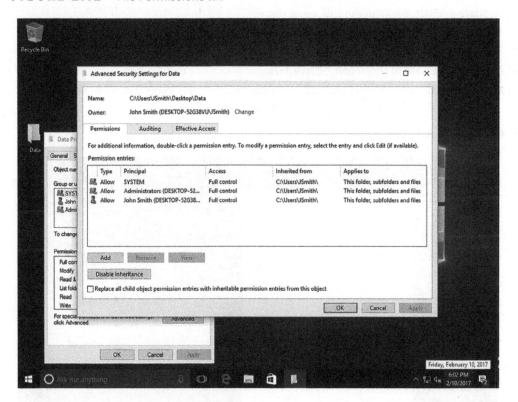

4. In the Owner section, click Change.

5. In the Select User or Group dialog box, in the Enter the object name to select text box, type the name of the user, such as **JSmith**, and click OK.

6. To close the Advanced Security Settings for Data dialog box, click OK.

7. To close the Properties dialog box, click OK.

Sharing Drives and Folders

Most users are not going to log on to a server directly to access their data files. Instead, a drive or folder will be shared (known as a *shared folder*), and they will access the data files over the network. To help protect against unauthorized access, use *share permissions* along with NTFS permissions (if the shared folder is on an NTFS volume). When a user needs to access a network share, they would use the UNC, which is \\servername\sharename.

Share a Folder

To share a folder, perform the following steps:

1. In Windows Server 2016, right-click the drive or folder, choose Properties, click the Sharing tab, and then click the Advanced Sharing button.

2. Select the "Share this folder" check box.

3. In the Advanced Sharing dialog box, in the "Share name" text box, type the name of the shared folder, such as **Data2** (see Figure 2.13).

FIGURE 2.13 Sharing a folder

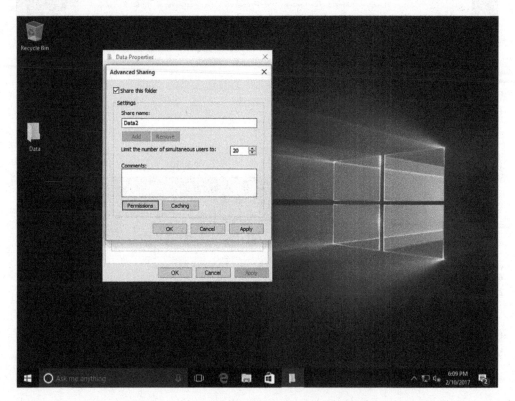

4. If necessary, specify the maximum number of people that can access the shared folder at the same time.

5. Click the Permissions button.

6. By default, Everyone is given Allow Read permission. If you don't want everyone to access the folder, remove Everyone and assign additional permissions or add additional people. See Figure 2.14.

FIGURE 2.14   Specifying share permissions

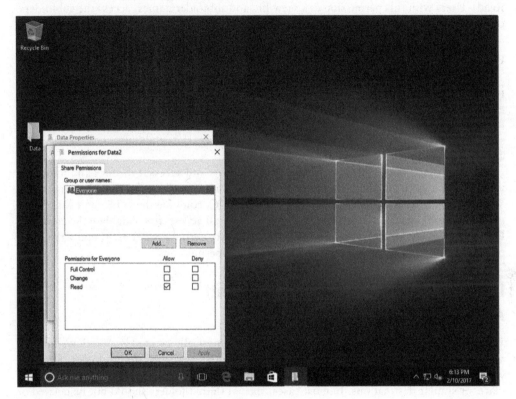

7. After the users and groups have been added with the proper permissions, click OK to close the Permissions dialog box.

8. To close the Advanced Sharing dialog box, click OK.

9. Click Close to close the Properties dialog box.

The share permissions that are available are:

Full Control   Users allowed this permission have Read and Change permissions, as well as the additional capabilities to change file and folder permissions and take ownership of files and folders.

Change   Users allowed this permission have Read permissions and the additional capability to create files and subfolders, modify files, change attributes on files and subfolders, and delete files and subfolders.

Read   Users with this permission can view file and subfolder names, access the subfolders of the share, read file data and attributes, and run program files.

It should be noted that share permissions always apply when accessed remotely using a UNC, even if it is on the FAT, FAT32, or NTFS volume.

Much like NTFS, you can allow or deny each share permission. To simplify managing share and NTFS permissions, Microsoft recommends giving Everyone Full Control and then controlling access using NTFS permissions. In addition, because a user can be a member of several groups, it is possible for the user to have several sets of permissions to a shared drive or folder. The effective share permissions are the combination of the user and all group permissions for which the user is a member.

When a person logs on directly to the server console and accesses the files and folders without using the UNC, only the NTFS permissions apply and not the share permissions. When a person accesses a shared folder using the UNC, combine the NTFS and share permissions to see what a user can do. To figure the overall access, first calculate the effective NTFS permissions. Then, determine the effective share permissions. Lastly, apply the more restrictive permissions between the NTFS and share permissions.

Understanding Special Shares and Administrative Shares

There are several special shared folders that are automatically created by Windows for administrative and system use. Different from regular shares, these shares do not show when a user browses the computer resources using Network Neighborhood, My Network Place, or similar destinations. In most cases, special shared folders should not be deleted or modified. For Windows Servers, only members of the Administrators, Backup Operators, and Server Operators groups can connect to these shares.

An *administrative share* is a shared folder typically used for administrative purposes. To make a shared folder or drive into a hidden share, the share name must have a $ at the end of it. Because the share folder or drive cannot be seen during browsing, use a UNC name that will include the share name and the trailing $. By default, all volumes with drive letters automatically have administrative shares (C$, D$, E$, and so on). Other administrative shares can be created as needed for individual folders.

In addition to the administrative shares for each drive, the following special shares are also available:

ADMIN$ A resource used by the system during remote administration of a computer. The path of this resource is always the path to the Windows 10 system root (the directory in which Windows 10 is installed—for example, C:\Windows).

IPC$ A resource sharing the named pipes that are essential for communication between programs. It is used during remote administration of a computer and when viewing a computer's shared resources.

PRINT$ A resource used during remote administration of printers.

Introducing the Registry

The *registry* is a central, secure database in which Windows stores all hardware configuration information, software configuration information, and system security policies. Components that use the registry include the Windows kernel, device drivers, setup programs, hardware profiles, and user profiles.

Certification Ready

What is used to specify who can access specific registry settings? Objective 2.1

Most of the time, it is not necessary to access the Windows registry because programs and applications typically make all the necessary changes to the registry automatically. For example, when changing the desktop background or changing the default color for Windows, access the Display settings within Control Panel and Windows will save the changes to the registry.

 If it is necessary to access and make changes to the registry, closely follow the instructions from a reputable source, because an incorrect change to your computer's registry could render your computer inoperable.

There may be a time when it is necessary to make a change in the registry because there is no interface or program to make the change. To view and manually change the registry, use the Registry Editor (Regedit.exe), which can be executed from the command prompt, Start search box, or Run box. See Figure 2.15.

FIGURE 2.15   The Registry Editor

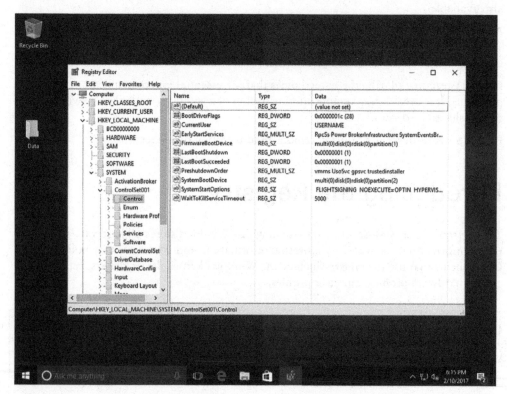

The registry is split into several logical sections, often referred to as hives, which are generally named by their Windows API definitions. The hives begin with HKEY are often abbreviated to a three- or four-letter short name starting with HK. For example, HKCU refers to HKEY_CURRENT_USER and HKLM refers to HKEY_LOCAL_MACHINE. Windows 10 has five root keys/HKEYs:

HKEY_CLASSES_ROOT   Stores information about registered applications, such as file association that tells which default program opens a file with a certain extension.

HKEY_CURRENT_USER   Stores settings that are specific to the currently logged-on user. When a user logs off, the HKEY_CURRENT_USER is saved to HKEY_USERS.

HKEY_LOCAL_MACHINE   Stores settings that are specific to the local computer.

HKEY_USERS   Contains subkeys corresponding to the HKEY_CURRENT_USER keys for each user profile actively loaded on the machine.

HKEY_CURRENT_CONFIG   Contains information gathered at runtime. Information stored in this key is not permanently stored on disk, but rather regenerated at the boot time.

Registry keys are similar to folders, which can contain values or subkeys. Navigating the keys within the registry follows a syntax similar to Windows folders or a file path, using backslashes to separate each level. For example:

`HKEY_LOCAL_MACHINE\Software\Microsoft\Windows`

refers to the subkey "Windows" of the subkey "Microsoft" of the subkey "Software" of the HKEY_LOCAL_MACHINE key.

Registry values include a name and a value. There are multiple types of values. Some of the common registry key types are shown in Table 2.2.

TABLE 2.2   Common Registry Key Types

Name	Data Type	Description
Binary Value	REG_BINARY	Raw binary data. Most hardware component information is stored as binary data and is displayed in Registry Editor in hexadecimal format.
DWORD Value	REG_DWORD	Data represented by a number that is 4 bytes long (a 32-bit integer). Many parameters for device drivers and services are this type and are displayed in Registry Editor in binary, hexadecimal, or decimal format.
Expandable String Value	REG_EXPAND_SZ	A variable-length data string. This data type includes variables that are resolved when a program or service uses the data.
Multi-String Value	REG_MULTI_SZ	A multiple string. Values that contain lists or multiple values in a form that people can read are generally this type. Entries are separated by spaces, commas, or other marks.
String Value	REG_SZ	A fixed-length text string.
QWORD Value	REG_QWORD	Data represented by a number that is a 64-bit integer. This data is displayed in Registry Editor as a Binary Value and was introduced in Windows 2000.

Reg files (also known as Registration entries) are text files for storing portions of the registry. They have a .reg file name extension. Double-click a reg file to add the registry entries into the registry. To export any registry subkey, right-click the subkey and choose Export. To back up the entire registry to a reg file, right-click Computer at the top of Regedit and choose export; or, back up the system state with Windows Backup.

Access Registry Permissions

Similar to NTFS permissions, the registry uses registry permissions that are stored in ACLs. To access the registry permissions, perform the following steps:

1.   Open Registry Editor.
2.   Click the key to which you want to assign permissions.
3.   Click Edit ➤ Permissions.

Then, add the affected user or group and assign either allow or deny Full Control or Read permission.

Using Encryption to Protect Data

Encryption is the process of converting data into a format that cannot be read by another user. Once a user has encrypted a file, it automatically remains encrypted when the file is stored on disk. *Decryption* is the process of converting data from encrypted format back to its original format.

Certification Ready

List and contrast the three primary methods of encryption. Objective 2.5

With commonly used encryption methods, the encryption algorithm needs to provide a high level of security, while being available to the public. Because the algorithm is made available to the public, the security resides in the key, and not in the algorithm itself.

One of the simplest cipher algorithms is the substitution cipher, which changes one character or symbol into another. For example, if you have:

```
clear text
```

And you substitute each *e* with the *y* and each *c* with the letter *j* and the letter *t* with *y*, you would get the following ciphertext:

```
jlyar yyxy
```

Another simple technique is based on the transposition cipher, which involves transposing or scrambling the letters in a certain manner. For example, if you have:

```
clear text
```

and you switch each two letters, you get:

```
lcae rettx
```

A *key*, which can be thought of as a password, is applied mathematically to plain text to provide cipher or encrypted text. A different key produces a different encrypted output. With computers, encryption is often based on bits, not characters. For example, if you have the Unicode letters *cl*, it would be expressed in the following binary format:

```
01100011 01101100
```

and if you mathematically add the binary form of *z* (01111010), which is the key, you get:

```
  01100011    01101100
 +01111010   +01111010
  11011101    1110 0110
```

which would show as strange Unicode characters: Ýæ.

Similar to a password, the longer the key (usually expressed in bits), the more secure it is. For a hacker to figure out a key, they would also have to use a brute force attack, which means the hacker would have to try every combination of bits until they figure out the correct key. While a key could be broken given enough time and processing power, long keys are chosen so that it would take months, maybe even years, to calculate. Of course, similar to passwords, some encryption algorithms change the key frequently. Therefore, a key length of 80 bits is generally considered the minimum for strong security with symmetric encryption algorithms. Today, 128-bit keys are commonly used and considered very strong.

Types of Encryption

Encryption algorithms can be divided into three classes: Symmetric, Asymmetric, and Hash function. Symmetric and Asymmetric encryption can encrypt and decrypt data. A Hash function can only encrypt data; that data cannot be decrypted.

Symmetric Encryption

Symmetric encryption uses a single key to encrypt and decrypt data. Therefore, it is also referred to as secret-key, single-key, shared-key, and private-key encryption. To use symmetric key algorithms, you need to initially exchange the secret key with both the sender and receiver.

Symmetric-key ciphers can be divided into block ciphers and stream ciphers. A block cipher takes a block of plain text and a key and outputs a block of ciphertext of the same size. Two popular block ciphers include the Data Encryption Standard (DES) and the Advanced Encryption Standard (AES), which have been designated cryptography standards by the U.S. government.

The Data Encryption Standard was selected by the National Bureau of Standards as an official Federal Information Processing Standard (FIPS) for the United States in 1976. It is based on a symmetric-key algorithm that uses a 56-bit key.

Because DES is based on a relatively small 56-bit key size, DES was subject to brute force attacks. Therefore, without designing a completely new block cipher algorithm, Triple DES (3DES) was developed, which uses three independent keys. DES and the more secure 3DES are still popular and used across a wide range of applications, including ATM encryption, email privacy, and secure remote access.

While DES and 3DES are still popular, a more secure encryption called Advanced Encryption Standard (AES) was announced in 2001 and is growing in popularity. The standard comprises three block ciphers, AES-128, AES-192, and AES-256, used on 128-bit blocks, with key sizes of 128, 192, and 256 bits, respectively. The AES ciphers have been analyzed extensively and are now used worldwide, including being used with Wi-Fi Protected Access 2 (WPA2) wireless encryption.

Stream ciphers create an arbitrarily long stream of key material, which is combined with plain text bit-by-bit or character-by-character. RC4 is a widely used stream cipher, used in Secure Sockets Layer (SSL) and Wired Equivalent Privacy (WEP). While RC4 is simple and is known for its speed, it can be vulnerable if the key stream is not discarded, nonrandom or related keys are used, or a single key stream is used twice.

Asymmetric Encryption

Asymmetric encryption uses two keys for encryption. Asymmetric key, also known as public key cryptography, uses two mathematically-related keys. One key is used to encrypt the data, while the second key is used to decrypt the data. Unlike symmetric key algorithms, it does not require a secure initial exchange of one or more secret keys to both sender and receiver. Instead, you can make the public key known to anyone and use the other key to encrypt or decrypt the data. The public key could be sent to someone or could be published within a digital certificate via a Certificate Authority (CA). Secure Sockets Layer (SSL)/Transport Layer Security (TLS) and Pretty Good Privacy (PGP) use asymmetric keys. Two popular asymmetric encryption protocols are Diffie-Hellman and RSA.

For example, say you want a partner to send you data. Therefore, you send the partner the public key. The partner will then encrypt the data with the key and send you the encrypted message. Then, you use the private key to decrypt the message. If the public key falls into someone else's hands, they still could not decrypt the message.

Hash Function Encryption

The last type of encryption is the hash function. Different from the symmetric and asymmetric algorithms, a *hash function* is meant as a one-way encryption. This means that after data has been encrypted, it cannot be decrypted. It can be used to encrypt a password that is stored on disk and for digital signatures. Anytime a password is entered, the same hash calculation is performed on the entered password, and it is compared to the hash value of the password stored on disk. If the two passwords match, the user must have typed the correct password. This avoids having to store the passwords in a readable format, where a hacker might try to access them.

Introducing Public Key Infrastructure (PKI)

When surfing the Internet, there are times when it is necessary to transmit private data over the Internet, such as credit card numbers, Social Security numbers, and so on. During these times, use HTTP over SSL (HTTPS) to encrypt the data sent over the Internet. By convention, URLs that require an SSL connection start with https: instead of http.

A *public key infrastructure (PKI)* is a system consisting of hardware, software, policies, and procedures that create, manage, distribute, use, store, and revoke digital certificates. Within the PKI, the certificate authority (CA) binds a public key with respective user identities and issues digital certificates containing the public key. For this system to work, the CA must be trusted. Typically, within an organization, you may install a CA on a Windows server, specifically on a domain controller, and it would be trusted within the organization. If it is necessary to have a CA trusted outside of your organization, use a trusted third-party CA, such as VeriSign or Entrust. Established commercial CAs charge to issue certificates that will automatically be trusted by most web browsers. See Figure 2.16.

FIGURE 2.16   Trusted CAs within Internet Explorer

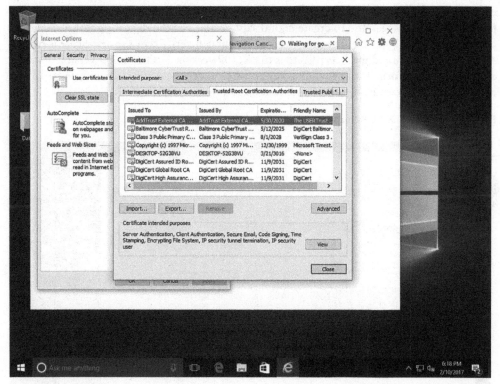

The registration authority (RA), which may or may not be the same server as the CA, is used to distribute keys, accept registrations for the CA, and validate identities. The RA does not distribute digital certificates; instead, digital certificates are distributed by the CA.

Besides having an expiration date, a digital certificate can also be revoked if it was compromised or the situation has changed for the system to which the digital certificate was assigned. A *certificate revocation list (CRL)* is a list of certificates (or more specifically, a list of serial numbers for certificates) that have been revoked or are no longer valid and therefore should not be relied upon.

Windows servers can host a certificate authority. The Enterprise Root CA is at the top level of the certificate authority hierarchy. Once an Enterprise Root CA is configured, it registers automatically within Active Directory and all computers within the domain will trust it. It will support auto-enrollment and auto-renewal of digital certificates.

To support outside clients and customers, you would most likely build a standalone CA. Different from an Enterprise Root CA, the standalone CA does not use Active Directory. Because standalone CA does not support auto-enrollment, all requests for certificates are pending until an administrator approves them.

Digital Certificate

A digital certificate is an electronic document that contains a person's or organization's name, a serial number, an expiration date, a copy of the certificate holder's public key (used for encrypting messages and to create digital signatures), and the digital signature of the CA that assigned the digital certificate so that a recipient can verify that the certificate is real.

The most common digital certificate is the X.509 version 3. The X.509 version 3 standard specifies the format for the public key certificate, certificate revocation lists, attribute certificates, and a certificate path validation algorithm. See Figure 2.17.

FIGURE 2.17   X.509 digital certificate

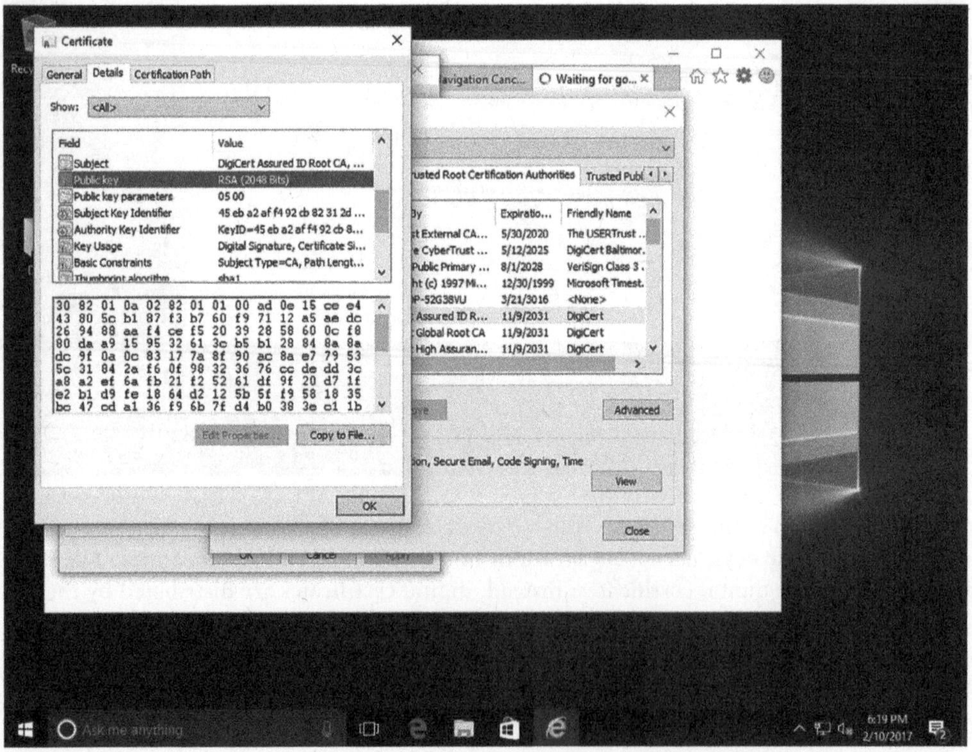

Digital certificates can be imported and exported via an electronic file. Four common formats are:

Personal Information Exchange (PKCS #12)   The Personal Information Exchange format (PFX, also called PKCS #12) supports secure storage of certificates, private keys, and all certificates in a certification path. The PKCS #12 format is the only file format that can be used to export a certificate and its private key. It will usually have a .p12 file name extension.

Cryptographic Message Syntax Standard (PKCS #7)   The PKCS #7 format supports storage of certificates and all certificates in the certification path. It will usually have a .p7b or .p7c file name extension.

DER-encoded binary X.509   The Distinguished Encoding Rules (DER) format supports storage of a single certificate. This format does not support storage of the private key or certification path. It will usually have a .cer, .crt, or .der file name extension.

Base64-encoded X.509   The Base64 format supports storage of a single certificate. This format does not support storage of the private key or certification path.

Acquire a Digital Certificate

To acquire a digital certificate using IIS 7/7.5, perform the following steps:

1. Request an Internet server certificate from the IIS server. To request an Internet server certificate, click the server from within IIS Manager and double-click Server Certificates in Features View. Then click Create Certificate Request from the Actions pane.

2. Send the generated certificate request to the CA, usually using the vendor's website.

3. Receive a digital certificate from the CA and install it on the IIS server. Again, open IIS Manager, double-click the server from within IIS Manager, and then double-click Server Certificates in Features View. Then, select the Complete Certificate Request.

If you have a farm that consists of multiple web servers, it is necessary to install the digital certificate from the first server and then export the digital certificate to a .pfx format needed to copy the public and private key to the other servers. Therefore, export the key from the first server and import to the other servers.

Export a Digital Certificate

To export a digital certificate, perform the following steps:

1. Open IIS Manager and navigate to the level you want to manage.

2. In the Features View, double-click Server Certificates.

3. In the Actions pane, click Export.

4. In the Export dialog box, type a file name in the Export to box or click the Browse button to navigate to the name of a file in which to store the certificate for exporting.

5. Type a password in the Password box if you want to associate a password with the exported certificate. Retype the password in the Confirm Password box.

6. Click OK.

Import a Digital Certificate

To import a digital certificate, perform the following steps:

1. Open IIS Manager and navigate to the level you want to manage.

2. In the Features View, double-click Server Certificates.

3. In the Actions pane, click Import.

4. In the Import Certificate dialog box, type a file name in the Certificate File box or click the Browse button to navigate to the name of a file where the exported certificate is stored. Type a password in the Password box if the certificate was exported with a password.

5. Select "Allow this certificate to be exported" if you want to be able to export the certificate, or clear "Allow this certificate to be exported" if you want to prevent additional exports of this certificate.

6. Click OK.

Certificate Chain

There are only so many root CA certificates that are assigned to commercial third-party organizations. Therefore, when acquiring a digital certificate from a third-party organization, it might be necessary to use a certificate chain to obtain the root CA certificate. In addition, it might be necessary to install an intermittent digital certificate that will link the assigned digital certificate to a trusted root CA certificate. The *certificate chain*, also known as the certification path, is a list of certificates used to authenticate an entity. It begins with the certificate of the entity and ends with the root CA certificate. See Figure 2.18.

FIGURE 2.18   A certificate chain

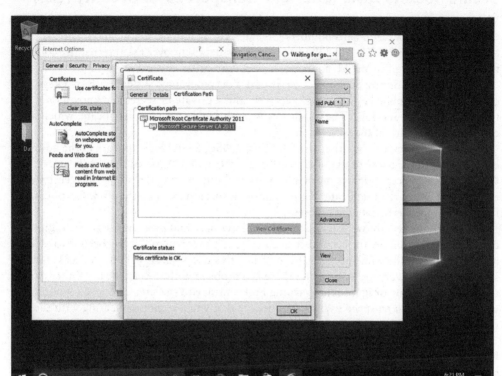

Digital Signature

A *digital signature* is a mathematical scheme that is used to demonstrate the authenticity of a digital message or document. It is also used to confirm that the message or document has not been modified. The sender uses the receiver's public key to create a hash of the message, which is stored in the message digest. The message is then sent to the receiver. The receiver will then use her private key to decrypt the hash value, perform the same hash function on the message, and compare the two hash values. If the message has not been changed, the hash values will match.

To prove that a message comes from a particular person, perform the hashing function with your private key and attach the hash value to the document to be sent. When the document is sent and received by the receiving party, the same hash function is completed. Then, use the sender's public key to decrypt the hash value included in the document. If the two hash values match, the user who sent the document must have known the sender's private key, proving who sent the document. It will also prove that the document has not been changed.

Secure Sockets Layer (SSL) and Transport Layer Security (TLS)

When surfing the Internet, there are times when it is necessary to transmit private data over the Internet such as credit card numbers, Social Security numbers, and so on. During these times, use SSL over HTTP (HTTPS) to encrypt the data sent over the Internet. By convention, URLs that require an SSL connection start with https: instead of http:.

SSL is short for *Secure Sockets Layer*. It uses a cryptographic system with two keys to encrypt data—a public key known to everyone and a private or secret key known only to the recipient of the message. The public key is published in a digital certificate, which also confirms the identity of the web server.

When connecting to a site that is secured using SSL, a gold lock appears in the address bar, along with the name of the organization to which the CA issued the certificate. Clicking the lock icon displays more information about the site, including the identity of the CA that issued the certificate. For even more information, click the View Certificate link to open the Certificate dialog box.

When visiting certain websites, Internet Explorer may find problems with the digital certificate. For example, the certificate has expired, it is corrupted, it has been revoked, or it does not match the name of the website. When this happens, IE will block access to the site and display a warning stating that there is a problem with the certificate. Either close the browser window or ignore the warning and continue to the site. Of course, ignore the warning only if you trust the website and believe that you are communicating with the correct server.

Transport Layer Security (TLS) is an extension of SSL, which is supported by the Internet Engineering Task Force (IETF) so that it could be an open, community supported standard, which could then be expanded with other Internet standards. While TLS is often referred to as SSL 3.0, it does not interoperate with SSL. While TLS is usually the default for most browsers, it has a downgrade feature that allows SSL 3.0 to run as needed.

Encrypting Email

Because email is sent over the Internet, one may be concerned with the data packets being captured and read. Therefore, there is a need to encrypt emails that contain confidential information.

There are multiple protocols that can be used to encrypt emails. They include:

- Secure/Multipurpose Internet Mail Extensions (S/MIME)
- Pretty Good Privacy (PGP)

Secure/Multipurpose Internet Mail Extensions (S/MIME) is the secure version of MIME, used to embed objects within email messages. It is the most widely supported standard used to secure email communications, which uses the PKCS #7 standard. S/MIME is included with popular web browsers and has also been endorsed by other vendors that make messaging products.

Pretty Good Privacy (PGP) is a freeware email encryption system that uses symmetrical and asymmetrical encryption. When an email is sent, the document is encrypted with the public key and a session key. The session key is a one-use random number used to create the ciphertext. The session key is encrypted into the public key and sent with the ciphertext. When the message is received, the private key is used to extract the session key. The session key and the private key are used to decrypt the ciphertext.

Encrypting Files with EFS

If someone steals a hard drive that is protected by NTFS permissions, they could take the hard drive, place it in a system in which they are an administrator, and access all files and folders on the hard drive. Therefore, to truly protect a drive that could be stolen or accessed illegally, encrypt the files and folders on the drive.

Windows 10 offers two file encrypting technologies—Encrypting File System (EFS) and BitLocker Drive Encryption. EFS protects individual files or folders, while BitLocker protects entire drives.

Encrypting File System (EFS) can encrypt files on an NTFS volume that cannot be used unless the user has access to the keys required to decrypt the information. After a file has been encrypted, it is not necessary to manually decrypt an encrypted file before using it. After encrypting a file or folder, work with the encrypted file or folder as with any other file or folder.

EFS is keyed to a specific user account, using the public and private keys that are the basis of the Windows public key infrastructure (PKI). The user who creates a file is the only person who can read it. As the user works, EFS encrypts the files he creates using a key generated from the user's public key. Data encrypted with this key can be decrypted only by the user's personal encryption certificate, which is generated using his private key.

Encrypting File System (EFS) allows an administrator or user to secure files or folders using encryption. Encryption uses the user's security identification (SID) number to secure the file or folder. To implement encryption, open the Advanced Attributes dialog box for a folder, and check the Encrypt Contents To Secure Data box.

There are two ways for an administrator to unencrypt files if they are encrypted using EFS. First, they can log in using the user's account (the account that encrypted the files) and unencrypt the files. Or, they can become a recovery agent and manually unencrypt the files.

Encrypt a Folder or File using EFS

To encrypt a folder or file using EFS, perform the following steps:

1. Right-click the folder or file you want to encrypt and choose Properties.
2. Click the General tab and click Advanced. See Figure 2.19.
3. Select the "Encrypt contents to secure data" check box, click OK, and then click OK again.

FIGURE 2.19   Encrypting data with EFS

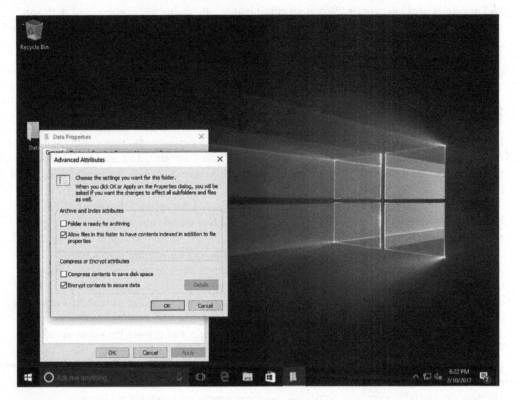

 You cannot encrypt a file with EFS while also compressing a file with NTFS.

Decrypt a Folder or File

To decrypt a folder or file, perform the following steps:

1. Right-click the folder or file you want to decrypt and choose Properties.

2. Click the General tab and click Advanced.

3. Clear the "Encrypt contents to secure data" check box, click OK, and then click OK again.

The first time a folder or file is encrypted, an encryption certificate is automatically created. If the certificate and key are lost or damaged and there isn't a backup, you won't be able to use the encrypted files. Therefore, always back up your encryption certificate.

Back Up an EFS Certificate

To back up an EFS certificate, perform the following steps:

1. Execute the `certmgr.msc` program. If prompted for an administrator password or confirmation, type the password or provide confirmation.

2. In the left pane, double-click Personal.

3. Click Certificates.

4. In the main pane, click the certificate that lists Encrypting File System under the Intended Purposes column. If there is more than one EFS certificate, you should back up all of them.

5. Click Action ➤ All Tasks ➤ Export.

6. In the Certificate Export Wizard, click Next, click Yes, export the private key, and then click Next.

7. Click Personal Information Exchange and click Next.

8. Type the password, confirm the password, and then click Next. The export process will create a file to store the certificate.

9. Type a name for the file and the location (include the whole path); or, click Browse, navigate to a location, type a file name, and then click Save.

10. Click Next, click Finish, and then click OK.

   Place the certificate in a safe place. If for some reason, a person leaves the company and you cannot read encrypted files, set up a recovery agent who can recover encrypted files for a domain.

Add Users as Recovery Agents

To add new users as recovery agents, they must first have recovery certificates issued by the enterprise CA structure. Perform the following steps:

1. Using Server Manager, on a domain controller, click Tools ➤ Group Policy Management.

2. In the Group Policy Management window, navigate to Forest: Adatum.com ➤ Domains ➤ Adatum.com. Then, right-click the Default Domain Policy and choose Edit.

3. In the Group Policy Management Editor, expand Computer Configuration\Policies\Windows Settings\Security Settings\Public Key Policies.

4. Right-click Encrypting File System and choose Add Data Recovery Agent.

5. In the Add Recovery Agent Wizard, click Next.

6. Click Browse Directory. Locate the user and click OK.

7. Click Next.

8. Click Finish.

9. Close the Group Policy Editor.

If copying a file or folder, the new folder and file will automatically acquire the encryption attribute of the original drive or folder. If the folder or file is moved within the same volume, the folder or file will retain the original assigned encryption attribute. Thus, if it is encrypted, it will remain encrypted at the new location. When the file or folder is moved from one volume to another, it copies the folder or file to the new location and then deletes the old location. Therefore, the moved folder and files are new to the volume and acquire the new encryption attribute.

Encrypting Disks in Windows

Different from EFS, BitLocker allows encryption of entire disks. Therefore, if a drive or laptop is stolen, the data is still encrypted even if they install the drive or laptop into another system in which they are an administrator.

BitLocker Drive Encryption is the feature in Windows 10 that makes use of a computer's TPM. A Trusted Platform Module (TPM) is a microchip that is built into a computer. It is used to store cryptographic information, such as encryption keys. Information stored on the TPM can be more secure from external software attacks and physical theft. BitLocker Drive Encryption can use a TPM to validate the integrity of a computer's boot manager and boot files at startup and to guarantee that a computer's hard disk has not been tampered with while the operating system was offline. BitLocker Drive Encryption also stores measurements of core operating system files in the TPM.

 BitLocker is a feature of Windows 10 Pro, Enterprise, and Education editions. It is not supported on Windows 10 Home edition.

The system requirements of BitLocker include the following:

- Because BitLocker stores its own encryption and decryption key in a hardware device that is separate from the hard disk, one of the following is required:
  - A computer with Trusted Platform Module (TPM): If the computer was manufactured with TPM version 1.2 or higher, BitLocker will store its key in the TPM.
  - A removable USB memory device, such as a USB flash drive: If the computer doesn't have TPM version 1.2 or higher, BitLocker will store its key on the flash drive.
- Have at least two partitions—a system partition (which contains the files needed to start the computer, and must be at least 200 MB) and an operating system partition (which contains Windows). The operating system partition will be encrypted and the system partition will remain unencrypted so the computer can start. If the computer doesn't have two partitions, BitLocker will create them. Both partitions must be formatted with the NTFS file system.
- The computer must have a BIOS that is compatible with TPM and supports USB devices during computer startup. If this is not the case, it will be necessary to update the BIOS before using BitLocker.

BitLocker has five operational modes, which define the steps involved in the system boot process. These modes, in descending order from most to least secure, are as follows:

TPM + Startup PIN + Startup Key The system stores the BitLocker volume encryption key on the TPM chip, but an administrator must supply a personal identification number (PIN) and insert a USB flash drive containing a startup key before the system can unlock the BitLocker volume and complete the system boot sequence.

TPM + Startup Key The system stores the BitLocker volume encryption key on the TPM chip, but an administrator must insert a USB flash drive containing a startup key before the system can unlock the BitLocker volume and complete the system boot sequence.

TPM + Startup PIN The system stores the BitLocker volume encryption key on the TPM chip, but an administrator must supply a PIN before the system can unlock the BitLocker volume and complete the system boot sequence.

Startup Key Only The BitLocker configuration process stores a startup key on a USB flash drive, which the administrator must insert each time the system boots. This mode does not require the server to have a TPM chip, but it must have a system BIOS that supports access to the USB flash drive before the operating system loads.

TPM Only The system stores the BitLocker volume encryption key on the TPM chip, and accesses it automatically when the chip has determined that the boot environment is unmodified. This unlocks the protected volume and the computer continues to boot. No administrative interaction is required during the system boot sequence.

When enabling BitLocker using the BitLocker Drive Encryption control panel, select the TPM + startup key, TPM + startup PIN, or TPM only option. To use the TPM + startup PIN + startup key option, it is necessary to first configure the Require additional authentication at startup Group Policy setting, found in the Computer Configuration\Policies\ Administrative Templates\Windows Components\BitLocker Drive Encryption\Operating System Drives container.

Determine Whether a Computer Has TPM

To find out if a computer has Trusted Platform Module (TPM) security hardware, perform the following steps:

1. Right-click Start and choose Control Panel.

2. Click System and Security ➢ BitLocker Drive Encryption.

3. In the left pane, click TPM Administration. If prompted for an administrator password or confirmation, type the password or provide confirmation.

The TPM Management on Local Computer snap-in indicates whether the computer has the TPM security hardware. See Figure 2.20. If the computer doesn't have it, a removable USB memory device is necessary to turn on BitLocker and store the BitLocker startup key that will be needed whenever you start the computer.

FIGURE 2.20   The TPM Management console

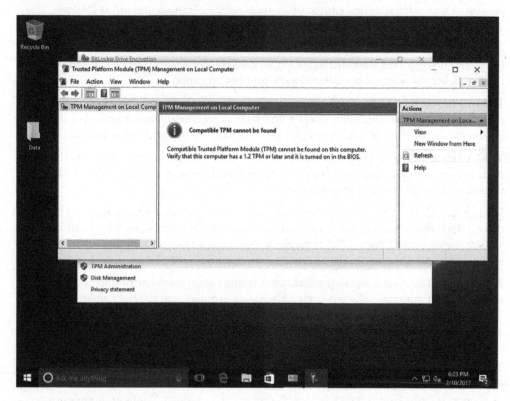

Turn on BitLocker

Log on to Windows 10 using an account with administrative privileges. To turn on BitLocker, perform the following steps:

1. Right-click Start and choose Control Panel.

2. Click System and Security ➤ BitLocker Drive Encryption. The BitLocker Drive Encryption window appears, as shown in Figure 2.21.

3. For the E: drive, click Turn On BitLocker for your hard disk drives. The Set BitLocker Startup Preferences page appears.

FIGURE 2.21   Turning on BitLocker

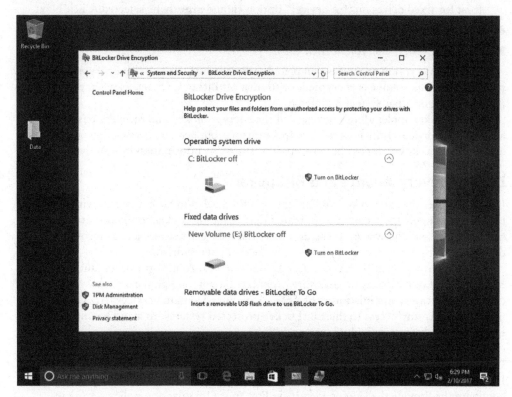

 If a computer has a TPM chip, Windows 10 provides a Trusted Platform Module (TPM) Management console that can be used to change the chip's password and modify its properties.

4. On the "Choose how you want to unlock this drive" page, click the "Use a password to unlock the drive" option. Then, in the Enter Your Password text box and the Reenter Your Password text box, type **Pa$$w0rd**. Click Next.

5. On the "How do you want to back up your recovery key" page, click the "Save to a file" option and click Next. The Save Your Startup Key page appears.

6. In the Save BitLocker recovery key as dialog box, specify the path for the text file, such as **\\LON-DC1\Software**. Then, click Save. Click Next.

7. On the "Choose which encryption mode to use" page, the "New encryption mode (best for fixed drives on this device)" option should already be selected. Click Next.

8. On the "Are you ready to encrypt this drive" page, click Start Encrypting.

9. When the disk is encrypted, click Close.

Once the encryption process is completed, open the BitLocker Drive Encryption window to ensure that the volume is encrypted, or to turn off BitLocker, such as when performing a BIOS upgrade or other system maintenance.

The BitLocker applet allows recovery of the encryption key and recovery password at will. Consider carefully how to store this information, because it will allow access to encrypted data. It is also possible to escrow or store this information into Active Directory.

Data Recovery Agents and BitLocker

If the user loses the startup key and/or startup PIN needed to boot a system with BitLocker, the user can supply the recovery key created during the BitLocker configuration process and gain access to the system. If the user loses the recovery key, use a data recovery agent designated with Active Directory to recover the data on the drive.

A data recovery agent (DRA) is a user account that an administrator has authorized to recover BitLocker drives for an entire organization with a digital certificate on a smart card. In most cases, administrators of Active Directory Domain Services (AD DS) networks use DRAs to ensure access to their BitLocker-protected systems, to avoid having to maintain large numbers of individual keys and PINs.

To create a DRA, first add the user account you want to designate to the Computer Configuration\Policies\Windows Settings\Security Settings\Public Key Policies\BitLocker Drive Encryption container in a GPO or to the system's Local Security Policy. Then, configure the Provide the Unique Identifiers For Your Organization policy setting in the Computer Configuration\Policies\Administrative Templates\Windows Components\ BitLocker Drive Encryption container with unique identification fields for your BitLocker drives.

Finally, enable DRA recovery for each type of BitLocker resource to be recovered by configuring the following policies:

▪   Choose How BitLocker-Protected Operating System Drives Can Be Recovered

▪   Choose How BitLocker-Protected Fixed Drives Can Be Recovered

▪   Choose How BitLocker-Protected Removable Drives Can Be Recovered

These policies enable you to specify how BitLocker systems should store their recovery information and enable you to store it in the AD DS database.

Using BitLocker To Go

BitLocker To Go is a feature introduced with Windows 7 that enables users to encrypt removable USB devices, such as flash drives and external hard disks. While BitLocker has always supported the encryption of removable drives, BitLocker To Go allows use of the encrypted device on other computers without having to perform an involved recovery process. Because the system is not using the removable drive as a boot device, a TPM chip is not required.

To use BitLocker To Go, insert the removable drive and open the BitLocker Drive Encryption window. The device appears in the interface, with a Turn on BitLocker link just like that of the computer's hard disk drive.

Understanding IPsec

IP Security, more commonly known as *IPsec*, is a suite of protocols that provide a mechanism for data integrity, authentication, and privacy for the Internet Protocol. It is used to protect data that is sent between hosts on a network by creating secure electronic tunnels between two machines or devices and it can be used for remote access, VPN, server connections, LAN connections, or WAN connections.

Certification Ready

What technology protects data transmitted on the wire or over the air? Objective 3.3

Certification Ready

What security features does IPsec offer? Objective 3.3

IPsec was designed to provide interoperable, high quality, cryptographically-based security for IPv4 and IPv6, and it provides a comprehensive set of security services, including the following:

- Access control
- Connectionless data integrity checking
- Data origin authentication
- Replay detection and rejection
- Confidentiality using encryption
- Traffic flow confidentiality

IPsec ensures that data cannot be viewed or modified by unauthorized users while being sent to its destination. Before data is sent between two hosts, the source computer encrypts the information by encapsulating each data packet in a new packet that contains the information necessary to set up, maintain, and tear down the tunnel when it is no longer needed. The data is then decrypted at the destination computer.

There are a couple of modes and a couple of protocols available in IPsec, depending on whether they are implemented by the end hosts, such as the server, or implemented on the routers and the desired level of security. IPsec can be used in one of two modes:

Transport Mode (Host-to-Host)   In transport mode, only the data packet payload is encapsulated. Because the packet header is left intact, the original routing information is used to transmit the data from sender to recipient. When used in conjunction with AH, this mode cannot be used in a NAT environment, as the encryption of the header is not compatible with the translated addressing.

Tunnel Mode (Gateway-to-Gateway or Gateway-to-Host)   In the tunnel mode, the IP packet is entirely encapsulated and given a new header. The host/gateway specified in the new IP header decapsulates the packet. This is the mode used to secure traffic for a remote access VPN connection from the remote host to the VPN concentrator on the internal network. This is also the mode used to secure site-to-site IPsec connections.

The IPsec protocols are:

Encapsulating Security Payload (ESP)   Provides confidentiality, authentication, integrity, and anti-replay for the IP payload only, not the entire packet. ESP operates directly on top of IP.

Authentication Header (AH)   Provides authentication, integrity, and anti-replay for the entire packet (both the IP header and the data payload carried in the packet). It does not provide confidentiality, which means that it does not encrypt the payload. The data is readable, but protected from modification. Some fields that are allowed to change in transit are excluded because they need to be modified as they are relayed from router to router. AH operates directly on top of IP.

Internet Key Exchange (IKE)   IKE is used to negotiate, create, and manage security associations (SA), which means that it is the protocol that establishes the secure communication channel between two network hosts.

ESP and AH can be combined to provide authentication, integrity, and anti-replay for the entire packet (both the IP header and the data payload carried in the packet) and confidentiality for the payload.

While AH and ESP provide the means to protect data from tampering, preventing eavesdropping, and verifying the origin of the data, it is the Internet Key Exchange (IKE) that defines the method for the secure exchange of the initial encryption keys between the two endpoints. IKE allows nodes to agree on authentication methods, encryption methods, the keys to use, and the lifespan of the keys.

The information negotiated by IKE is stored in a Security Association (SA). An SA is like a contract laying out the rules of the VPN connection for the duration of the SA. An SA is assigned a 32-bit number that, when used in conjunction with the destination IP address, uniquely identifies the SA. This number is called Security Parameters Index (SPI).

In order for IPsec to work in conjunction with NAT, the following protocols need to be allowed across the firewall:

Internet Key Exchange (IKE)   User Datagram Protocol (UDP) port 500

Encapsulating Security Payload (ESP)   IP protocol number 50

Authentication Header (AH)   IP protocol number 51

IPsec can be used with Windows in various ways. To enable IPsec communications for a Windows Server 2008 or higher computer, create group policies and assign them to individual computers or groups of computers. You can also use the Windows Firewall with Advanced Security.

Encrypting with VPN Technology

Today, it is very common for an organization to use remote access server (RAS), which enables users to connect remotely using various protocols and connection types. By connecting to RAS over the Internet, users can connect to their organization's network so that they can access data files, read email, and access other applications just as if they were sitting at work. Because the Internet is considered an insecure medium, encryption must be used to secure the data.

A *virtual private network (VPN)* links two computers through a wide-area network, such as the Internet. To keep the connection secure, the data sent between the two computers is encapsulated and encrypted. In one scenario, a client connects to the RAS server to access internal resources from offsite. Another scenario is to connect one RAS server on one site or organization to another RAS server on another site or organization so that the site or organizations can communicate with each other.

The three types of tunneling protocols used with a VPN server/RAS server running on Windows Server 2008 R2 include:

Point-to-Point Tunneling Protocol (PPTP)   A VPN protocol based on the legacy Point-to-Point protocol used with modems. Although PPTP is easy to set up, it is considered weak encryption technology.

Layer 2 Tunneling Protocol (L2TP)   Used with IPsec to provide security. It is the industry standard when setting up secure tunnels.

Secure Socket Tunneling Protocol (SSTP)   Introduced with Windows Server 2008, which uses the HTTPS protocol over TCP port 443 to pass traffic through firewalls and web proxies that might block PPTP and L2TP/IPsec.

IKEv2 (Short for Internet Key Exchange Version 2)   This protocol uses IPsec for encryption while supporting VPN Reconnect (also called Mobility), which enables VPN connections to be maintained when a VPN client moves between wireless cells or switches, and to automatically reestablish broken VPN connectivity. Different from L2TP with IPsec, IKEv2 client computers do not need to provide authentication through a machine certificate or a pre-shared key.

When using VPNs, Windows 10 and Windows Server 2016 support the following forms of authentication:

Password Authentication Protocol (PAP)   Uses plain text (unencrypted passwords). PAP is the least secure authentication and is not recommended.

Challenge Handshake Authentication Protocol (CHAP)   A challenge-response authentication that uses the industry standard md5 hashing scheme to encrypt the response. CHAP was an industry standard for years and is still quite popular.

Microsoft CHAP Version 2 (MS-CHAP v2)   Provides two-way authentication (mutual authentication). MS-CHAP v2 provides stronger security than CHAP.

Extensible Authentication Protocol (EAP)   EAP is a universal authentication framework that allows third-party vendors to develop custom authentication schemes, including retinal scans, voice recognition, fingerprint identification, smart cards, Kerberos, and digital certificates. It also provides a mutual authentication method that supports password-based user or computer authentication.

Create a VPN Tunnel

To create a VPN tunnel on a computer running Windows 10 so that you can connect to a Remote Access Server, perform the following steps:

1. In Control Panel, click Network and Internet ➢ Network And Sharing Center.
2. Click "Set up a new connection or network."
3. In the Set Up A Connection Or Network window, click "Connect to a workplace" and click Next.
4. In the Connect To A Workplace window, click Use My Internet connection (VPN).
5. On the next screen (see Figure 2.22), select your VPN connection or specify the Internet address for the VPN server and a Destination name. Optionally, select the Use A Smart Card, Remember My Credentials, and "Allow other people to use this connection" check boxes.

FIGURE 2.22   Setting up a VPN connection

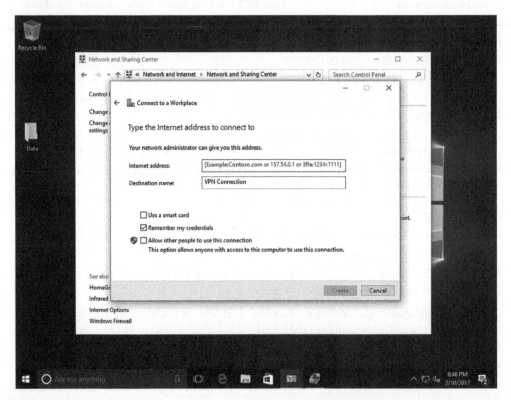

Often, additional configuration of your VPN connection may be needed, such as specifying the type of protocol, which authentication protocol to use, and the type of encryption.

When the VPN connection is created and configured to connect using the VPN, open the Network and Sharing Center and click "Change adapter settings." Then, right-click the VPN connection and choose Connect to open the Connect to a Workplace dialog box, as shown in Figure 2.23.

FIGURE 2.23   Connecting to a VPN

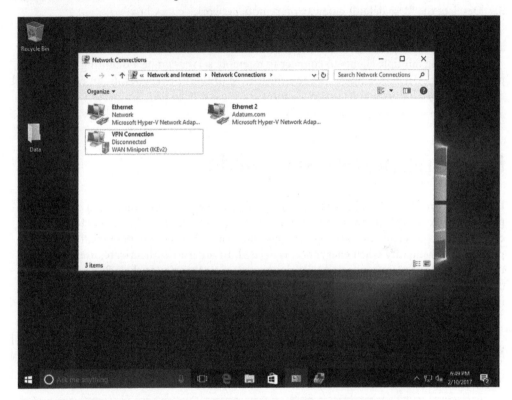

Another method for Windows 10 is to right-click the network status icon on the taskbar and choose the VPN connection. In the Settings window, click the VPN connection and click Connect.

By default, when connecting to a VPN using the previous configuration, all web browsing and network traffic go through the default gateway on the Remote Network unless you are communicating with local home computers. Having this option enabled helps protect the corporate network, because all traffic will also go through firewalls and proxy servers and help prevent a network from being infected or compromised.

To route your browsing through a home Internet connection rather than going through the corporate network, disable the "Use default gateway on remote network" option. When disabling this option, it is called using split tunnel.

Enable Split Tunneling

To enable split tunneling, perform the following steps:

1. Right-click a VPN connection and choose Properties.

2. Click the Networking tab.

3. Double-click Internet Protocol Version 4 (TCP/IPv4).

4. Click the Advanced button.

5. Deselect the "Use default gateway on remote network" check box.

It can be a lot of work to configure multiple clients to connect to a remote access server and may be too complicated for a computer novice.

Configuring multiple clients to connect to a remote server can be a daunting task that is prone to errors. To help simplify the administration of the VPN client into an easy to install executable, use Connection Manager Administration Kit (CMAK). To install CMAK on Windows Server 2016, install it as a feature.

Introducing Smart Cards

Used with a smart card reader attached to a computer, smart cards contain an embedded processor that is used to communicate with the host computer and the card reader. They can be used to authenticate users, ensure data integrity when signing documents, and provide confidentiality when encryption is needed. In order to authenticate, users insert their cards into readers connected to their computers and then type their PINs. The smart card holds the user's logon information, private key, digital certificate, and other private information.

Certification Ready

How does virtual smart card resemble a physical smart card? Objective 2.1

To deploy smart cards, it is necessary to use a public key infrastructure (PKI), which includes digital certificates, CAs, and other components that are used to create, distribute, validate, and revoke certificates. Smart cards can be credit card–sized devices or a token style (USB) device. Information stored on the cards cannot be extracted from the device— all communication with the card is encrypted to protect against malicious software intercepting it, and brute force attempts to hack the PIN will result in the card being blocked until an administrator can unlock it. Because both the smart card and a PIN are required, it is much less likely that someone will be able to steal both.

Windows 8 introduced *virtual smart cards (VSCs)*, which make additional hardware (smart card readers and smart cards) unnecessary. These cards emulate the functionality of regular smart cards, but require a *Trusted Platform Module (TPM) chip*—an international standard for a secure cryptoprocessor—to protect the private keys. The TPM is used to encrypt the information, which is then stored on the computer's hard drive. If the user needs to access multiple computers using the VSC, the user will need a new VSC for each system.

It is also possible to use multiple VSCs (one for each user) on multi-use computers. If a computer is lost or stolen, the user can contact an administrator, who can revoke the certificate associated with the VSC on the user's computer.

Set Up a Virtual TPM Smart Card Environment

To set up a virtual TPM smart card environment, you must have a computer running Windows 10 (TPM supported), you must be connected to a domain, and you must have access to a domain server with a functional CA in place. Perform the following steps:

1. Create a certificate template (on the domain controller). This is the certificate that will be requested in Step 3 on the client.
2. Create the VSC on the Windows 10 client machine using the TPM VSC Manager and then type a PIN.
3. Use the Certificate console on the Windows 10 client machine to request a new certificate and then select the certificate that was created in Step 1.

After these steps are completed, use the VSC the next time you boot your system.

For authentication, virtual smart cards use two-factor authentication. The user must have the computer with the virtual smart card and the user must know the PIN associated with the smart card.

Besides the TPM chip, the computer must be running Windows 8 or higher, must be part of the domain, and must have access to the certificate authority (CA). Then, follow these steps:

1. Create the certificate template, which is based on the Smartcard Logon.
2. Create the TPM virtual smart card.
3. Enroll the certificate on the TPM virtual smart card.

Create a Certificate Template

To create a certificate template on the Certificate Authority, perform the following steps:

1. On LON-DC1, click Start and type **mmc** to open the Microsoft Management Console (MMC).
2. Click File ➤ Add/Remove Snap-in.
3. In the available snap-ins list, double-click Certificate Templates and click OK.
4. Double-click Certificate Templates to view all available certificate templates.
5. Right-click the Smartcard Logon template and choose Duplicate Template.

6. On the Compatibility tab, under Certification Authority, click Windows Server 2003.

7. On the General tab, specify the following:

   ▪ For the name, type **TPM Virtual Smart Card Logon.**

   ▪ Set the validity period to the desired value.

8. On the Request Handling tab, set the Purpose to "Signature and smartcard logon." Click "Prompt the user during enrollment."

9. On the Cryptography tab, set the minimum key size to 2048. Click "Requests must use one of the following providers" and select the Microsoft Base Smart Card Crypto Provider check box.

10. On the Security tab, add the security group to which you want to provide enroll access. If you want to give access to all users, select the Authenticated users group and give them Enroll permissions.

11. Click OK to close the Properties Of New Template dialog box.

12. Using Server Manager, click Tools ➤ Certificate Authority.

13. In the left pane of the MMC, expand Certification Authority (Local), and then expand your CA within the Certification Authority list.

14. Right-click Certificate Templates and choose New ➤ Certificate Template To Issue.

15. From the list, select TPM Virtual Smart Card Logon and click OK.

Create a TPM Virtual Smart Card

To create a TPM virtual smart card on a domain-joined computer running Windows 10, perform the following steps:

1. On LON-DC1, open a command shell with administrative privileges.

2. At the command prompt, execute the following command:

   ```
   tpmvscmgr.exe create /name tpmvsc /pin default /adminkey random /generate
   ```

3. When prompted for a PIN, type a PIN that is at least eight characters in length and then confirm it.

4. Wait several seconds for the process to finish.

   Upon completion, tpmvscmgr.exe will provide the device instance ID for the TPM VSC. Store this ID for later reference; it will be needed to manage or remove the VSC.

Enroll for the Certificate on the TPM Virtual Smart Card

To enroll for the certificate on the TPM virtual smart card on the domain-joined computer running Windows 10, perform the following steps:

1. On LON-DC1, click Start and type **certmgr.msc** to open the Certificates console.

2. Right-click Personal and choose All Tasks ➤ Request New Certificate.

3. On the Before You Begin page, click Next.

4. On the Select Certificate Enrollment Policy page, click Next.

5. On the Request Certificates page, select TPM Virtual Smart Card Logon and click Enroll.

6. If prompted for a device, select Microsoft Virtual Smart Card.

7. Type the PIN for the TPM smart card that you entered when creating the VSC and click OK.

8. Wait for the enrollment to finish and then click Finish.

Configuring Biometrics, Windows Hello, and Microsoft Passport

In the past, administrators had to struggle with managing third-party software and hardware to support biometrics. With each vendor providing different drivers, software, and management tools, it became very labor-intensive to support. Fortunately, Microsoft introduced native support for biometric technologies through its *Windows Biometric Framework (WBF)*. WBF enables users to manage device settings for biometric devices through Control Panel, provides support for managing device drivers, and manages Group Policy settings that can be used to enable, disable, or limit use of biometric data for a local computer or domain.

Certification Ready

Describe what is meant by biometrics. Objective 2.1

A fingerprint reader is the most commonly used biometric device in corporate networks. These devices can be purchased separately or can be built in to new laptops. The reader captures an image of your fingerprint and then saves it to the computer. This process is called enrolling. When you log on, the reader scans your fingerprint and compares it to the fingerprint on file.

Windows Hello is a Windows 10 biometric authentication system that uses a user's face, iris, or fingerprint to unlock devices. To use Windows Hello, specialized hardware is needed, including a fingerprint reader, illuminated infrared (IR) sensor, or other biometric sensors. Windows Hello will not work with an ordinary webcam, but it will work with an existing fingerprint sensor.

Set Up Windows Hello Facial Recognition

To set up Windows Hello facial recognition on a computer running Windows 10, perform the following steps:

1. On LON-CL1, click Start ➤ Settings.

2. Click Accounts.

3. Click Sign-in Options.

4. Under Windows Hello, select the Infrared IR Camera option. If a Windows Hello section is not shown, you do not have compatible hardware.

5. On the Welcome to Windows Hello page, click the Get Started button.

6. Set up a PIN code if prompted to do so.

7. To scan your face, for best results, hold your face six to eight inches away from the front of the camera.

8. Click Finish to complete scanning or click Improve Recognition to continue scanning.

Set Up Windows Hello Fingerprint Reader

To set up a Windows Hello fingerprint reader on a computer running Windows 10, perform the following steps:

1. On LON-CL1, click Start ➤ Settings.

2. Click Accounts.

3. Click Sign-in Options.

4. Under Windows Hello, select the Fingerprint option and click Set Up. If a Windows Hello section is not shown, you do not have compatible hardware.

5. On the Welcome To Windows Hello page, click the Get Started button.

6. Repeatedly place your preferred finger on the fingerprint ID sensor on your type cover. The system will tell you when setup is complete. You can set up multiple fingers to be read by the scanner.

7. Click Finish to complete scanning.

   Microsoft Passport is a two-factor authentication that consists of an enrolled device (such as a smartphone) and a Windows Hello (biometric) or PIN. The two factors are an encrypted key stored on the device combined with Windows Hello or a PIN. Microsoft Passport lets users authenticate to a Microsoft account, an Active Directory account, a Microsoft Azure Active Directory (AD) account, or a non-Microsoft service that supports Fast ID Online (FIDO) authentication.

Don't confuse Microsoft Passport used with Windows 10 with the Microsoft Account, which was previously known as Microsoft Passport. Microsoft Account is a single sign-on web server developed and provided by Microsoft that allows users to log on to websites, devices, and applications using one account. It is also known as .NET Passport, Microsoft Passport Network, or Windows Live ID.

To implement Microsoft Passport, one of the following is needed:

- Microsoft account
- Azure Active Directory
- Windows Server 2016 Active Directory

To implement Microsoft Passport using a Microsoft account, perform the following steps:

1. Log on with a Microsoft account on a computer running Windows 10.
2. Configure a PIN or Windows Hello.

After performing the initial two-step verification during Microsoft Passport enrollment, a Microsoft Passport is set up on the user's device and the user gets a gesture, which can be Windows Hello or a PIN.

To implement Microsoft Password in your organization, create a Group Policy that will implement Microsoft Passport on devices running Windows 10. The GPO settings are located at:

Computer Configuration ➢ Policies ➢ Administrative Templates ➢ Windows Components ➢ Microsoft Passport For Work

Using Auditing to Complete the Security Picture

As mentioned before, security can be divided into three areas. Authentication is used to prove the identity of a user while authorization gives access to the user that was authenticated. To complete the security picture, enable auditing so that you can have a record of the users who have logged on and what the users accessed or tried to access.

Certification Ready

Explain why auditing is so important to security. Objective 2.4

It is important to protect your information and service resources from people who should not have access to them and at the same time make those resources available to authorized users. Along with authentication and authorization, enable auditing so that you can have a record of the following:

- Who has successfully logged on
- Who has attempted to log on, but failed
- Who has changed accounts in Active Directory
- Who has accessed or changed certain files
- Who has used a certain printer
- Who restarted a system
- Who has made some system changes

In Windows, auditing is not enabled by default. To enable auditing, specify what types of system events to audit using group policies or the local security policy (Security Settings\ Local Policies\Audit Policy). See Figure 2.24. Table 2.3 shows the basic events to audit that are available in Windows Server 2016. Windows Server 2008 and higher have additional options for more granular control. After you enable logging, open the Event Viewer security logs to view the security events. By default, the security logs can only be seen and managed by the Administrators group.

FIGURE 2.24 Enabling auditing using group policies

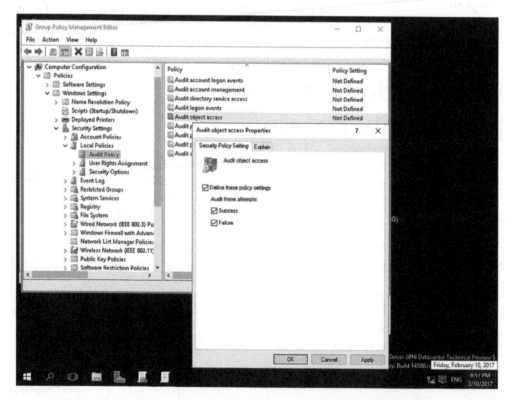

TABLE 2.3 Audit Events

Event	Explanation
Account Logon	Determines whether the OS audits each time the computer validates an account's credentials, such as account logon.
Account Management	Determines whether to audit each event of account management on a computer, including changing passwords, and creating or deleting user accounts.
Directory Service Access	Determines whether the OS audits user attempts to access Active Directory objects.
Logon	Determines where the OS audits each instance of a user attempting to log on, or log off, her computer.
Object Access	Determines whether the OS audits user attempts to access non–Active Directory objects, including NTFS files and folders and printers.
Policy Change	Determines whether the OS audits each instance of attempts to change user rights assignments, auditing policy, account policy, or trust policy.
Privilege Use	Determines whether to audit each instance of a user exercising a user right.
Process Tracking	Determines whether the OS audits process-related events, such as process creation, process termination, handle duplication, and indirect object access. This is usually used for troubleshooting.
System	Determines whether the OS audits if the system time is changed, system startup or shutdown, attempts to load extensible authentication components, loss of auditing events due to auditing system failure, and security logs exceeding a configurable warning threshold level.

Auditing NTFS files, NTFS folders, and printers is a two-step process. First, enable Object Access using group policies. Then, specify which files or folders you want to audit or which printer you want to audit. After you enable logging, open the Event Viewer security logs to view the security events.

Because Windows is only part of what makes up a network, also look at other areas to audit. For Microsoft's web server, IIS, enable logging of who visits each site. For Microsoft's Internet Security and Acceleration (ISA) and Microsoft's Threat Management Gateway (TMG) servers, enable logging to record who accesses your network through a VPN or what is accessed through the firewall. If your company has Cisco routers and firewalls, enable auditing so that if someone reconfigures the router and firewall, there is a record of it.

To audit non-Microsoft products, it might be necessary to use Syslog. *Syslog* is a standard for logging program messages that can be accessed by devices that would not otherwise have a method for communications. For example, Cisco firewalls and routers, computers running Linux and UNIX, and many printers can use Syslog. Syslog can be used for computer system management and security auditing as well as generalized informational, analysis, and debugging messages.

Lastly, make sure there is a change management system and a ticket system. A change management system will record what changes are made. It gives the IT department a method to review the changes before they are implemented so that if the change could cause problems with a system, it can be raised as a concern. In addition, if a problem does occur, all the changes made to your environment will be listed in a single place.

The ticket system will provide a record of all problems and requests by users. A ticket system helps to determine the most common problems and identify trends.

Audit Files and Folders

Assuming object auditing has been enabled, to audit files and folders, perform the following steps:

1. Open File Explorer.

2. Right-click the file or folder that you want to audit, choose Properties, and then click the Security tab.

3. Click Advanced.

4. In the Advanced Security Settings For *<object>* dialog box, click the Auditing tab.

5. Do one of the following:

   ▪ To set up auditing for a new user or group, click Add. In the Enter the object name to select box, type the name of the user or group and click OK.

   ▪ To remove auditing for an existing group or user, click the group or user name, click Remove, click OK, and then skip the rest of this procedure.

   ▪ To view or change auditing for an existing group or user, click its name and click Edit.

6. In the Apply Onto box, click the location where auditing should take place.

7. In the Access box, indicate what actions should be audited by selecting the appropriate check boxes:

   ▪ To audit successful events, select the Successful check box.

   ▪ To stop auditing successful events, clear the Successful check box.

   ▪ To audit unsuccessful events, select the Failed check box.

   ▪ To stop auditing unsuccessful events, clear the Failed check box.

   ▪ To stop auditing all events, click Clear All.

8. If you want to prevent subsequent files and subfolders of the original object from inheriting these audit entries, select the "Apply these auditing entries to objects and/or containers within this container only" check box.

9. Click OK to close the Advanced Security Settings dialog box.

10. Click OK to close the Properties dialog box.

Understanding Dynamic Access Control

An advantage of Windows Server 2016 and Windows 10 is that they have the ability to apply data governance to their file servers. This helps control who has access to information and auditing with the use of Dynamic Access Control (DAC).

DAC provides:

- An administrator to identify data by using data classifications either automatic or manual and then control access to these files based upon these classifications.

- An administrators with the ability to control file access by using a central access policy, which allows them to set up audit access to files for reporting and forensics investigations.

- An administrator to set up Active Directory Rights Management Service (AD RMS) encryption for Microsoft Office documents.

- An administrator has the flexibility to configure file access and auditing to domain-based file servers. The DAC controls claims in the authentication token, resource properties, and conditional expressions within permission and auditing entries.

- An administrator has the ability to give users access to files and folders based on Active Directory attributes.

Securing Access to Files and Folders

On NTFS partitions, an administrator can specify the access each user has to specific folders or files on the partition based on the user's logon name and group associations.

Access control consists of rights and permissions. The owner of an object or any user who has the necessary rights to modify the permissions can apply permissions to NTFS objects. If permissions are not explicitly granted within NTFS, then they are implicitly denied. Permissions can also be explicitly denied; explicit denials override explicitly granted permissions.

Skill Summary

In this lesson, you learned:

- In security, AAA (Authentication, Authorization, and Accounting) is a model for access control.

- Authentication is the process of identifying an individual.

- After a user is authenticated, users can access network resources based on the user's authorization. Authorization is the process of giving individuals access to system objects based on their identity.

- Accounting, also known as auditing, is the process of keeping track of a user's activity while accessing the network resources, including the amount of time spent on the network, the services accessed while there, and the amount of data transferred during the session.

- Nonrepudiation prevents one party from denying actions they carried out.

- A user can authenticate using what they know, what they own or possess, and who they are.

- When two or more authentication methods are used to authenticate someone, a multi-factor authentication system is being implemented.

- The most common method of authentication with computers and networks is the password.

- A password is a secret series of characters that enables a user to access a file, computer, or program.

- To hack a password, users will try obvious passwords, brute force attacks, and dictionary attacks.

- To make a password more secure, be sure to choose a password that nobody can guess. Therefore, it should be lengthy and should be considered a strong or complex password.

- A personal identification number (PIN) is a secret numeric password shared between a user and a system that can be used to authenticate the user to the system.

- The digital certificate is an electronic document that contains an identity such as a user or organization and a corresponding public key.

- A smart card is a pocket-sized card with embedded integrated circuits consisting of non-volatile memory storage components and perhaps dedicated security logic.

- A smart card can contain digital certificates to prove the identity of someone carrying the card and may also contain permissions and access information.

- Biometrics is an authentication method that identifies and recognizes people based on voice recognition or physical traits such as a fingerprint, face recognition, iris recognition, and retina scan.

- Because administrators have full access to a computer or the network, it is recommended that a standard non-administrator user should perform most tasks.

- Active Directory is a technology created by Microsoft that provides a variety of network services, including LDAP, Kerberos-based and single sign-on authentication, DNS-based naming and other network information, and central location for network administration and delegation of authority.

- Kerberos is the default computer network authentication protocol, which allows hosts to prove their identity over a non-secure network in a secure manner.

- Single sign-on (SSO) allows a user to log on once and access multiple, related, but independent software systems without having to log on again.
- A user account enables a user to log on to a computer and domain.
- The local user account is stored in the Security Account Manager (SAM) database on the local computer.
- A group is much like it sounds; it is used to group users and computers together so that when rights and permissions are assigned, they are assigned to the group rather than to each user individually.
- A right authorizes a user to perform certain actions on a computer, such as logging on to a system interactively or backing up files and directories on a system.
- A permission defines the type of access that is granted to an object (an object can be identified with a security identifier) or object attribute.
- Explicit permissions are permissions granted directly to the file or folder.
- Inherited permissions are permissions that are granted to a folder (parent object or container) that flow into child objects (subfolders or files inside the parent folder).
- The owner of the object controls how permissions are set on the object and to whom permissions are granted.
- Encryption is the process of converting data into a format that cannot be read by another user. Once a user has encrypted a file, it automatically remains encrypted when the file is stored on disk.
- Decryption is the process of converting data from encrypted format back to its original format.
- Encryption algorithms can be divided into three classes: Symmetric, Asymmetric, and Hash function.
- Symmetric encryption uses a single key to encrypt and decrypt data. Therefore, it is also referred to as secret-key, single-key, shared-key, and private-key encryption.
- Asymmetric encryption, also known as public key cryptography, uses two mathematically related keys. One key is used to encrypt the data, while the second key is used to decrypt the data.
- Different from the symmetric and asymmetric algorithms, a hash function is meant as a one-way encryption. This means that after it has been encrypted, it cannot be decrypted.
- A public key infrastructure (PKI) is a system consisting of hardware, software, policies, and procedures that create, manage, distribute, use, store, and revoke digital certificates.
- The most common digital certificate is the X.509 version 3.
- The certificate chain, also known as the certification path, is a list of certificates used to authenticate an entity. It begins with the certificate of the entity and ends with the root CA certificate.

- A digital signature is a mathematical scheme that is used to demonstrate the authenticity of a digital message or document. It is also used to confirm that the message or document has not been modified.

- When surfing the Internet and needing to transmit private data over the Internet, use SSL over HTTPS (HTTPS) to encrypt the data sent over the Internet. By convention, URLs that require an SSL connection start with https: instead of http:.

- IP Security, more commonly known as IPsec, is a suite of protocols that provide a mechanism for data integrity, authentication, and privacy for the Internet Protocol.

- Virtual private network (VPN) links two computers through a wide-area network, such as the Internet.

- Windows Hello is a Windows 10 biometric authentication system that uses a user's face, iris, or fingerprint to unlock devices.

- Syslog is a standard for logging program messages that can be accessed by devices that would not otherwise have a method for communications.

Knowledge Assessment

Multiple Choice

1. Which of the following is not a method for authentication?
   A. Something the user knows
   B. Something the user owns or possesses
   C. Encryption
   D. Something a user is

2. Which of the following would not be a biometric device?
   A. Password reader
   B. Retina scanner
   C. Fingerprint scanner
   D. Face scanning

3. Which service is used for centralized authentication, authorization, and accounting?
   A. VPN
   B. PGP
   C. RADIUS
   D. PKI

4. Which of the following is the primary authentication used on Microsoft Active Directory?
   A. LDAP
   B. Kerberos
   C. NTLAN
   D. SSO

5. Which of the following is the master time keeper and master for password changes in an Active Directory domain?
   A. PDC Emulator
   B. RID
   C. Infrastructure master
   D. Schema master

6. Local user accounts are found in which of the following?
   A. Active Directory
   B. Registry
   C. SAM
   D. LDAP

7. Which of the following authorizes a user to perform certain actions on a computer?
  A. Permissions
  B. An encryption algorithm
  C. Authentication protocol
  D. A right

8. Which file system offers the best security?
  A. FAT
  B. FAT32
  C. NTFS
  D. EFS

9. Which NTFS permission is needed to change attributes and permissions?
  A. Full Control
  B. Modify
  C. Read & Execute
  D. Write

10. Which permission is granted directly to the file or folder?
  A. Explicit
  B. Inherited
  C. Effective
  D. Share

11. When copying a file or folder to a new volume, which permissions are acquired?
  A. The same permissions that it had before
  B. The same permissions as the target folder
  C. The same permissions as the source folder
  D. No permissions

12. Which of the following uses an ACL? (Choose all that apply.)
  A. NTFS folder
  B. Active Directory user
  C. Registry key
  D. Logon rights

13. Which type of key has one key for encryption and a different key for decryption?
  A. Symmetric
  B. Asymmetric
  C. Hash function
  D. PKI

14. Which infrastructure is used to assign and validate digital certificates?

    A. Asymmetric algorithm

    B. Active Directory

    C. PKI

    D. VPN

15. Which technology is used to encrypt an individual file on an NTFS volume?

    A. BitLocker

    B. BitLocker To Go

    C. PPTP

    D. EFS

16. Which physical device is used to authenticate users based on what a user has?

    A. Smart card

    B. Windows Hello

    C. Universal Windows Platform

    D. Device Guard

17. Which of the following is a two-factor authentication that uses an enrolled device and Windows Hello?

    A. Device Guard

    B. Credential Guard

    C. Virtual secure mode

    D. Microsoft Passport

Fill in the Blank

1. A(n) _____ is a secret numeric password shared between a user and a system that can be used to authenticate the user to the system.

2. A pocket-sized card with embedded integrated circuits used for authentication is known as a(n) _____.

3. A device that may provide a second password to log on to a system is a(n) _____.

4. The _____ holds a copy of the centralized database used in Active Directory.

5. By default, a computer clock should not be off more than _____ minutes or there might be problems with Kerberos authentication.

6. A(n) _____ defines the type of access over an object or the properties of an object such as an NTFS file or printer.

7. The _____ permissions flow from the parent object to the child object.

8. When a folder cannot be accessed because someone removed the permissions so that no one can access it, it is necessary to take _____ of the folder.

9. The centralized database that holds most of the Windows configurations is known as the _____.

10. To track a user's activities in Windows, it is necessary to enable _____.

Business Case Scenarios

Scenario 2-1: Understanding Biometrics

As an IT administrator for the Contoso Corporation, your CIO wants you to investigate the corporation using biometrics. The CIO understands what biometrics is and how it can be used. But he does not understand the disadvantages of using biometrics. Describe your recommended solution.

Scenario 2-2: Limiting Auditing

As an IT administrator for the Contoso Corporation, your CIO needs to know when a particular user accessed a folder. However, the information was not available because auditing was not enabled. To ensure that this does not happen in the future, the CIO asks you to enable auditing for everything. Describe your recommended solution.

Scenario 2-3: Assigning NTFS Permissions

As an IT administrator for the Contoso Corporation, you are tasked with assigning NTFS permissions. You will need to log on as an administrator on a computer running Windows 10. Create a group called Managers on your computer. Create a user account called JSmith and assign it to the Managers group. Create another user account called JHamid. Create a folder called SharedTest. Create a text file called test.txt in the SharedTest folder. Share the folder. Assign Allow Full Control to Everyone, and assign Read & Execute to the Managers group. Log on as JHamid and try to access the \\localhost\SharedTest folder. Log on as JSmith and try to access the \\localhost\SharedTest folder. Describe the step-by-step procedure for assigning NTFS permissions.

Scenario 2-4: Using EFS

In this exercise, you will describe how to use EFS. Add JHamid to the Managers group. Log on as JSmith. Encrypt the test.txt file with EFS. Log on as JHamid and try to access the test.txt file.

Real World Scenario

Workplace Ready: Planning and Maintaining Security

When planning security, you need to consider the big picture. Security must be planned from the beginning. Therefore, define what the goals of the security need to be, determine what effect it will have on current access and network applications, and look at how it will affect the users. After security is implemented, maintain it by constantly monitoring the security of the system, making changes as needed, patching security holes, and constantly reviewing the security logs.

Lesson 3

Understanding Security Policies

Lesson Skill Matrix

Technology Skill	Objective Domain Description	Objective Domain Number
Using Password Policies to Enhance Security	Understand password policies	2.3
Protecting Domain User Account Passwords	Understand password policies	2.3

Key Terms

acceptable use policy

account lockout

cracked password

Credential Guard

Device Guard

fine-grained password policies

Group Policy Object (GPO)

password policy

Password Settings Object (PSO)

security policy

sniffers

strong passwords

virtual secure mode (VSM)

 Real World Scenario

Lesson 3 Case

One of the foundations of information security is the protection of networks, systems, and most important of all, data. At the foundation of all information security policies, procedures, and processes is the need to protect data.

At the foundation of much of today's data protection is the password. Think about your life. Passwords are used to secure voice mail, ATM access, an email account, a Facebook account, and a host of other things. In order to keep these accounts secure, it is important to select strong passwords. In this lesson, we will be discussing what goes into creating a strong password and how to configure password settings to ensure that passwords in an environment stay secure.

Let's take a minute and think about a specific instance where a strong password is critical. A good example is an ATM password—that's the password (or PIN) that is needed to keep someone from using your ATM card to steal your money.

Using Password Policies to Enhance Security

There are a variety of configuration settings that can be used on systems to ensure that users are required to set and maintain strong passwords. As hard as it can be to believe, left to their own devices, many users will still select weak passwords when securing their accounts. With user education and system controls, users can reduce the risk of weak passwords compromising their applications.

Certification Ready

How can a company enforce the use of stronger passwords? Objective 2.3

A basic component of an information security program is ensuring that employees select and use *strong passwords*. The strength of a password can be determined by examining the length, complexity, and randomness of the password.

Microsoft provides several controls that can be used to ensure the security associated with passwords is maintained. These include:

- Password complexity
- Account lockout
- Password length
- Password history
- Time between password changes
- Group Policies that enforce password security
- Education on common attack methods

Using Password Complexity to Make a Stronger Password

Password complexity deals with the characters used to make up the password. A complex password will use characters from at least three of the following categories:

- English uppercase characters (A through Z)
- English lowercase characters (a through z)
- Numeric characters (0 through 9)
- Non-alphanumeric characters (such as !, @, #, $, %, ^, &)

Microsoft's password complexity settings, when enabled, require characters from three of these categories by default on domain controllers, and the domain can be configured to require this setting for all passwords.

The password complexity settings can be either enabled or disabled. There are no additional configurations available.

There is one very important thing to be aware of when enforcing password complexity. It is not a guarantee that users will not still use easily guessable passwords. The password "Summer2010" meets the current complexity guidelines required by the Windows password complexity setting. It's also a terrible password, because it is very easily guessable and memorable should someone only catch a quick glimpse of it.

Some password selection methods that should be avoided include words that can be found in a dictionary, derivatives of user IDs, and common character sequences such as "123456" or "QWERTY." Likewise, personal details such as a spouse's name, license plate, Social Security number, and birthday should be avoided. Finally, avoid passwords that are based on proper names, geographical locations, common acronyms, and slang terms.

Some methods for selecting strong passwords include:

- Bump characters in a word a certain number of letters up or down the alphabet. A shift three letters translation of "AArdvark!!" becomes "DDvgzdvn!!"

- Create acronyms from words in a song, a poem, or another known sequence of words. The phrase "Ask not what you can do for your country?" yields the password "Anwycdfyc?" Add $$ to arrive at the strong password $$Anwycdfyc?

- Combine a number of personal facts like birthdates and favorite colors, foods, and so on, with special characters to create passwords like: "##Yell0w419" or "$^327p!zZ@"

> One of the easiest ways to set a complex password is to start with a dictionary word and use character substitution to make it complex. For example, *computer* becomes C0mput3r. However, be sure to not use words that are easy to guess—like *computer*!

Using Account Lockout to Prevent Hacking

Account lockout refers to the number of incorrect logon attempts permitted before the system will lock the account. Each bad logon attempt increments the bad logon counter, and when the counter exceeds the account lockout threshold, no further logon attempts will be permitted.

This setting is critical because one of the most common password attacks (discussed later in the lesson) involves repeatedly attempting to logon with guessed passwords. Microsoft provides three separate settings with respect to account lockout:

Account Lockout Duration   This setting determines the length of time a lockout will remain in place before another logon attempt can be made. This can be set from 0 to 99,999 minutes. If set to 0, an administrator will need to manually unlock the account; no automatic unlocking will occur.

Account Lockout Threshold   This setting determines the number of failed logons permitted before the account lockout occurs. This can be set from 0 (no account lockouts) to 999 attempts before lockout.

Reset account lockout counter after: This setting determines the period of time, in minutes, that must elapse before the account lockout counter is reset to 0 bad logon attempts. If an account lockout threshold is set, the reset account lockout threshold must be less than or equal to the account lockout duration.

Commonly, account lockout settings range from 3 to 10 attempts, with the account lockout duration setting and the reset account lockout counter after setting usually set anywhere from 30 to 60 minutes. While some users complain when they don't get as many attempts to log on as they can use, this is a critical configuration to set to ensure that an environment remains secure.

Examining Password Length

The length of a password is a key component of ensuring the strength of a password. Password length is the number of characters used in a password. A password with 2 characters is considered very insecure, because there is a very limited set of unique passwords that can be made using 2 characters. A 2- character password is considered trivial to guess.

On the other side of the spectrum is the 14-character password. While extremely secure relative to a 2-character password, a 14-character password is very difficult for most users to remember. This is when they generally start breaking out the note paper and writing the passwords down, defeating any security benefits that might have been gained from requiring a 14-character password in the first place.

The trick to setting a minimum password length is balancing usability with security. Microsoft permits setting a minimum password length ranging from 1 to 14 characters (a setting of 0 means no password is required, which is never the appropriate setting in a production environment). The generally accepted minimum password length is 8 characters.

Using Password History to Enforce Security

Password history is the setting that determines the number of unique passwords that must be used before a password can be reused. This setting prevents the recycling of the same passwords through a system. The longer the period of time a password is used, the greater the chance it can be compromised.

Microsoft allows a password history setting between 0 and 24. A fairly common setting in standard environments is 10, although Windows Server 2008 and higher defaults to 24 for domain controllers and domain member computers.

Setting Time Between Password Changes

The final password setting to be aware of is the time between password changes. Two settings are available:

Minimum Password Age   The minimum password age setting controls how many days a user must wait before they can reset their password. This can be set to a value from 1 to 998 days. If set to 0, passwords can be changed immediately. Using a setting that is too low could allow users to defeat the password history settings. For example, if this is set to 0 and the password history is set to 10, all a user would need to do is reset their password 10 times, one right after another, and then they could go back to their original password. This setting must be set to a lower value than the maximum password age, unless the maximum password age is set to 0, which means passwords never expire. A good setting is typically 10 days or more, although this can vary widely depending on administrator preferences.

Maximum Password Age   The maximum password age setting controls the maximum period of time permitted before a user is forced to reset their password. This can be set from 1 to 999 days, or to 0 if passwords are set to never expire. A general rule for this setting is 90 days for user accounts, although for administrative accounts, it's generally a good idea to reset the passwords more frequently. In high security areas, 30 days is not an uncommon setting.

Passwords should always expire, unless under unique circumstances, such as service accounts for running applications. While this may add some additional administrative overhead to some processes, passwords that don't expire can be a serious security issue in virtually all environments.

We have discussed the different settings that can be used to ensure the best password security for an environment. Let's look at how to review those settings on a Windows 10 workstation.

Review the Password Settings on a Windows 10 Workstation

Before you begin these steps, launch the Administrative Tools, Local Security Policy (see Figure 3.1). To review the password settings on a Windows 10 workstation, perform the following steps.

FIGURE 3.1   The Local Security Policy window

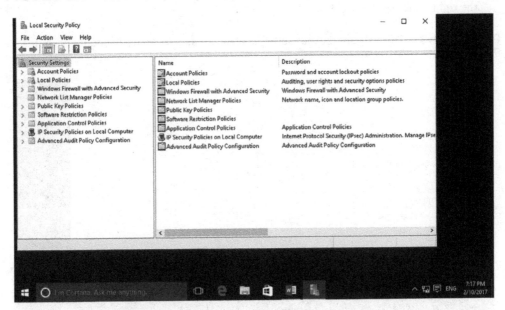

1. In the Local Security Policy snap-in, click Account Policies.
2. Double-click Password Policy. The password settings we've discussed appear in the right pane. See Figure 3.2.

FIGURE 3.2   The password settings available as part of the Password Policy

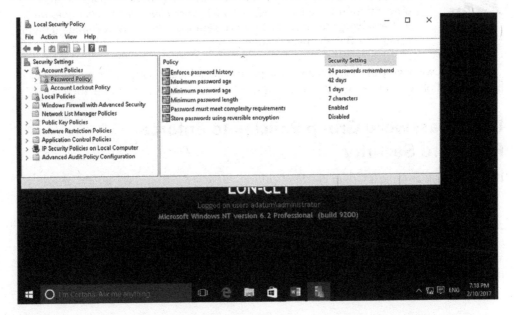

3. Click Account Lockout Policy. The account lockout settings we've discussed appear in the right pane. See Figure 3.3.

FIGURE 3.3   The account lockout settings available as part of the Account Lockout Policy

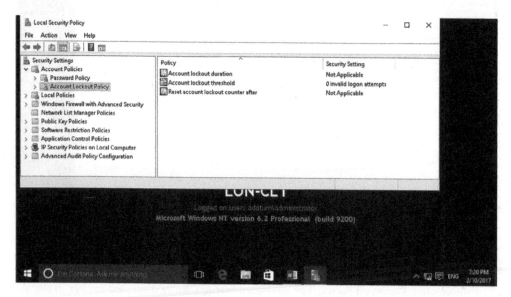

 The password settings for a Windows Server 2016 domain are configured differently than on a standalone host or client. In the example, we are reviewing the current password settings. We'll look at changing them using a GPO in the next section.

Now that we have looked at setting these policies on a local client, let's take a look at how Group Policies can be used to set these properties for members of a domain.

Using Password Group Policies to Enforce Password Security

Before we look at using a Group Policy to enforce password settings, we should probably discuss the details of a Group Policy (also known as a Group Policy Object).

A *Group Policy Object (GPO)* is a set of rules which allow an administrator granular control over the configuration of objects in Active Directory (AD), including user accounts, operating systems, applications, and other AD objects. GPOs are used for centralized management and configuration of the Active Directory environment. Let's look at how we can use GPOs to enforce password controls in Active Directory.

Windows Server 2008 fundamentally changed the mechanism for setting password attributes in Active Directory. We will look at the legacy GPO model for enforcing password controls as well as a high-level example of how to perform a similar function in a Windows Server 2016 Active Directory.

Use a Group Policy to Enforce Password Controls on Systems in a Domain

Before you begin these steps, be sure to log on to a Windows Server 2016 domain controller as domain administrator. To use a group policy to enforce password controls on systems in a domain, perform the following steps:

1. In Server Manager, click Tools ➤ Group Policy Management.
2. In the Group Policy Management window, if necessary, expand Forest: Adatum.com ➤ Domains ➤ Adatum.com.
3. Right-click the Default Domain Policy GPO and choose Edit.
4. In the Group Policy Management Editor window, navigate to the Computer Configuration\Policies\Windows Settings\Security Settings\Account Policies\ Password Policy node.
5. Click the Account Lockout Policy node.
6. After configuring the settings as needed, close the Group Policy Object Editor.
7. Close the Group Policy Management window.

Configuring and Applying Password Settings Objects

If it is necessary to use different password policies for different sets of users, use fine-grained password policies, which are applied to user objects or global security groups.

Certification Ready

Which Active Directory feature provides fine-grained password policies? Objective 2.3

Fine-grained password policies allow you to specify multiple password policies within a single domain so that different restrictions for password and account lockout policies can be applied to different sets of users in a domain. To use a fine-grained password policy, the domain functional level must be at least Windows Server 2008. To enable fine-grained password policies, first create a *Password Settings Object (PSO)*. Then, configure the same settings that are configured for the password and account lockout policies. In the Windows Server 2016 environment, PSOs can be created and applied by using the Active Directory Administrative Center (ADAC) or Windows PowerShell.

Create and Configure the Password Settings Container

To create and configure the Password Settings Container, perform the following steps:

1. Open Server Manager.

2. Click Tools ➢ Active Directory Administrative Center. The ADAC opens.

3. In the ADAC navigation pane, click the arrow next to the domain and click the System folder. Then, scroll down and double-click Password Settings Container.

4. In the Tasks pane, click New ➢ Password Settings. The Create Password Settings window opens (see Figure 3.4).

FIGURE 3.4   Creating a new Password Settings Container

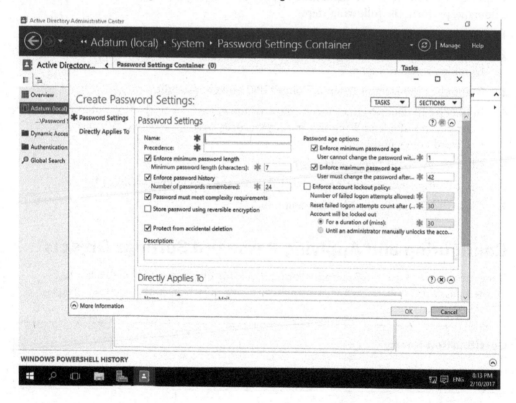

5. In the Name text box, type a name for the Password Settings Container.

6. In the Precedence text box, type a Precedence number. Passwords with a lower precedence number overwrite the Password Settings Containers with a higher precedence number.

7. Fill in or edit the appropriate fields for the settings that you want to use.

8. Under Directly Applies To, click Add. In the Select Users or Groups dialog box, specify the name of the user or group that the Password Settings Container should affect and click OK.

9. Click OK to submit the creation of the PSO.

10. Close the ADAC.

Establishing Password Procedures

Passwords are the most common form of authentication, and IT help desks spend a lot of time managing calls from users who cannot log on because they forgot their passwords or their accounts have been compromised.

Certification Ready

How can you establish a password reset procedure that allows passwords to be changed quickly, but securely? Objective 2.3

Every organization should develop a *security policy*, which is a written document that describes how a system, organization, or other entity is secured. The security policy should include an *acceptable use policy*, which describes the constraints and practices that users must agree to in order to access the corporate network, corporate resources, and the Internet. It is also important to specify a *password policy*, which dictates the length and complexity requirements for passwords and how often a password should be changed. It can also specify whether multi-factor authentication should be used and whether a lock-out policy is used when a user has attempted to log on several times using the incorrect password.

It is important that users periodically change their passwords. They should also change their passwords when their accounts have been compromised. When a user cannot access a system and their password needs to be changed, be careful with how the password change is communicated to the user. As a general rule, forgotten or new passwords should not be emailed to the user, because they can be intercepted by anyone who has control of their email account. If email absolutely must be used, send a password reset link that contains a token that will expire after a short period of time and can be used only once. If a caller calls in or sends an email to request a new password, use a procedure that requires the caller to prove their identity as an authorized user. Users should not use secret questions (such as their mother's maiden name or their pet's name), because many of these answers can be guessed through social engineering or by searching the Internet for user profiles.

One way to authorize users is to use voicemail. When a user needs to use a PIN to retrieve phone messages, inform the user that you will call them back and that they are *not* to answer the phone (so that you can leave a voice mail). Because the user should be the only one who knows the PIN to retrieve her voicemail, their use of the PIN to retrieve their voicemail will be used to prove the user's identity. Alternatively, provide the password to their manager, who is local to the user account. In both situations, indicate that the password must be changed as soon as the user logs on. When changing an application password, also send emails or messages to all the user's devices, notifying the user of the password change. If an unauthorized user attempts to get the password changed, the authorized user will be notified and he should be trained to contact the help desk to report that he did not request a password change.

Understanding Common Attack Methods

Passwords have long been recognized as one of the weak links in many security programs. While tokens, smart cards, and biometrics are gaining traction in the business world for securing key systems and data, a significant amount of confidential and private data is still being secured with passwords. Passwords are considered a weak link for two main reasons.

First, users select their own passwords. While many users will select strong passwords in line with your standards, and some tools exist to enforce password attributes like password complexity and minimum password length, there are going to be users who will continue to select weak passwords. Attackers are aware of this and will try to exploit those users.

Second, even strong passwords are vulnerable to attack through a variety of different mechanisms, including those discussed in the following sections.

Dictionary Attack/Brute Force Attack

A dictionary attack (also known as a brute force attack) uses a dictionary containing an extensive list of potential passwords that the attacker then tries in conjunction with a user ID to attempt to guess the correct password. This is known as a dictionary attack because the earliest versions of this attack actually used lists of words from the dictionary as the basis of their attacks. Now, custom dictionaries with likely passwords are available for download from the Internet, along with applications that can use them against your systems.

Another, more crude type of brute force attack doesn't rely on lists of passwords, but instead tries all the combinations of the permitted character types. While this type of attack was historically considered ineffective, improvements in processor and network performance have made it more usable, although not nearly as effective as a dictionary attack.

These types of attacks tend to be more successful when the password length is 7 characters or less. Each additional character adds a significant number of possible passwords. These attacks are often successful because users will sometimes use common words with the first letter capitalized and then append a number to meet the complexity guidelines. These are the easiest passwords for users to remember, but they are also the easiest for an attacker to compromise.

The account lockout settings discussed earlier in the lesson are a critical defense against this type of attack, because an account lockout will either slow or stop a brute force attack in its tracks after the configured number of incorrect logon attempts is reached.

| **More Info** |
| Lesson 1 contains more details on keylogging. |

Physical Attack

Any time a computer can be physically accessed by an attacker, the computer is at risk. Physical attacks on a computer can completely bypass almost all security mechanisms, by capturing the passwords and other critical data directly from the keyboard when a software or hardware keylogger is used. In fact, if an encryption key passes through a keylogger, even the encrypted data can be jeopardized.

Some other physical attacks include the use of a hidden camera to tape keystrokes, or even the removal and duplication (or direct theft) of a hard drive. While not specifically a password attack, by removing a hard drive, attackers can frequently bypass password controls by mounting the drive remotely, and accessing data directly from the drive, without an intervening operating system.

Leaked or Shared Passwords

While not strictly an attack, another challenge that is commonly encountered when dealing with users in an office environment is the leaked or shared password. Users tend to trust their co-workers. They all work for the same company, and in many cases, they have access to similar information within the company. As a result, a user could easily be convinced to share their password with a co-worker who felt they "needed it." This practice is especially problematic in environments with high turnover, because there is no way to tell who in the last crop of employees might be someone who still has a friend's user ID and password for continued access to the production network. Users will frequently justify the sharing of account information as critical to "getting the job done" or stating that it's "more convenient."

Even if the user doesn't deliberately provide their password to another employee, the casual work environment frequently makes it easy for an employee to watch as their co-worker keys in their user ID and password.

Finally, employee spouses, children, and other relatives could end up with access to an environment because of their close relationship with that employee.

User awareness is the best way to combat this type of attack. Providing users with a greater understanding of the risks and impact of these types of behaviors can go a long way towards keeping passwords under the control of only authorized users. In addition, the minimum password age and maximum password age settings, as well as the password history setting, will help mitigate this risk. Even if someone does get a password they shouldn't have, when the maximum password age limit hits, you can force a reset of all passwords, including shared ones.

Cracked Passwords

A *cracked password* frequently relies on more than just a password attack. In a cracked password attack, the attacker gets access to an encrypted password file from a workstation or server. Once they have access, the attacker will start running password cracking tools against the file, with an eye towards breaking as many passwords as possible, then leveraging them to further compromise the company's network and systems.

Passwords that are stored in an encrypted state are harder to break than passwords that are stored in clear text or in a hashed state. With today's computing power, even encrypted password stores are being compromised by password cracking attacks.

If a password store has been compromised, every employee with an account on the compromised system should change their passwords immediately.

It is possible to use the same tools that potential attackers might use to audit the security of your password stores. Trying to crack your own password file is a common practice for testing the security of a password store. In addition, if any passwords are found to be compromised and are weak, the users can be asked to change them to more secure passwords.

Network/Wireless Sniffer

If an attacker can gain access to your internal network, your wireless network, or even an Internet access point used by your employees, they have the ability to use a specialized tool known as a sniffer to try to intercept unencrypted passwords. While applications have become more secure in recent years, there are still a number of applications that pass sensitive information like passwords across the network in clear text, where they can be read by anyone with the ability to view the data as it traverses the network.

Sniffers are specially designed software (and in some cases hardware) applications that capture network packets as they traverse the network and display them for the attacker. Sniffers are valid forms of test equipment, used to identify network and application issues, but the technology was rapidly co-opted by attackers as an easy way to grab logon credentials.

In addition to attacks against a wired network, there are now sniffers that can capture wireless data as well. When connected to a business wireless network at the local coffee shop or while attending a meeting at a hotel, a user is potentially at risk of having their data pulled literally out of the air and made available to an attacker. The use of encryption remains the best mechanism for combating this type of attack.

Another area of concern with sniffers is wireless keyboards. At its core, a wireless keyboard is a broadcast technology that sends keystrokes from the keyboard to the receiver connected to the computer. If a receiver is tuned to the same frequency close enough to the computer, every keystroke entered into the wireless keyboard can be captured, without needing a keylogger installed. Most wireless keyboards now support additional security like encrypted connections, but they are still broadcasting any information that is input, and as long as we enter most data through the keyboard, this will be a significant potential source for an attacker to exploit. Many companies will only permit their employees to use wired keyboards in the office to mitigate this risk.

Guessed Passwords

While not as prevalent an issue as it was in times past, there is still the possibility that someone could sit down at your computer and guess your password. As we have seen in countless movies, the attacker is familiar with the person whose system they are trying to compromise, or they look around the office and see a postcard from a trip, or pictures of the kids with their names on them to ascertain the password. If the user does not follow the corporate rules and set a strong, not easily guessable password, and instead selects a password based on a spouse, child's, or pet's name and birthday, the attacker could guess the password and access the employee's data.

That being said, this type of attack is almost never seen these days. With the widespread availability of password cracking tools, the type of individual targeting required to guess someone's password is seldom worth the effort. It is generally much easier to leverage an attack against one of the other vectors available. Typically, only co-workers or close friends will try to guess a user's password.

Protecting Domain User Account Passwords

Over the years, malware has changed dramatically and has become quite sophisticated. Microsoft developed Device Guard and Credential Guard, which complement each other in protecting the system against malware.

Certification Ready

Which mechanisms used with Windows 10 helps protect the domain user account passwords? Objective 2.3

Device Guard helps harden a computer system against malware by running only trusted applications, thereby preventing malicious code from running. *Credential Guard* isolates and hardens key system and user security information. Both technologies are available only through Windows 10 Enterprise.

Device Guard and Credential Guard use Windows 10 *virtual secure mode (VSM)*, which, in turn, uses the processor's virtualization to protect the PC, including data and credential tokens on the system's disks. By using hardware virtualization, Windows 10 is organized into multiple containers. Windows runs one container; the Active Directory security tokens that allow access to your organization's resources run in another container. Each container is isolated from the other. Therefore, if Windows is compromised by malware, the tokens are protected because they are isolated in their own encrypted container.

Following are requirements for using VSM:

- UEFI running in Native Mode (not Compatibility/CSM/Legacy mode)
- 64-bit version of Windows 10 Enterprise
- 64-bit processor that supports Second Layer Address Translation (SLAT) and Virtualization Extensions (such as Intel VT or AMD V)

A Trusted Platform Module (TPM) is recommended.

Use the following procedure to install Hyper-V and Isolated User Mode after meeting these requirements.

Install Hyper-V and Isolated User Mode on Windows 10

To install Hyper-V and Isolated User Mode on Windows 10 Enterprise, perform the following steps:

1. On LON-CL1, right-click the Start button and choose Programs And Features.

2. Click the "Turn Windows features on or off" option.

3. In the Windows Features dialog box, select Isolated User Mode and Hyper-V Platform, and then click OK.

    Next, enable Device Guard and Credential Guard with group policy.

Enable Device Guard and Credential Guard

To enable Device Guard and Credential Guard, perform the following steps:

1. Open a GPO and then navigate to Computer Configuration\Administrative Templates\ System\Device Guard\Turn On Virtualization Based Security (as shown in Figure 3.5).

FIGURE 3.5   Turning on virtualization based security

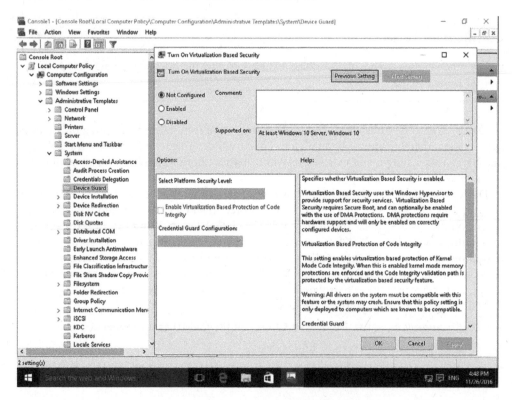

2. Click Enabled.

3. To enable Device Guard, select Enable Virtualization Based Protection of Code Integrity.

4. To enable Credential Guard, select Enable Credential Guard.

5. Close the Turn On Virtualization Based Security window by clicking OK.

Skill Summary

In this lesson, you learned:

- The strength of a password can be determined by examining the length, complexity, and randomness of the password.

- A complex password will use characters from at least three of the following categories: uppercase characters, lowercase characters, numeric characters, and non-alphanumeric characters.

- Account lockout refers to the number of incorrect logon attempts permitted before the system will lock the account.

- The length of a password is a key component of ensuring the strength of a password.

- The minimum password age setting controls how many days a user must wait before they can reset their password.

- The maximum password age setting controls the maximum period of time permitted before a user is forced to reset their password.

- A Group Policy Object (GPO) is a set of rules that allow an administrator granular control over the configuration of objects in Active Directory (AD), including user accounts, operating systems, applications, and other AD objects.

- Passwords have long been recognized as one of the weak links in many security programs.

- A dictionary attack (also known as a brute force attack) uses a dictionary containing an extensive list of potential passwords that the attacker then tries in conjunction with a user ID to attempt to guess the correct password.

- A brute force attack tries all the combinations of the permitted character types.

- Physical attacks on a computer can completely bypass almost all security mechanisms, by capturing the passwords and other critical data directly from the keyboard when a software or hardware keylogger is used.

- In a cracked password attack, the attacker gets access to an encrypted password file from a workstation or server. Once they have access, the attacker will start running password cracking tools against the file.

- If an attacker can gain access to your internal network, your wireless network, or even an Internet access point used by your employees, they have the ability to use a specialized tool known as a sniffer to try to intercept unencrypted passwords.

- While not as prevalent an issue as it was in times past, there is still the possibility that someone could sit down at your computer and guess your password.

- Device Guard helps harden a computer system against malware by running only trusted applications, thereby preventing malicious code from running.

- Credential Guard isolates and hardens key system and user security information. The Credential Guard and Device Guard technologies are available only through Windows 10 Enterprise.

Knowledge Assessment

Multiple Choice

1. Which of the following are not valid password controls? (Choose all that apply.)
   - **A.** Minimum Password Age
   - **B.** Maximum Password Age
   - **C.** Maximum Password Length
   - **D.** Account Lockout Threshold
   - **E.** Password History

2. Which of the following would be an acceptable password on a Windows 10 Pro system with Password Complexity enabled and a minimum password length set to 8? (Choose all that apply.)
   - **A.** Summer2010
   - **B.** $$Thx17
   - **C.** ^^RGood4U
   - **D.** Password
   - **E.** St@rTr3k

3. Which of the following is the maximum setting for Minimum Password Age?
   - **A.** 14
   - **B.** 999
   - **C.** 998
   - **D.** 256

4. Which of the following corresponds with the minimum and maximum password history settings for securing a Windows 10 Pro workstation image? (Choose the best answer.)
   - **A.** 0, 14
   - **B.** 1, 14
   - **C.** 0, 24
   - **D.** 1, 24
   - **E.** 0, 998

5. Which of the following are common password attacks? (Choose all that apply.)
   - **A.** Cracking
   - **B.** Phreaking
   - **C.** Phishing
   - **D.** Leaking
   - **E.** Brute force

6. Which of the following refers to a form of brute force password attack that uses an extensive list of pre-defined passwords? (Choose the best answer.)

   A. Bible

   B. Cracking

   C. Guessing

   D. Dictionary

7. Which setting should be applied to ensure that a possible dictionary attack against a Windows application server has a limited chance at success? (Choose the best answer.)

   A. Minimum Password Length

   B. Account Lockout Threshold

   C. Password History

   D. Maximum Password Age

8. Which Administrative Tool should be used to configure password control settings on a new standalone server?

   A. Active Directory Users and Computers

   B. Computer Management

   C. Security Service

   D. Local Security Policy

9. Which two features in Windows Server 2008 and higher permit the use of fine-grained password policies? (Choose two.)

   A. Global Policy Object

   B. Password Settings Container

   C. Password Settings Object

   D. Password Policy

10. Which of the following explains why a minimum password age would be set?

   A. To ensure that no one can guess a password

   B. To stop someone from trying over and over to guess a password

   C. To make sure a user cannot reset a password multiple times until he or she can reuse his or her original password

   D. To automatically reset a password

11. Which of the following uses the processor's virtualization to protect the PC, including data and credential tokens on the system's disks?

   A. Virtual smart cards

   B. Device Guard

   C. Credential Guard

   D. Windows Hello

12. In Windows 10, which component is used by Device Guard and Credential Guard to protect the PC?

   A. Windows Store

   B. Virtual smart cards

   C. Windows Hello

   D. Virtual secure mode

Fill in the Blank

1. A set of rules that allow an administrator granular control over the configuration of objects in Active Directory (AD), including user accounts, operating systems, applications, and other AD objects is known as a _____.

2. The number of incorrect logon attempts permitted before the system will lock the account is known as _____.

3. The setting that determines the number of unique passwords that must be used before a password can be reused is the _____.

4. A type of attack that uses an extensive list of potential passwords is known as a _____.

5. Using special software to read data as it is broadcasted on a network is called _____ the network.

6. The _____ option needs to be less than or equal to the Account Lockout Duration.

7. The highest setting that account lockout duration can use is _____.

8. In a Windows Server 2016 Active Directory, the _____ automatically applies in the event that a fine-grained password policy has not been set.

9. The three configuration settings for account lockout are _____, _____, and _____.

10. A _____ is a type of account that might be configured so that the password will not expire.

Business Case Scenarios

Scenario 3-1: Understanding Long Passwords

For each scenario, specify the number of possible passwords based on the number of possible combinations.

a. Let's say you have a four-digit personal identification number (PIN). Each digit can be 0, 1, 2, 3, 4, 5, 6, 7, 8, or 9, giving a total of 10 possible numbers for each digit. If a PIN is 4 digits, each digit can be any one of the 10 possible numbers. How many combinations can you have?

b. Let's say you can use a 4-letter password and each password can be a lowercase letter (a-z). There are 26 letters. If you have 4 letters, how many combinations do you have?

c. Let's say you have 6-letter passwords and each password can be a lowercase letter (a-z). How many combinations are there?

d. Let's say you have 8-letter passwords and each password can be a lowercase letter (a-z). How many combinations are there?

e. Let's say you have 8-letter passwords and each password can be a lowercase letter (a-z) or uppercase letter (A-Z). How many combinations are there?

f. Let's say you have 8-letter passwords, each password can be a lowercase letter (a-z), uppercase letter (A-Z), a digit (0-9), or a special character ~ ` ! @ # $ % ^ & * ( ) _ - + = { [}] | \ : ; " ' < , > . ? or / . How many combinations are there?

Scenario 3-2: Using Keys and Passwords

The CIO at Contoso Corporation indicates that he just received a message on his computer stating that he must change his password. He wants to know why he should change the password to a relatively long password on a regular basis. Describe your explanation.

Scenario 3-3: Managing User Accounts

As an administrator with the Contoso Corporation, you have been tasked with managing user accounts. Describe the steps necessary to creating a standard account for John Adams on a computer running Windows 10. You will then change John Adams (JAdams) to an administrator account and then set the password for John Adams to Pa$$w0rd.

Scenario 3-4: Configuring a Local Security Policy

As an administrator with the Contoso Corporation, you have been tasked with configuring a local security policy. On a computer running Windows 10, open the Group Policy Management window to access the Local Group Policy. View the Password Policy and Account Lockout Policy and record the default settings for Password Policy and Account Lockout Policy.

 Real World Scenario

Workplace Ready: Understanding Group Policies

Group Policies refers to one of the most powerful features that is included with Active Directory. Besides configuring password policies and account lockout policies, it can be used to assign user rights that define what a user can do on a computer. It can also be used to install software, prevent other software from being installed, lock down a computer, standardize a working environment, and preconfigure Windows. With Group Policies configuration, there are thousands of possible settings.

Lesson 4

Understanding Network Security

Lesson Skill Matrix

Technology Skill	Objective Domain Description	Objective Domain Number
Using Dedicated Firewalls to Protect a Network	Understand dedicated firewalls	3.1
Using Isolation to Protect the Network	Understand network isolation	3.2
Protecting Data with Protocol Security	Understand protocol security	3.3
Understanding Denial-of-Service Attacks	Understand protocol security	3.3
Securing the Wireless Network	Understand wireless security	1.4

Key Terms

application-level firewalls

ARP spoofing

Back door attack

Buffer overflow attack

circuit-level firewalls

cross-site scripting (XSS) attack

denial-of-service (DoS) attack

distributed denial-of-service (DDoS) attack

demilitarized zone (DMZ)

DNS poisoning

DNS Security Extensions (DNSSEC)

DNS spoofing

email bomb

firewall

honey net

honeypot

host firewall

HTTP flood

ICMP (ping) flood

IEEE 802.1x

intrusion detection systems (IDS)

intrusion prevention systems (IPS)

IP address spoofing

MAC address

Man-in-the-middle attacks

network firewall

Open Systems Interconnect (OSI) reference model

personal firewalls

ping of death

remote code execution attack

replay attack

social engineering

spoofing

SQL injection attack

stateful inspection

stateless inspection

SYN flood

tunneling

UDP flood

User Datagram Protocol (UDP)

Wired Equivalent Privacy (WEP)

Wi-Fi Protected Access (WPA)

Wi-Fi Protected Access version 2 (WPA2)

zero-day attacks

⊕ **Real World Scenario**

Lesson 4 Case

Traditionally, when looking at building information security infrastructure, the first point of focus is the network. As soon as networks began interconnecting, it was obvious that the network offered the main vector of attack. It was the one way to get to an internal network from the outside.

The philosophy around network protection was originally reminiscent of the castles of old. The best way to secure a castle was to build strong walls, dig moats, and control access to the castle through the main gate. In network terms, this meant deploying multiple layers of firewall and then controlling who could enter the network with firewall rules, access controls, and DMZs. This practice is known as securing the perimeter, or defense in depth.

This model worked quite well until the next round of technology evolution came about. In the late 1990s, the concept of virtual private networks (VPNs) was introduced. VPNs allowed companies to securely extend their network across untrusted networks like the Internet, but also impacted the perimeter of the network.

Next came wireless network technologies, moving the perimeter that needed to be protected literally into the air, offering additional challenges to the network perimeter and the layered security model.

The good news is that as network technologies have evolved that have made securing the perimeter more challenging, the security technologies available for addressing those challenges have evolved as well. In this lesson, we will discuss these security solutions and how they can be used to address the challenges you may encounter.

Using Dedicated Firewalls to Protect a Network

Firewalls remain the foundation of network security technologies. There are a number of options, types, and technologies associated with selecting, implementing, and maintaining the firewalls in a network. There are also a number of factors that help determine the proper solution to meet business requirements.

Certification Ready

Where would most companies place their dedicated firewall? Objective 3.1

One of the first things that comes to mind when people talk about information security is the firewall. Firewalls have long been the foundation of a company's network security infrastructure. But what exactly is a firewall?

A *firewall* is a system that is designed to protect a computer or a computer network from network-based attacks. A firewall does this by filtering the data packets traversing the network. A typical perimeter firewall is implemented with two (or more) network connections (see Figure 4.1):

- A connection to the network being protected
- A connection to an external network

FIGURE 4.1   Example of a firewall implementation

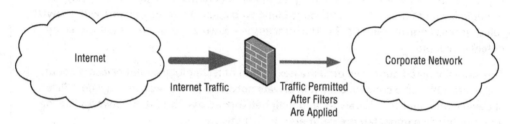

There are numerous variations on this model, but ultimately a firewall protects hosts on one network from hosts on another network.

These network connections may be referenced using different labels: internal and external, clean and dirty, secure and unsecure, local and remote, and so on. They all refer to the same model, but occasionally may need translation into familiar terminology.

In today's networks, firewalls are being used for a number of things beyond securing the perimeter. Many of today's corporate networks are being divided into security zones, secured by firewalls. Sometimes, these firewalls are not only securing Internet and extranet connections, but also creating secure zones for financial systems, to secure research and development servers, or sometimes even to secure the production network from the development and test networks.

Given the widely varying uses for firewalls in today's networks, there are a variety of different firewall types. But before we get into discussing the different types of firewalls, we need to discuss the OSI model.

Understanding the OSI Model

Any discussion about network security requires a discussion and understanding of the *Open Systems Interconnect (OSI) reference model*. The OSI model is a conceptual model, created by the International Organization for Standardization (ISO) in 1978 and revised in 1984, to describe a network architecture that allows data to be passed between computer systems. While never fully utilized as the model for a protocol, the OSI model is the standard for discussing how networking works.

As shown in Figure 4.2, the OSI model is built in the same way it is usually discussed, from the bottom to the top. The layers are: physical, data-link, network, transport, session, presentation, and application. When they are discussed, the physical layer is referred to as Layer 1, and the application layer is Layer 7. This is important to remember because in discussions, routers are often referred to as "Layer 3 devices," or a specific type of firewall might be called a "Layer 7 device." This nomenclature refers to where on the OSI model that device interacts. As a result, it is important to be familiar with the high-level concept of the OSI model and what occurs at each layer.

FIGURE 4.2   The seven-layer OSI model

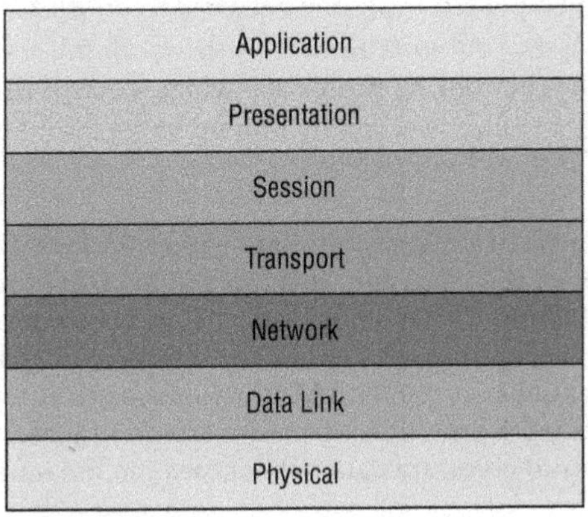

| Application |
| Presentation |
| Session |
| Transport |
| Network |
| Data Link |
| Physical |

Each layer of the OSI model has its own specific function. The following sections describe the function of each layer starting with the physical layer and working up the OSI model.

Physical Layer (Layer 1)

The physical layer of the OSI model is used to define the physical characteristics of the network, including the following specifications:

Media   Cabling types, voltage, signal frequency, speed, bandwidth, and so on.

Hardware   Type of connector, type of network interface card used, and so on.

Topology   The topology to be used in the network, such as ring, mesh, star, and bus.

Data-Link Layer (Layer 2)

The data-link layer connects the data layer to the physical layer so that the data can be transmitted across the network. The data-link layer handles error detection, error correction, and hardware addressing (for example, the address of a network interface card).

The data-link layer is broken into two sublayers—the Media Access Control (MAC) sublayer and the Logical Link Control (LLC) sublayer.

MAC Layer   The MAC address is defined at this layer. The *MAC address* is the physical or hardware address burned into each NIC (for example, 96-4C-E5-48-78-C7). The MAC sublayer also controls access to the underlying network media.

LLC Layer   The LLC layer is the layer responsible for the error and flow control mechanisms of the data-link layer. The LLC layer is specified in the IEEE 802.2 standard.

 The IEEE 802.x standards define a variety of networking technologies. For example, 802.1x defines a standard for wireless security. Ethernet is defined by the IEEE 802.3 standard.

Network Layer (Layer 3)

The network layer is primarily responsible for routing. The network layer defines the mechanisms that allow data to be passed from one network to another. To be clear, it doesn't specify how the data is passed, but instead defines the mechanisms that permit it. How the data is passed is defined by the routing protocols (which we will discuss in more detail later in the lesson.) As a result, a router is typically known as a Layer 3 device.

 It's important to remember that in addition to routing, that is, allowing traffic to select the best path, this layer of the OSI model specifies one other critical function. These protocols also set the addressing. In the case of TCP/IP, this is the layer where IP addresses are specified. While the data-link layer uses hard-coded MAC addresses to communicate on the physical layer, network protocols use software-configured addresses and routing protocols to communicate data across the network.

Transport Layer (Layer 4)

The transport layer does exactly what the name implies. It provides the mechanisms for carrying data across the network. It uses three main mechanisms to accomplish this:

Segmentation   Downloading an MP3 file from a favorite music site involves dealing with a large block of data. In order to get from the music site to a PC, this file needs to be broken down into smaller, more manageable blocks, so the network can handle it. This process performed by the transport layer is called segmentation.

Service Addressing   Network protocols (TCP/IP, for example) provide several network services. These services are identified by ports. The transport layer ensures that when data traverses the network, it is passed to the correct service.

Error Checking   Transport layer protocols also perform error checking on the data and ensure that data is sent and received correctly.

The protocols operating at the transport layer come in two types:

Connection Oriented   A connection-oriented protocol, such as the Transmission Control Protocol (TCP), requires an end-to-end connection between hosts before data can be transmitted. Think of this like a telephone call—you don't start speaking to the person at the other end of a phone call until you are successfully connected to the person at the other end.

Connectionless   A connectionless protocol, such as the User Datagram Protocol (UDP), allows for the transmission of data without requiring that a connection be established first. Connectionless protocols rely on the network to ensure the proper delivery of data from one host to another across the network. Think of a connectionless protocol like sending an email. You don't have to connect directly to the recipient before sending an email; instead you address the email, type it, and click Send. The network ensures that the email gets to the addressee.

The transport layer has an additional responsibility in the OSI model. It handles flow control of the data. Flow control determines how the receiving device accepts the data transmissions. There are two common methods of flow control—buffering and windowing:

Buffering   Buffering flow control temporarily stores data in a buffer and waits for the destination device to become available. Buffering can be problematic if the sending device is able to transmit data much faster than the receiving device is able to receive. Too high a transmit rate can overload a buffer, which has a limited size, causing data loss.

Windowing   In a windowing environment, data segments are grouped together, and when sent, require only one acknowledgment. The size of the window (that is, the number of segments that can be sent at one time) is agreed to by the two devices. In some cases, the window size is agreed to when the connection is first established; in others, the window size can vary based on network congestion and device resources. These types of windows are referred to as sliding windows. Windowing improves network performance by reducing the number of acknowledgments that need to be sent between devices.

 If you are familiar with PC hardware, you may recognize these flow control methods. They are the same methods used for flow control in a PC when moving data into and out of the different types of data storage—like a hard drive, cache, and RAM.

Session Layer (Layer 5)

The session layer is responsible for data synchronization between the applications on the two devices. The session layer establishes, maintains, and breaks sessions between devices. The transport layer is responsible for connections between the two devices, and the session layer handles the same functions for the application transferring the data between the two devices.

Presentation Layer (Layer 6)

The presentation layer converts application layer data into a format that permits the data to be transmitted across the network. Data formatted for transport across the network is not always natively readable by applications. Some common data formats that are converted by the presentation layer include the following:

- Graphics files
- Text and data files
- Music and video files

The presentation layer is also the layer where encryption and decryption of data is done.

Application Layer (Layer 7)

Finally, at the top of the OSI model is the application layer. The application layer takes data from the user and passes the data to the lower layers of the OSI model for transport. Responses are passed up through the layers and are displayed back to the user.

It's important to remember that the application layer of the OSI model is not the actual application displayed on the computer. The application layer is used to define how the applications running on a computer can take advantage of the network. For example, to print a document to a network printer, the word processing application would take the file information and pass it to the application layer, which would pass it down the layers so the data could be transmitted to the printer. Of course, there are applications that may use the network service or application that runs at application layer services, like web browsers.

While the OSI model gives us a framework to categorize technology, it is not fully implemented on today's networks. Instead, today's networks follow a simplified model usually consisting of the following four layers:

Link Layer   The link layer is the lowest layer of the TCP/IP model and is designed to be hardware independent. It is responsible for linking to the hardware network technology and transmits data. TCP/IP has been implemented on top of virtually any hardware networking technology in existence.

Internet Layer   The Internet layer is responsible for connecting multiple networks together and for routing of packets between networks.

Transport Layer   The transport layer is responsible for end-to-end message transfer capabilities independent of the underlying network. It also handles error control, segmentation, flow control, congestion control, and application addressing (port numbers).

Application Layer   The application layer refers to the higher-level network protocols and services such as SMTP or FTP.

Now that you have an understanding of the OSI model, we can discuss the various networking technologies and their impact on your information security program.

Types of Hardware Firewalls and Their Characteristics

In today's network environment, the clear majority of production firewalls are hardware based. A hardware firewall is a firewall that runs on a dedicated platform, specifically designed, optimized, and hardened (the process of securing a system) to run the firewall application software.

While there are a variety of types of firewalls, with varying characteristics, firewalls share some basic functions. Firewalls filter traffic based on a set of configured rules. Generally, these rules are based on information contained in the data packets that are traveling across the network. The header information contained in those data packets provides the firewall the information it needs to properly apply these rules.

These rules are generally defined by a company's security policies and business requirements. While it is possible to configure a firewall to permit all traffic and block specific traffic based on rules, virtually all firewalls will work based on the deny-all, permit-specific philosophy. This means that the firewall will by default deny all traffic. Any traffic permitted to traverse the firewall will need to be explicitly configured in the firewall's rules.

There are a variety of different firewall types, and different people sometimes define firewall types in different ways. The key is to thoroughly understand the basics, because besides passing the certification test, you will generally not be called upon to identify firewall types in your day-to day-duties.

Don't get too hung up on the definitions of firewall types. Understand the functionality of the firewall types instead. What they are called is not as important as how the different flavors of firewalls function.

Understanding Packet Filtering

The first type of firewall is known as the packet-filtering firewall. This type of firewall is considered the first-generation firewall, because the first firewalls functioned as packet filters. As we have discussed, the primary purpose of a firewall is to filter traffic. A packet-filtering firewall inspects the data packets as they attempt to traverse the firewall, and based on the rules that have been defined on the firewall, the firewall allows or denies each packet.

One of the very first versions of this firewall was the packet-filtering router. Routers can do some rudimentary packet filtering, such as permitting all outbound traffic while denying all inbound traffic, or blocking specific protocols from passing through the router, like Telnet or FTP.

Firewalls significantly improve on the capabilities of a packet-filtering firewall, as they permit more granular rules. You might configure a packet-filtering firewall to block web browsing on the Internet, except to your company's Internet website, while permitting outbound web traffic from your internal network to the Internet. Another option is to set up a rule that would drop any ping requests, unless they originate from someone on the network team's workstation.

When configuring a packet-filtering firewall rule, one (or more) of the following TCP/IP attributes should generally be used:

- Source IP addresses
- Destination IP addresses
- IP protocol (Telnet, FTP, HTTP, HTTPS, and so on)
- Source TCP and UDP ports (for example, the HTTP protocol runs on TCP port 80)
- Destination TCP and UDP ports
- The inbound firewall network interface
- The outbound firewall network interface

Some of the more common protocols and ports that will be encountered in a production network include the following:

FTP (file transfer): 20/tcp and 21/tcp

Telnet (Terminal logon): 23/tcp

DNS: 53/udp and 53/tcp

HTTP (web): 80/tcp

HTTPS (web): 443/tcp

SMTP (email): 25/tcp

POP3 (email): 110/tcp

IMAP3 (email): 220/tcp

IMAP4 (email): 143/tcp

LDAP (directory services): 389/tcp

SQL Server: 1433/tcp

RDP (Terminal Services): 3389/tcp

This is not a comprehensive list, as there are thousands of different protocols and ports, but these are common protocols you will see when configuring rules on a packet-filtering firewall. For a comprehensive list, visit the following website:

`http://www.iana.org/assignments/port-numbers`

Understanding Circuit-Level Firewalls

Circuit-level firewalls are typically considered a second-generation firewall technology. They work similarly to packet-filtering firewalls, but they operate at the transport and session layers of the OSI model.

Instead of analyzing each individual packet, a circuit-level firewall monitors TCP/IP sessions by monitoring the TCP handshaking between packets to validate the session. Traffic is filtered based on specified session rules and may be restricted to authorized computers only. When the session is established, the firewall maintains a table of valid connections and lets data pass through when session information matches an entry in the table. The table entry is removed, and the circuit is closed when the session is terminated. One unique feature of circuit-level firewalls is that sessions that cross this type of firewall appear to originate from that firewall. This allows the internal network to be hidden from the public network.

This type of firewall is also known as a transparent proxy, because all sessions appear to originate from the firewall. Circuit-level firewalls are almost always used in conjunction with other types of firewalls, because they are only able to permit sessions from authorized computers. Additional granularity is typically required in most production environments.

Understanding Application-Level Firewalls

Application-level firewalls (also known as proxy servers) work by performing a deep inspection of application data as it traverses the firewall. Rules are set based on analyzing client requests and application responses, then enforcing correct application behavior.

Application-level firewalls can block malicious activity, log user activity, provide content filtering, and even protect against spam and viruses. Microsoft Internet Security and Acceleration Server is an example of an application-level firewall.

Now for the downside—deep inspection of application data is a resource-intensive activity and can require significant processing power to reduce the chances of the firewall impacting network performance. The deeper the inspection, the higher the resource requirements, and the higher the possibility for network performance impacts. When deploying an application-level firewall, it is important to size it appropriately. Cutting corners on processor and RAM on your application-level firewall is an excellent formula for creating unhappy users, and it is always a better idea to go a little more powerful than your immediate needs. Remember to always plan for growth. Network utilization very seldom decreases over time. You usually don't want to go back to management in a year to fund an upgrade.

One capability available on some application-level firewalls that can help offset performance impacts of the deep inspection of application data is the addition of caching. Caching allows the firewall to store commonly downloaded data and provide it in response to requests from a user rather than having to retrieve the data from the Internet. Most web browsers have this capability for local storage of commonly used pages; a caching firewall extends this capability to all users on the network. For example, if 50 employees all read the front page of the online Wall Street Journal when they come into the office, the firewall caches the first visit to the site and then serves the stored page to the next 49 visitors.

Caching was a much more effective technology during the early days of the Internet, when most of the content was static. With the advent of customizable views, mashups, and interactive content, the effectiveness of caching is becoming more and more limited.

Understanding Stateful Multi-level Firewalls

Stateful multi-level firewalls are designed to provide the best features of both packet-filtering and application-level firewalls. This type of firewall provides network-level packet filtering and is also capable of recognizing and processing application-level data. When configured correctly, these firewalls can provide the highest level of security of the firewall types discussed, but are typically the most expensive firewalls. In addition, with all the available features, they can also be very complex to configure and maintain.

Understanding When to Use a Hardware Firewall Instead of a Software Firewall

Before we can look at when it's appropriate to utilize a hardware firewall instead of a software firewall, we need to look at what is meant by a software firewall. There are two basic types of software firewall:

Host Firewall   One type of software firewall is a firewall application installed on a host, used to protect the host from network-based attacks. An example of this type of software firewall would be the Windows firewall included with recent versions of Microsoft operating systems. Host firewalls are also known as *personal firewalls*.

Network Firewall   The other type of software firewall is a firewall application installed on a server used to protect network segments from other network segments. These types of firewalls offer similar functionality to a hardware firewall. The most popular network firewalls are those produced by Cisco.

The one circumstance where it clearly doesn't make sense to use a hardware firewall is to protect a single host. To protect a single host, the best solution would be to install a software firewall on the host, with a specific set of rules based on what needs to be protected. If the host is part of a larger network, which they virtually always are, it will also be protected by any network firewalls deployed on the network.

Host firewalls aside, there are a variety of factors that will impact the decision on whether to use a software solution to protect a network. Many of these factors are related to some of the challenges associated with software firewalls. These factors include the following:

Host Hardware   Software firewalls run on the already busy server's general-purpose hardware. This can lead to bottlenecks (such as processor, memory, or network), especially if the hardware hasn't been sized appropriately to address the traffic requirements associated with running a firewall application.

Host Operating System   While both hardware and software firewalls run operating systems, a hardware firewall runs a hardened operating system, providing a smaller attack surface than an unhardened operating system. In order to match the security level of the hardened OS provided by a hardware firewall, the software firewall server needs to be similarly hardened. This can require specialized expertise and additional investments in time and resources. As a result, most software firewalls have larger attack surfaces than their hardware counterparts.

Other Applications   Software firewalls must compete for resources with any other processes running on the host. A hardware firewall has dedicated hardware resources that are not shared with any other service. As a result, additional hardware may be needed to match the performance of the hardware firewall, due to the added resource requirements.

Availability/Stability   One of the potential issues associated with using a software firewall is that its reliability is tied to the reliability of the underlying operating system and associated hardware. While the hardware components in a host will generally be as reliable as the components found in a hardware firewall, they are not always available in a redundant configuration as hardware firewalls are. Operating systems have come a long way in terms of stability, but a general-purpose operating system that would be used with a software firewall is typically not as stable as the hardened operating system used on a hardware firewall.

With all the potential challenges associated with software firewalls, there are a couple of compelling reasons to use software firewalls. First, they are very cost effective. Second, they are generally less complex to install and support than their hardware counterparts.

So, in a medium to large network environment, where performance, availability, and reliability are critical, a hardware firewall is the best solution. Hardware firewalls exist in virtually every enterprise network.

For a small network, when trying to keep costs down or trying to secure a single host, using a software firewall may be the right answer.

Understanding Stateful Inspection and Stateless Inspection

As we have discussed, the most basic firewall system works by filtering packets. A packet-filtering firewall inspects the data packets as they attempt to traverse the firewall, and based on the rules that have been defined on the firewall, the firewall allows or denies each packet. The firewall doesn't consider any other information related to the packets when determining which packets are permitted to cross the firewall and which packets are blocked. This type of data packet inspection is known as stateless inspection.

In *stateless inspection*, the data traversing the firewall are examined for information like:

- The IP address of the sending device
- The IP address of the receiving device
- The type of packet (TCP, UDP, and so on)
- The port number

Stateful inspection takes packet filtering to the next level. In addition to examining the header information of a packet traversing the firewall, a stateful inspection firewall also considers other factors when determining if traffic should be permitted across the firewall.

Stateful inspection also determines whether a packet is part of an existing session, and that information can be used to determine whether to permit or deny a packet. The existing session is referred to as the state and frequently occurs at Layer 4 of the OSI model, the transport layer. Many of today's stateful inspection firewalls can also track communications across Layers 5–7 as well.

It may sound simple, but it's a very complex process, which is why stateful inspection firewalls are typically more expensive and more challenging to configure. A stateful inspection firewall keeps track of all current sessions in a state table stored in memory. In other words, when a user initiates a connection to the MSN website to check today's headlines, the firewall stores the information regarding the session in a table. The same is done for every other connection occurring across the firewall.

As each packet is encountered by the firewall, it will be analyzed to determine whether it is part of an existing session (state) or not. If it is, and the session is permitted based on the current firewall rules, then it is passed. If it is not part of an existing session, and it is not a packet being used to initiate a permitted session, it will be dropped.

Another benefit of stateful inspection is that once a session is established, the firewall manages access based on the sessions rather than on the packets. This permits a simpler set of firewall rules when compared to traditional packet-filtering firewalls. A packet-filtering firewall requires a rule for each authorized packet. To permit a connection between Host A and Host B across a packet-filtering firewall, you need a rule that permits packets from Host A to Host B, and another rule that permits packets from Host B to Host A. Using a stateful inspection firewall, a rule can be defined that permits a connection from Host A to Host B, and then the firewall's state table management will automatically allow the return traffic.

Stateful inspection firewalls make excellent perimeter firewalls for protecting an internal network from the Internet, for protecting DMZ-based hosts (discussed in more detail later in this lesson) from the Internet, and for protecting extranets from connections to customers, vendors, or business partners.

Using Isolation to Protect the Network

In addition to protecting the perimeter of the network, there are other techniques that can be used to protect computing resources on an internal network. These technologies allow you to isolate portions of your network, provide a special use for your firewalls, or even supplement the security provided by your firewalls. Virtual local area networks (VLANs) and routing are network technologies that can help to segregate a network into security zones. Also, deploying technologies like honeypots helps to distract attackers from the important portions of the network. Firewalls can also play a part if it is necessary to create DMZs on the network. VPN, NAT, Server isolation, and Domain isolation are additional network concepts that can be used to secure the network.

Certification Ready

Which feature can be used to isolate a subnet, with all of its servers, from the rest of the network? Objective 3.2

Understanding VLANs

Before we can discuss what a virtual LAN (VLAN) is, we need to quickly review what is meant by local area network (LAN). A LAN is a network of hosts covering a small physical area, like an office, a floor in a building, or a small group of buildings. LANs are used to connect multiple hosts. These LANs are then connected to other LANs using a router, which is a Layer 3 device.

One of the challenges with LANs as they grow larger is that each device on each LAN subnet broadcasts traffic onto that subnet. While these broadcasts will not cross a router, if there are enough hosts, the aggregate broadcast traffic can saturate a network. One solution is to deploy more routers as a way to divide the network into more manageable segments. But routers add latency to network traffic and require a routing protocol (which we will discuss in the next section) for traffic to find its way from one part of the network to another.

Virtual LANs (VLANs) were developed as an alternate solution to deploying multiple routers. VLANs are logical network segments used to create separate broadcast domains, but still allow the devices on the VLANs to communicate at Layer 2, without requiring a router. VLANs are created by switches and traffic between VLANs is switched, not routed, which creates a much faster network connection, as there is no need for a routing protocol to be involved. Even though the hosts are logically separated, the traffic between the hosts is switched directly as if the hosts were on the same LAN segment.

VLANs provide several benefits over a routed network, including the following:

- Higher performance on medium or large LANs due to reduced broadcast traffic

- Organized devices on the network for easier management

- Additional security because devices can be put on their own VLAN

There are several different ways to assign hosts to VLANs. These methods include the following:

VLAN Membership by Port   The ports on the switch are defined as belonging to a specific VLAN, so any device plugged into a port would be assigned to the corresponding VLAN. For example, a 32-port switch might have ports 1–4 assigned to VLAN1, ports 5–16 assigned to VLAN2, and ports 17–32 assigned to VLAN3. While this seems like a straightforward method for organizing ports, it can be problematic if, for example, you work in an environment where users change office locations frequently. If the ports have been assigned in one section of cubes to Sales, and next week they decide to move Sales to the other side of the floor, the switch needs to be reconfigured to support them. In a relatively static environment, this model works very well.

VLAN Membership by MAC Address   Under this model, membership in a VLAN is based on the MAC address of the host. When the VLAN is set up on the switch, the hosts are assigned based on their MAC address. When a workstation moves to another location and connects to a different switch port, the switch automatically assigns the host to the appropriate VLAN based on the MAC address of the workstation. Because the MAC address is generally hard-coded into the host's NIC, this model is generally more usable in an environment where hosts move. One downside to this model is that it does require more initial work to set up, because it is necessary to obtain all the MAC addresses from the hosts and associate them with the appropriate VLAN.

Membership by IP Subnet Address   In this type of VLAN association, membership is based on the Layer 3 header. The switch reads the Layer 3 IP address and associates the address range with the appropriate VLAN. Even though the switch accesses Layer 3 information in the header, the VLAN assignment is still done at Layer 2 of the OSI model, and no routing takes place. This model is also conducive to an environment where there are frequent user moves. There can be an impact to performance, because the switch needs to read the Layer 3 header to determine which VLAN to assign the host to. This is generally not an issue with today's switch technologies, but it is good to be aware that there is additional overhead associated with this model.

Membership by Protocol   VLANs can also be organized based on protocol. This was a very useful solution when many LANs ran multiple network protocols, but with the dominance of TCP/IP in virtually every network, this model is almost never used on a modern network.

The next question to think about is, "How do VLANs help with security?" There are two basic ways to leverage VLANs in support of security.

First, because a VLAN provides logical separation, traffic on one VLAN is not directly accessible to hosts on another VLAN. However, this is of minimal use because there are techniques called VLAN hopping which can get access to traffic on other VLANs.

The second use of VLANs from a security perspective is to use VLANs to organize the hosts for assigning access permissions. This technique is used in conjunction with firewalls or access control lists. For example, create a VLAN for the section of the building in which the administrators work, and give it access through your firewalls so these employees can access all sections of the network. The Sales department might be on a VLAN with its access restricted to the Sales application servers, but is blocked from getting to the HR and Finance applications.

Understanding Routing

Routing takes one step up the OSI model from the VLAN—taking place at Layer 3. Routing is the process of forwarding a packet based on the packet's destination address. At each step in the route a packet takes across the network, a decision has to be made about where the packet is to be forwarded.

To make these decisions, the IP layer consults a routing table stored in the memory of the routing device. Routing table entries are created by default when TCP/IP initializes, and then additional entries are added either manually by a system administrator or automatically through communication with routers.

But what exactly is a router? Above, we defined routing as the process of forwarding a packet based on the packet's destination address. In its simplest form, a router is any device that forwards packets from one interface to another. This is a very simple description for a very complex process.

Routers come in two basic types: software and hardware. A software router is a computer running an operating system and multiple services, including a routing service. Windows Server 2016 supports routing, for example. Some benefits of a software router include the following:

Tight Integration with the OS   The routing service is frequently integrated with the operating system and other services.

Consistent/Easier User Interface   No retraining is required on a new interface/operating system—the routing functions are configured through the standard user interface.

Low Cost   When adding routing to an existing server, it is not necessary to pay for dedicated hardware. This reduces the overall cost, although if you were to dedicate a software router for just routing, any cost savings would be negligible.

Flexibility   Software routers allow multiple services to be configured and run on a single platform.

When is it a good idea to use a software router? Typically, software routers can be found in small offices that usually need an inexpensive, easy-to-manage solution. While there are a number of benefits to software-based routers, the drawbacks frequently outweigh them during the selection process. A hardware router will not typically be impacted by a virus or be prone to performance problems due to a runaway process. Another circumstance in which you might use a software router is between two LAN segments, where traffic requirements are expected to be low. An example of this might be a lab segment, where you want to isolate the lab hosts, but do not want to invest in a dedicated hardware router.

While there are benefits to using a software router, there are also some significant drawbacks when compared to a hardware router. These drawbacks of a software router include the following:

Performance   Due to the additional overhead associated with the operating system and any additional running services, software routers are typically slower than a hardware router.

Less Reliable   Any software router has the potential for issues with the operating system and other running services, as well as with the greater number of hardware components compared to a hardware router. As a result, software routers are typically less reliable than hardware routers.

Limited Scalability   Scaling a software router to multiple high-speed interfaces will be subject to the limitations of the computer hardware. Because most PC-based servers are not designed to route multiple high-speed network interface cards, software routers will generally not scale as easily or as much as a hardware router. Also, adding additional services like access control lists or firewall services impact a software router's performance to a greater degree than a comparable hardware router.

Limited Protocol Support   Software routers typically do not support as many routing protocols as a hardware router. Windows Server 2016 is limited to the IP routing protocols RIP, OSPF, and BGP, and does not presently support any of the more advanced IP-based routing protocols, like BGP4.

A hardware router is a dedicated hardware device whose main function has been to route packets. This description is not as true as it was in years past. Many of today's hardware routers are multi-function devices, having additional functionality like VPN, DHCP, firewall, caching, or in some cases even intrusion detection services. The benefits of a hardware router include the following:

Higher Performance   Hardware routers run on custom-built, single-purpose hardware platforms with highly optimized hardware and operating systems.

Highly Reliable   Hardware routers are typically more reliable than their software counterparts, due in large part to the limited software capabilities, and dedicated hardware. A hardware router will typically have higher modularity than a software router. Hardware routers also support more high availability capabilities, where they can be deployed in pairs—one will take over if the other fails. While this is theoretically possible with a software router, it is very seldom done.

Wide Routing Protocol Support   Hardware routers can typically be configured to support a larger range of routing protocols, as long as the appropriate functions are purchased. They also support a greater number of routing algorithms than a software router. In a larger network environment, this can be critical.

Using hardware routers is not always advantageous—sometimes there are drawbacks to using a hardware router:

Higher Cost   Hardware routers are typically dedicated platforms, which tends to make them more expensive than a software router that is also providing other services. This line is blurring as additional features continue to become available on hardware routers. However, a small hardware router can be relatively inexpensive.

Less User Friendly   Hardware routers are typically configured using a Secure Shell (SSH) connection, and are managed through a command-line interface. While there are graphical tools for managing routers, a lot of router configuration is still done through the command line, using an extremely complex list of commands. An experienced router support engineer can configure or troubleshoot a router without too much difficulty, but for someone new to routers, there is a steep learning curve.

More Complex   While an individual router may not actually be that much more complex than its software-based counterpart, when scaling to large networks, a hardware router environment can rapidly become very complex. This issue would also apply to a software router, but software routers are not common in the real world. In most network environments, hardware routers are used almost exclusively, with software routers being reserved for only the smallest networks or locations.

How Does Routing Work?

When a router receives a packet that must be forwarded to a destination host, the router needs to make a decision. It needs to determine if it can deliver the packet directly to the destination host or whether it needs to forward the packet to another router. To make this decision, the router examines the destination network address. If the router has an interface that is connected to the same network as the destination host, it can deliver the packet directly. Where it gets interesting is when the router is not connected to the same network as the destination host and it needs to determine the best route to the destination host so it can forward the packet correctly.

When one router needs to forward a packet to another router, it uses the information in its routing tables to choose the best path for forwarding the packet. The decision as to which router to forward the packet to is determined by a number of variables about each of the network paths to the destination host, including the number of hops, the cost of each hop, and so on.

Just because there is a route to a destination, there is no guarantee there is a route back. While not a common problem in networks with dynamic routing enabled, it can happen, particularly when working in a heavily firewalled network environment.

When a router needs to forward a packet to another router for delivery to a remote network, it consults a database of information known as the routing table. This database is stored in the router's memory to ensure this lookup process can be performed very quickly.

As the packet travels across the network toward its destination, each router along the way decides about where to forward the packet by consulting its routing table. When a destination host sends a reply packet, it is possible that the same path may not be used to reach the original sender. This depends on the metrics of each path along the route. In other words, the way to the destination host may not be the best path back.

Information in the routing table can be generated in one of two ways. The first method is to manually configure the routing table with the routes for each destination network. This is known as static routing. Static routing is more suited to small environments where the amount of information to configure is small, and the overhead of generating the routing information dynamically is unacceptable. Static routers do not scale well to large or frequently changing internetworks because of the requirement for manual administration.

The second method for generating routing table information is to make use of a dynamic routing protocol. Because dynamic routing protocols are quite a bit more complex than static routing, we need to take a more in-depth look at the subject.

A general definition of a protocol is an agreed-upon method for exchanging data between two devices. A routing protocol defines the method for exchanging routing information between two routing devices. A dynamic routing protocol is used to exchange routing information that is created and maintained in the routing table automatically. When using a dynamic routing protocol, routing information is exchanged between routers to update the information kept in their routing tables. This can be done either periodically (at scheduled intervals) or on demand. If set up correctly at the outset, dynamic routers will require little administration after they have been configured, outside of ensuring software updates are applied in a timely fashion. Because they learn routing information dynamically and can route around failures when the network architecture will support it, dynamic routing is generally used in large network environments where it would not be practical to use static routing.

Remember—routers need to be patched too. Because routers run an operating system, there are security and functionality updates that need to be applied on a regular basis.

Understanding Routing Protocols

Routing protocols are based either on a distance vector or link-state algorithm. The differences between the two algorithms include when routing information is exchanged, what information is sent when the routing information is exchanged, and how quickly the protocol can route around outages, when the network topology will support it.

Path selection involves applying a routing metric to multiple routes, in order to select the best route. Some of the metrics used are bandwidth, network delay, hop count, path cost, load, reliability, and communication costs. The hop count is the number of routers traversed by a packet between its source and destination.

Distance vector-based routing protocols require that each router inform its neighbors of its routing table. This is done by sending the entire routing table when the router boots and then at scheduled intervals afterward. Each router receives changes from its neighboring routers and then updates their own routing tables based on the information they receive. Using the information from these updates, a router can build a network map in its routing table and determine hop counts (the distance to any network) for each network entry in the routing table. RIP is an example of a distance vector-based routing protocol and is supported by Windows Server 2016. Routing updates sent using a distance vector-based routing protocol are unacknowledged and unsynchronized, which is one of the drawbacks of these protocols. Some other drawbacks of this type of routing protocol include the following:

High Overhead Because every router on the network sends its entire routing table when it sends an update, distance vector-based protocols produce very large routing tables. This adds overhead to the router memory needed to store these tables, and the router processing power needed to maintain these tables. Large routing tables can also hamper an administrator trying to determine the source of an issue when problems arise.

Not Scalable Distance vector-based networks are limited to 15 hops (router traversals) for any given route. In a large network (like the Internet) it is very easy to have network segments that are greater than 15 hops away, and these would be unreachable in a distance vector-based network.

Network Bandwidth Intensive Distance vector-based protocols require that routers exchange their entire routing table whenever they do an update. On a large network, with large routing tables, these routing updates can utilize significant amounts of bandwidth, especially across slower WAN connections or demand-dial links.

Long Convergence Time Convergence is the amount of time it takes a routing algorithm to detect and route around a network failure. Distance vector-based protocols typically have longer convergence times than link-state-based protocols.

Routing Loop Issues Distance vector-based protocols can also suffer from routing loop issues when there are multiple paths to a network.

Count-to-Infinity Issues (routing loops) Count-to-infinity issues occur when there is a network outage, and the routing algorithm cannot calculate a new router. One router will broadcast a route and increment the hop count for the router, then a second router will broadcast the same route to the first router, also incrementing the hop count, and so on, until the route metric (hop count) reaches 16 and the route is discarded.

Distance vector-based routing protocols have additional mechanisms that allow them to avoid the count-to-infinity issues as well as improving convergence. These mechanisms include the following:

Split Horizon The split horizon mechanism prevents routes from being broadcast out the interface from which they were received. Split horizon eliminates count-to-infinity issues and routing loops during convergence in single-path internetworks and reduces the chances of count-to-infinity issues in multipath internetworks.

Split Horizon with Poison Reverse The split horizon with poison reverse mechanism allows routes to be broadcast back to the interface from which they were received, but they are announced with a hop count of 16, which indicates that the network is unreachable (in other words, the route has been poisoned and is unusable through that interface).

Triggered Updates   Triggered updates allow a router to announce changes in metric values almost immediately, rather than waiting for the next periodic announcement. The trigger is a change to a metric in an entry in the routing table. For example, networks that become unavailable can be announced with a hop count of 16 through a triggered update. If triggered updates were sent by all routers immediately, each triggered update could cause a cascade of broadcast traffic across the IP internetwork.

The advantages of distance vector-based routing are that it requires low maintenance and is easy to configure, making it popular in small network environments.

Link-state routing was designed to overcome the disadvantages of distance vector-based routing. Routers using link-state routing protocols learn about their network environment by "meeting" their neighboring routers. This is done through a "hello" packet, which tells the neighboring router what networks the first router can reach. Once the introduction is complete, the neighboring router will send the new network information to each of its neighboring routers using a link-state advertisement. Open Shortest Path First (OSPF) is an example of a link-state routing protocol. The neighboring routers copy the contents of the packet and forward the link-state advertisement to each attached network, except for the one on which the link-state advertisement was received. This is known as flooding.

Routers using a link-state routing protocol build a tree, or map, of shortest paths with itself as the root. The tree is based on all the link-state advertisements seen. The tree contains the route to each destination in the network. Once this tree has been built, routing information is only sent when changes to the network occur, instead of periodically as in the distance vector-based protocols.

There are a few advantages to this method, especially when compared to the distance vector-based routing protocols. These advantages include the following:

Smaller Routing Tables   Because the router only maintains a table of link states, rather than a copy of every route on the network, it needs to maintain much smaller routing tables.

Highly Scalable   Link-state protocols do not suffer from the 15-hop issue that distance vector-based protocols do, so they are able to scale to much larger networks.

More Efficient Use of Network Bandwidth   Because link-state information is not exchanged after the network has converged, routing updates do not consume precious bandwidth, unless there is an outage that forces the network to re-converge.

Faster Convergence   Link-state routing protocols will converge faster than distance vector-based protocols, because updates are sent as soon as a change to the network occurs, instead of having to wait for the periodic update used in the distance vector-based protocols.

The disadvantages of link-state-based protocols are that they are more complex to understand and configure than distance vector-based protocols. They also require additional processing power on the router, due to the need to calculate the routing tree.

Routing can be a key component of network security because it lets you determine which parts of the network can be accessed by other parts of the network. For example, if you have a business partner connection to a third-party network, the third-party network will need to have routing information in order to access any systems that have been advertised on your extranet DMZ for them to access. While a firewall is the best way to secure this connection, you can add an additional layer of security by restricting the routing available to the third party. In other words, if you only tell the third party's network the routes to the extranet, they will not be able to send packets to those parts of your network where they should not have access.

Understanding Intrusion Detection Systems (IDS) and Intrusion Prevention Systems (IPS)

Two other security technologies available to secure networks are *intrusion detection systems (IDS)* and *intrusion prevention systems (IPS)*. An IDS is a solution designed to detect unauthorized user activities, attacks, and network compromises.

An intrusion prevention system (IPS) is very similar to an IDS, except that in addition to detecting and alerting, an IPS can also take action to prevent the breach from occurring.

There are two main types of IDS/IPS technologies:

Network-Based   A network-based IDS (NIDS) monitors network traffic using sensors that are located at key locations within the network, often in the demilitarized zone (DMZ) or at network borders. These sensors capture all network traffic and analyze the contents of individual packets for malicious traffic. An NIDS will gain access to network traffic by connecting to a hub, a network switch configured for port mirroring, or a network tap.

Host-Based   A host-based IDS (HIDS) generally has a software agent that acts as the sensor. This agent monitors all activity of the host on which it is installed, including monitoring the file system, the logs, and the kernel, to identify and alert upon suspicious behavior. An HIDS is typically deployed to safeguard the host on which it is installed.

There are two common deployment methodologies used when placing an IDS/IPS to protect a network from the Internet. Each has its own advantages and disadvantages:

Unfiltered   An unfiltered IDS/IPS installation examines the raw Internet data stream before it crosses the firewall. This provides the highest amount of visibility to attacks, but also means that there is a significantly higher volume of data to be monitored, with a higher possibility of false positives. There is also a chance that during periods of high traffic, the IDS/IPS might not be able to process all the packets, and attacks can be missed.

Screened   A screened IDS/IPS solution monitors the traffic that gets through the screening firewall. The advantage to this model is it dramatically reduces the amount of traffic that needs to be monitored, reducing the chances of false positives and lost packets during high traffic volumes. There is a loss of visibility with this model, because attacks cannot be seen on the screening firewall.

IDS and IPS are solutions that have historically been used to secure or provide alerts on Internet connections, because those connections have typically presented the largest threat to the network. However, with the interconnectivity of networks beyond the Internet and the threat of an insider attack, it may make sense to deploy IDS/IPS in strategic locations on your internal network. Give this some serious consideration if your internal network has connections to third-party networks like customers, vendors, or business partners.

Understanding Honeypots

Honeypots, honey nets, and padded cells are complementary technologies to IDS/IPS deployments. A *honeypot* is a trap for hackers. A honeypot is designed to distract hackers from real targets, detect new vulnerabilities and exploits, and learn about the identity of attackers. A *honey net* is just a collection of honeypots used to present an attacker with an even more realistic attack environment. A padded cell is a system that waits for an IDS to detect an attacker and then transfers the attacker to a special host where they cannot do any damage to the production environment. They are all related technologies, used to add an additional layer to your security infrastructure.

A honeypot is valuable as a surveillance and early-warning tool. It is also a generic term to describe anything that would attract an attacker. While it is usually a reference to a host running special software for detecting and analyzing an attack, the term honeypot can refer to other things such as files or data records, or even unused IP address space.

There are a variety of different types of honeypots, including the following:

Production   A production honeypot is a relatively easy solution to deploy. They are used to distract attackers from potentially vulnerable production systems and are relatively easy to use. A production honeypot typically captures limited information and can generally be found in corporate networks. This type of honeypot is typically used as an additional form of early-warning system, as an enhancement to an IDS/IPS system.

Research   A research honeypot is more complex than a production honeypot and is more difficult to deploy and maintain. This type of honeypot is used to capture extensive information that is used to develop attack signatures, identify new attack techniques and vulnerabilities, and develop a better understanding of the attacker's mindset. Research honeypots are used primarily for research by universities, the military, or other government organizations.

When deploying a honeypot, ensure that there is no production information or purpose for the server. This not only ensures that production data is secure, but because there is no legitimate reason for traffic or activity on the system, the only thing that will touch the honeypot will be malicious activity.

Also, be aware that honeypots can create risks to the environment. Because a honeypot is essentially being used as bait for an attacker, attackers are being lured into the network environment. As a result, be absolutely certain that the honeypots are isolated from the production environment. If they are not, the attacker can jump from the honeypot to the production environment and compromise critical systems or infrastructure. It's somewhat like trying to lure a bear to an adjoining empty campsite, to keep them away from yours—there's always a chance the bear may find your campsite, anyway.

One area where honeypots are especially useful is in the battle against spam. One of the challenges associated with spam and spam filtering is that the spammers are constantly changing the techniques they use to bypass spam filters. They also have a variety of techniques for harvesting email addresses from websites for inclusion in their spam target lists.

As a result, the people who develop spam filters spend much of their time working to identify those techniques and develop new filters to combat the new spam methods. Honeypots are an essential component of this fight, and there are two types of honeypots that can be used to combat spam.

Email Address Honeypot   Any email address that is dedicated to receiving spam for analysis can be considered a spam honeypot. An example of this technique is Project Honey Pot, a distributed, open-source project that uses honeypot pages installed on websites around the world in conjunction with uniquely tagged email addresses for analyzing not only spam delivery, but also the email address harvesting techniques.

Email Open Relay Honeypot   Email open relays are servers that relay mail from one mail server to another mail server. An example of a mail relay server is using POP3 or IMAP to send an email through your personal ISP. In some instances, these servers are set up so they do not need credentials to send email, which is a significant prize for spammers. It allows them to relay their millions of spam emails anonymously. Setting up a honeypot that appears to be an open relay can potentially reveal the spammer's IP address and provide bulk spam capture. This allows for in-depth analysis of the spammers techniques, response URLs, email addresses, and other valuable information.

While these are all extremely exciting technologies, they do not get deployed in too many corporate environments. Generally, these are deployed by educational institutions and security research firms. Corporate information security professionals are so busy securing their environment from attacks that they don't spend a lot of time researching attack patterns. As long as the attack didn't succeed, they are satisfied. In cases of high-security environments, where there is extensive Internet-based activity and data requiring additional layers of security, honeypots may be used as part of the layered security defense.

Understanding DMZ

When most people hear the term *DMZ* (short for demilitarized zone), images of barbed wire and machine gun emplacements come to mind. While not entirely accurate in the scope of information security, the concept is not that far from reality. In computer networking, a DMZ is a firewall configuration used to secure hosts on a network segment. In most DMZs, the hosts on the DMZ are connected behind a firewall which is connected to a public network like the Internet. Another common configuration is to have the firewall connected to an extranet, with connections to customers, vendors, or business partners. DMZs are designed to provide access to systems without jeopardizing the internal network.

There are two typical DMZ configurations encountered in production environments:

Sandwich DMZ   In a sandwich DMZ model (see Figure 4.3), there is an outer firewall and an inner firewall. The outer firewall secures the DMZ network segment from the external (insecure) network. Servers that are meant to be accessed from the external network (like the Internet) have the appropriate rules configured to permit secure access. The inner firewall is used to add an additional layer of security between the servers on the DMZ and the internal (secure) network. The main benefit of this model is that in the event that the outer firewall and/or a server on the DMZ is compromised, there is an additional layer of firewall security protecting the internal network. Ideally, the outer and inner firewalls are from different vendors, in order to ensure that in the event an exploit is used to compromise the outer firewall, the same exploit cannot be used to compromise the inner firewall. The major drawbacks of this model are that it is a more complex architecture to implement and maintain, and it is more expensive, because additional training is needed for the different additional firewall.

FIGURE 4.3   An example of a sandwich DMZ

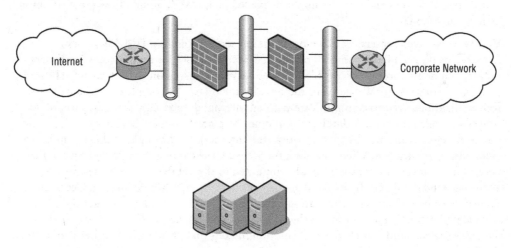

Single Firewall DMZ   In a single firewall DMZ (see Figure 4.4), the DMZ is an additional network connection from the firewall. This provides an external network connection, an internal network connection, and a DMZ network connection, all connected to the same firewall. While this architecture still allows the firewall to control access to DMZ resources, if the firewall is compromised, access to the internal network may be breached. This model is less expensive than the sandwich model, but does not provide as high a level of security.

FIGURE 4.4   An example of a single firewall DMZ

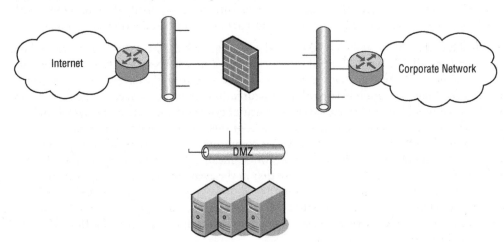

While it's easy to talk about the architecture of a DMZ, it's important to understand what types of servers and services might be placed on a DMZ. Some of the most common include the following:

Web Servers   Web servers are the most common servers found in DMZ networks. Accessed using HTTP over port 80 or HTTPS over port 443 for secure access, web servers are commonly Internet-accessible. All web servers accessed on the Internet are hosted on a DMZ somewhere. Web servers add an additional layer of complexity because many web applications need to communicate with an internal database or databases to provide some specialized services. A database would not be placed on the DMZ because it should not be accessed from the insecure network (the Internet). An example of this might be an e-commerce application. When reaching the website, the catalog data, including product descriptions, prices, and availability are contained in the database (sometimes referred to as the backend database). If the database server contains critical information like Social Security numbers, financial information, credit card data, and so on, it's a good idea to add an application firewall between the web server and the database server. While this increases the cost and complexity of a solution, it adds an extra layer of security to protect the database.

Email Relay Servers   Email servers are another type of server that needs to be accessed from the Internet, to allow for sending and receiving Internet email. In the early years of computer networking, it was not unusual for email to be restricted to the corporate network. Once companies and individuals got connected to the Internet, the ability to send and receive email from other companies over the Internet became critical to business success. By placing email relay servers, which communicate on port 25, on the DMZ, they can receive email from the Internet, and then relay it to mail servers on the internal network securely. Spam filtering capabilities are frequently included on these relay servers.

Proxy Servers   Proxy servers are used to proxy, or act as an intermediary, for user requests from the internal network to the Internet and are typically used to retrieve website information. These are placed on the DMZ to provide additional security for web browsing. Some proxy servers will filter content, including inappropriate websites, add virus protection and anti-spyware security, and even improve performance by caching web requests.

Reverse Proxy Servers   Reverse proxy servers are used to provide secure access to internal applications from an insecure network. While these have largely been replaced by VPN technologies, reverse proxy servers can be used to provide employees with access to web-based email servers on the internal network, provide access to internal web applications, and, in some cases, even provide secure terminal services connections to the internal network.

Understanding NAT

Network Address Translation (NAT) is a technique used to modify the network address information of a host while traffic is traversing a router or firewall. This technique is used to hide the network information of a private network, while allowing traffic to be transferred across a public network like the Internet.

NAT was originally created as a workaround for IP addressing issues. The Internet relies on the TCP/IP protocol suite for communications between hosts. A critical component of this protocol suite is the IP addressing. The explosive growth of the Internet threatened to exhaust the pool of IPv4 IP addresses, which would have crippled the expansion and use of the Internet. Without unique addresses, the Internet would be unable to successfully route TCP/IP traffic. NAT was the resultant workaround solution for preserving the number of IP addresses used on the Internet.

In the early days of the Internet, when the TCP/IP protocol and related addressing was being developed, the 32-bit addressing scheme (known as IPv4) was considered more than adequate for any potential network growth. Technically there were 4,294,967,296 unique addresses available using a 32-bit address, and even discounting the reserved ranges, there are still over 3 billion possible addresses. At the time, that was enough addresses to provide an address for every person on the planet, including children. Unfortunately, the designers of the addressing scheme dramatically underestimated the explosive growth of the Internet, as well as the widespread adoption of TCP/IP in business and home networks, resulting in the depleting of IP addresses.

The practical use for NAT is that it allows the use of one set of IP addresses on the internal LAN, and a second set of IP addresses for the Internet connection. There is a device (usually a router or firewall) in between the two networks that provides NAT services, managing the translation of internal addresses to external addresses. This allows companies to use large numbers of unregistered internal addresses while only needing a fraction of that number of addresses on the Internet, thus conserving the addresses. This allows for the re-use of addresses within private networks while ensuring that the addresses used on the Internet remain unique.

The long-term solution for this issue is IPv6 or Internet Protocol Version 6, the next generation protocol for the Internet. It's designed to provide several advantages over IPv4, including support for addresses that are 128 bits long. This permits 2^{128} unique IPv6 addresses, or over 340 trillion addresses.

However, the adoption of IPv6 has been slow, in large part to the successful use of NAT and proxy servers to conserve the number of IPv4 addresses used on the Internet today.

 Network Address Translation (NAT) is supported under Windows Server 2016 by the Routing and Remote Access Service.

There are two main types of NAT:

Static NAT   Static NAT maps an unregistered IP address on the private network to a registered IP address on the public network, using a one-to-one basis. This is used when the translated device needs to be accessible from the public network. For example, a web server on a DMZ network might have an unregistered address of 10.20.30.40 that is translated by a NAT-capable device to an Internet-facing address of 12.4.4.234. A user trying to connect to that website can enter 12.4.4.234, and the router or firewall at the other end will translate that address to 10.20.30.40 when the packet reaches it. This version of NAT is typically used in conjunction with DMZ or extranet networks.

Dynamic NAT   Dynamic NAT maps an unregistered IP address on the private network to a registered IP address that is selected by the routing device providing the NAT service from a pool of registered IP addresses. This is more commonly used when many hosts on the internal network need to access the Internet and don't have a requirement for a static address. The workstation's address is translated to the next available registered address in the pool as soon as it initiates a connection to the public network.

There are two major security implications associated with the use of NAT. First, NAT can be used to hide private network addresses, which makes it more difficult for an attacker to successfully penetrate a private network. The addresses that are visible to an Internet-based attacker are the NAT addresses typically stored on the firewall, which should be one of the more secure devices on a network.

NAT also presents a unique issue when working with the IPsec protocol, which we will be discussing in more detail later in the lesson. Early implementations of IPsec did not support NAT, so the IPsec protocol could not be used when NAT was enabled in the environment. NAT traversal capability was added in later versions of the IPsec protocol, but IPsec still requires that some special steps be taken in order to successfully work with NAT.

Understanding VPN

VPN (Virtual Private Network) is a technology that uses encrypted tunnels to create secure connections across public networks like the Internet. There are a variety of uses for this technology—three of the most common uses appear in Figure 4.5.

FIGURE 4.5   Some common uses for VPN

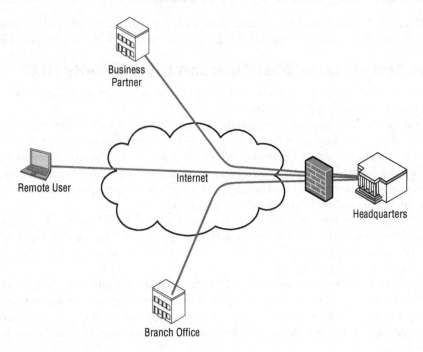

VPNs are commonly used by remote employees for access to the internal network, to create secure network-to-network connections for branch offices or business partner connections, or even to create secure host-to-host connections for additional security and isolation on an internal network. VPNs utilize encryption and authentication to provide confidentiality, integrity, and privacy protection for data.

Remote access VPNs were first introduced in the late 1990s and were initially used in conjunction with modems to provide more secure, more flexible connectivity to a corporate network. All that was required was a dial-up Internet connection and a VPN client, and a user could connect to the corporate network over an encrypted connection. No more modem banks in the data center, and no more toll-free modem lines to be managed. A user who could get to the Internet could get remote access up and running.

With the advent of high-speed Internet connections, the use of VPN technologies exploded. It was now possible in some cases to get a faster connection via a high-speed home Internet connection than typical dedicated network connections from branch offices. It also allows businesses to migrate from expensive dedicated network connections to less expensive Internet-based VPN connections.

The first standards-based VPNs were based on the IPsec protocol. The IPsec-based VPNs quickly overtook some of the proprietary-based VPNs that were the first products to market.

Understanding Other VPN Protocols

While IPsec can be considered the predominant protocol associated with VPNs, there are other protocols that can also be used to build VPNs, or provide VPN-like connectivity.

Secure Sockets Layer (SSL)/Transport Layer Security (TLS)

One of the key VPN protocols used today is SSL/TLS, which is the main alternative to IPsec for implementing a VPN solution.

The SSL protocol standard was originally proposed as a standard by Netscape. While this protocol is widely used to secure websites, it has since been formalized in the IETF standard known as Transport Layer Security (TLS). The SSL/TLS protocol provides a method for secure client/server communications across a network and prevents eavesdropping and tampering with data in transit. SSL/TLS also provides endpoint authentication and communications confidentiality using encryption.

HTTPS, the secure version of HTTP web browsing, uses the SSL protocol. This protocol provides 128-bit encryption and is currently the leading security mechanism for protecting web traffic including banking, e-commerce, secure email, and essentially any other secure website that might be encountered.

In typical end-user/browser usage, SSL/TLS authentication is one way. Only the server is authenticated—the client compares the information entered to access a server to information on the SSL certificate on the server. Thus, the client knows the server's identity. However, the server does not do this for the client—the client remains unauthenticated or anonymous.

SSL/TLS can also perform bi-directional authentication by using client-based certificates. This is particularly useful when using this protocol to access a protected network, as it adds an additional layer of authentication to the access.

As we discussed in the section on IPsec, a VPN creates a secure tunnel through a public network like the Internet. While SSL VPNs still leverage the concept of tunneling, they create their tunnels differently than IPsec. An SSL VPN establishes connectivity using the SSL protocol. IPsec works at Layer 3 of the OSI model, while SSH functions at Layers 4–5. SSL VPNs can also encapsulate information at Layers 6–7, which makes SSL VPNs very flexible.

One additional function of an SSL VPN is that an SSL VPN usually connects using a web browser, whereas an IPsec VPN generally requires that client software be installed on the remote system.

SSL VPNs are predominantly used for remote access VPN connections, where a client is connecting to applications on an internal network, as opposed to a site-to-site connection, where two gateways are used to connect disparate private networks across the Internet.

Some benefits of SSL/TLS VPNs over IPsec VPNs include:

Less Expensive   Because an SSL VPN is typically clientless, there aren't the costs for rolling out, supporting, and updating client software.

Platform Independent   Because the access to an SSL VPN is granted through the standard SSL interface, which is a component of virtually every web browser, virtually any OS that runs a browser is supported.

Client Flexibility   Generally, IPsec clients are usually installed only on corporate systems. Due to the additional configuration flexibility, SSL VPNs can be configured to allow access from a variety of clients, including corporate systems, home systems, customer or supplier systems, or even a kiosk machine in a library or an Internet cafe. This wider access can greatly increase employee satisfaction.

NAT Support   Historically Network Address Translation (NAT) can cause issues with IPsec VPNs. Virtually all IPsec vendors have created workarounds for this issue. An SSL VPN doesn't have these issues, because SSL works at a higher layer than IPsec and thus is not impacted by NAT.

Granular Access Control   This could be considered a benefit or, depending on the environment, it could be a drawback. SSL VPNs require a greater granularity of access than a typical IPsec VPN, because instead of creating a tunnel from the host to the internal network, SSL VPNs require that each resource accessed be explicitly defined. The upside is unless it has been explicitly defined, an SSL VPN user cannot access it, which has significant security benefits, but in a complex environment this could add significant overhead to VPN support.

Fewer Firewall Rules Required   In order to access an IPsec gateway across a firewall, open several ports to support the individual protocols for authentication and the tunnel. An SSL VPN only needs port 443 opened, which is generally easy to do, due to the prevalence of the HTTPS protocol.

Secure Shell (SSH)

The Secure Shell (SSH) protocol is a protocol for secure remote logon and other secure network services over the network. SSH can be used for several applications across multiple platforms, including UNIX, Microsoft Windows, Apple Mac, and Linux.

Some of the applications supported with SSH include the following:

- Secure logon
- Secure remote command execution
- Secure file transfer
- Secure backup, copy, and mirroring of files
- Creation of VPN connections (when used in conjunction with the OpenSSH server and client)

The SSH protocol consists of three major components:

Transport Layer Protocol   This provides server authentication, confidentiality, and integrity with perfect forward secrecy.

User Authentication Protocol: This provides authentication of the client to the server.

Connection Protocol   Multiplexes the encrypted tunnel into several logical channels.

Now that we've looked at some of the protocols that can be used to secure traffic across a network and usually across a public network like the Internet, we can look at a technique for providing additional security on an internal network.

Understanding Server and Domain Isolation

Security professionals are constantly being asked by businesses to allow greater and greater access to resources in order to facilitate business requirements. While wider and easier access to resources can increase the production of a business, it also presents significant security challenges. The risk of virus attacks, rogue users and devices, and unauthorized access to sensitive information associated with unauthorized or unmanaged devices is enough to keep an information security professional awake at night.

An example of this might be a developer's workstation. Many developers feel they have unique requirements to do their job, and as a result, they may run custom configurations, unsupported operating systems, open source applications, and not participate in the corporate patch and configuration management programs. In a typical environment, once this system is on the network, it would have access to any internal resources. Server and domain isolation provides some additional security options.

 To leverage isolation in an environment, be sure to take the time to do the appropriate planning. This can be a complex implementation and needs to be understood before protocols are enabled.

Server and domain isolation is a solution based on IPsec and the Microsoft Active Directory that enables administrators to dynamically segment their Windows environment into more secure and isolated logical networks. These logical networks are segmented based on policy and can be accomplished without needing to deploy firewalls, implement VLANs, or make other changes on the network. Through the use of authentication and encryption, internal servers and domains can be secured. This creates an additional layer of policy-driven protection and provides another alternative to the security controls we have discussed thus far in this lesson.

Figure 4.6 provides an example of server and domain isolation. The isolated network can only be accessed by computers with the appropriate IPsec and Active Directory configuration.

FIGURE 4.6   An example of server and domain isolation

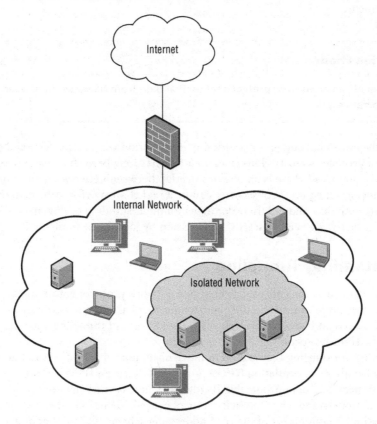

How does it work? Authentication to the isolated environment is based on the computer's machine credentials. The machine credentials can be an Active Directory–issued Kerberos ticket, or it can be an X.509 certificate automatically distributed to the computer by a Group Policy. Once the machine has authenticated, the associated isolation policies are enforced by the built-in IPsec functionality in Windows.

Recall that IPsec supports two modes. Tunnel mode is the most frequently used mode, because it supports the widely used remote access and site-to-site VPN solutions that are becoming ubiquitous in the corporate world. Transport mode is used for Server and Domain isolation, as it is the mode that supports secure host-to-host communications.

Protecting Data with Protocol Security

In this lesson, we have discussed several security protocols such as IPsec, SSL/TLS, and SSH. In this section, we are going to look at a couple more protocols that can be used to secure data. This includes looking at protocol spoofing, network sniffing, and some of the common attacks that might be encountered when working on securing a corporate computing environment.

Certification Ready

Which protocol can be used to protect confidential data from being sent between servers? Objective 3.3

One of the more challenging topics for any information security professional to tackle is the idea of protocol security. This is an area that has long been the area of networking professionals, and while there is an obvious overlap between networking and information security, understanding protocol security can be a real challenge for information security professionals both new and old. In order to get an understanding of how network protocols can impact security, we need to start the discussion by looking at tunneling.

Understanding Tunneling

Tunneling is defined as the encapsulation of one network protocol within another. Tunneling can be used to route an unsupported protocol across a network or to securely route traffic across an insecure network. VPNs use a form of tunneling when data is encapsulated in the IPsec protocol.

An example of tunneling that is used to move unsupported traffic across a network is the Generic Routing Encapsulation (GRE) protocol. GRE is an IP-based protocol frequently used to carry packets from unrouteable IP addresses across an IP network.

In order to understand why the GRE protocol is used, we need to discuss a little about IPv4 addressing. A component of the IPv4 addressing scheme is a set of addresses known as either private or reserved address ranges. These ranges include 10.0.0.0–10.255.255.255, 172.16.0.0–176.31.255.255, and 192.168.0.0–192.168.255.255. These ranges were assigned to help delay the exhaustion of the available IPv4 IP addresses, and are typically used for both home and office networks, where there is not a requirement for the addresses to be routed across a public network like the Internet. These networks generally use NAT to permit Internet access.

Another area where these addresses are used is for lab/development networks in an enterprise environment. Sometimes there is a requirement to route traffic from the lab/development network to another, but because these networks are addressed with private addresses, they may not be routable across the enterprise network. This is when GRE becomes useful. Traffic between the labs can be encapsulated in a GRE tunnel that can be routed over the enterprise network without requiring readdressing.

 What is PPP? PPP, the Point-to-Point Protocol, was a protocol defined in the late 90s that provided a standard transport mechanism for point-to-point data connections. This was largely used in conjunction with modem connections and has largely been phased out as modem connections have been replaced by high-speed Internet connections.

PPTP (Point-to-Point Tunneling Protocol) is a proprietary VPN protocol originally developed by the PPTP Forum, a group of vendors that included Ascend Communications, Microsoft Corporation, 3Com, ECI Telematics, and U.S. Robotics. PPTP was designed as an extension of the Point-to-Point Protocol (PPP) to allow PPP to be tunneled through an IP network. At one time PPTP was the most widely used VPN protocol, but the release of IPsec had a significant impact on PPTP's use.

Another tunneling protocol that was widely used was L2TP (Layer 2 Tunneling Protocol), which combined the best features of PPTP and the L2F (Layer Two Forwarding) protocol, an early competing protocol for PPTP that was developed by Cisco Systems. Like PPTP, L2TP was designed as an extension of PPP to allow PPP to be tunneled through an IP network. L2TP support was first included in a Microsoft server product with the release of Windows 2000 Server. Prior to Windows 2000, PPTP was the only supported protocol. A number of hardware VPN vendors, including Cisco, also supported PPTP.

Understanding DNS Security Extensions (DNSSEC)

Anyone who has ever connected to a website by name has used the Domain Name Service (DNS). The DNS is a service used on the Internet for resolving fully qualified domain names (FQDN) to their actual Internet Protocol (IP) addresses, using a distributed network of name servers. When entering a server name, like www.espn.com, DNS ensures the connection is directed to the appropriate servers. Although this service is largely invisible to end users, DNS is a critical element of how the Internet functions.

Let's say you want to check the scores from your favorite sport on ESPN's website. Before DNS, when asking "What's the address of ESPN's website?" the answer might be 199.181.132.250. Most people might remember that number for less than 30 seconds and then would probably never find those sports scores. With DNS, type the server name to go to a site such as www.espn.com, and the DNS infrastructure of the Internet will translate the name to the correct address. It's like a big phone book—put in a name to find the correct number.

However, DNS was developed during the early years of the Internet, when functionality was the goal, not security. As a result, DNS was built without security. In recent years, this lack of security has been exploited with forged DNS data, which, among other things, redirects connections to malicious websites. After typing the address of your bank, it appears you have reached your destination. You enter your user ID and password to access your accounts, but can't log on. Next month you find out that your account has been cleaned out. What happened was that the initial connection was the result of a bad DNS entry. Instead of connecting to the bank's website, you connected to a clever duplicate, which captured your logon information and let the bad guys steal your life savings.

DNS Security Extensions (DNSSEC) adds security provisions to DNS so that computers can verify that they have been directed to proper servers. This new standard was published in March 2005 and is slowly being adopted by the Internet domains. DNSSEC provides authentication and integrity checking on DNS lookups, ensuring that outgoing Internet traffic is always sent to the correct server. This removes the issues of forged DNS data, because there is no way to forge the appropriate authentication. This not only addresses the issue of website redirection but also addresses some challenges associated with spam and the use of faked mail domains.

DNSSEC provides authentication and integrity checking through the use of public key encryption. The domain name structure provides a hierarchy of authenticated keys, creating a chain of trust from the root of the DNS hierarchy to the domain being queried. DNSSEC will address many of the most problematic security issues associated with the Internet's core infrastructure, but it comes at a significant cost. As with any large-scaled public key implementation, rolling this out to the entire Internet will be an enormously complex, resource-intensive project. There are also challenges associated with maintaining the web of trust created by using public keys on such a large scale.

Understanding Protocol Spoofing

Another security area of concern with respect to protocols is the concept of protocol *spoofing*. The word spoof can be defined as a hoax. Protocol spoofing is the misuse of a network protocol to perpetrate a hoax on a host or a network device. Some common forms of protocol spoofing include:

ARP spoofing   ARP (Address Resolution Protocol) spoofing (or ARP poisoning) is an attack on the protocol used to determine a device's hardware address (MAC address) on the network when the IP address is known. This is critical for the proper delivery of network data once the data has reached the proper LAN segment. An ARP spoofing attack occurs when an attacker modifies the network's ARP caches and takes over the IP address of the victim host. This permits the attacker to receive any data intended for the original host.

DNS spoofing   DNS spoofing occurs when an attacker is able to intercept a DNS request and respond to the request before the DNS server is able to. As a result, the victim host is directed to the wrong website, where additional malicious activities can take place. This attack is frequently used in conjunction with network sniffing, which will be discussed in the next section.

IP address spoofing   In an IP address spoofing attack, the attacker creates IP packets with a forged source IP address either to conceal the identity of the attacking host or to impersonate the identity of a victim host. This attack was very popular in the early days of packet analysis firewalls—an attacker would spoof an internal IP address from the outside of a firewall, and if not configured correctly, the firewall would permit access to the internal network.

It is important to be aware that the term protocol spoofing has another definition within the computing arena. It's a term used to represent a technique associated with data compression and is used to improve network throughput and improve network performance. While a valuable tool in the appropriate circumstances, this form of protocol spoofing does not have information security implications.

Understanding Network Sniffing

Network sniffing is a type of network analysis that is a very useful tool for network administrators responsible for maintaining networks and identifying network issues. It involves connecting a device to the network with the appropriate software to allow access to the details of the packets traversing the network. Figure 4.7 shows an example of an open source network sniffing tool.

FIGURE 4.7   Wireshark—a commonly used open source network sniffing tool

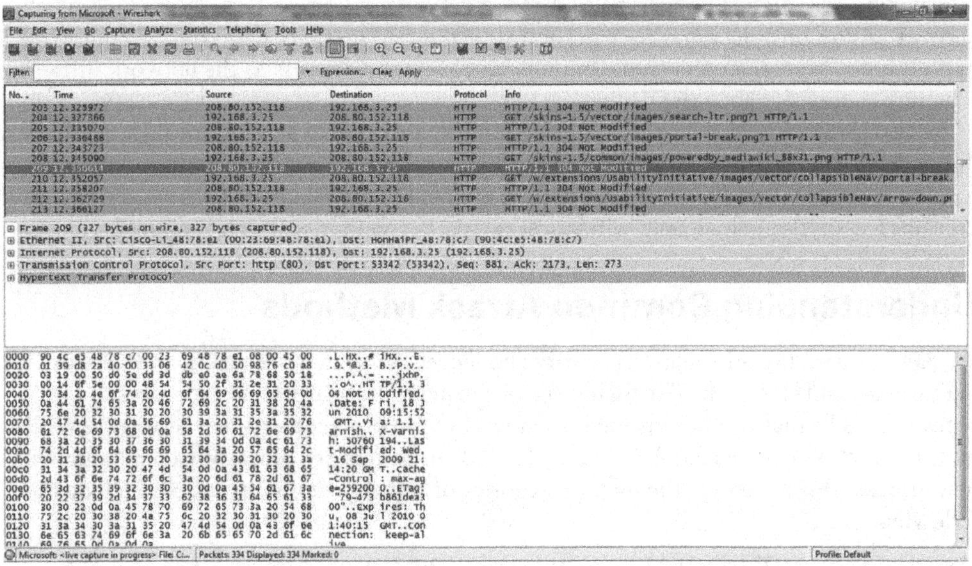

As shown in the figure, this tool reveals a significant amount of information about the packet being analyzed. To a network administrator with an in-depth understanding of networking, this information can be used to identify application issues, network latency, and a variety of other network errors.

Unfortunately, to an attacker with similar skills, the information offered by network sniffing provides equally valuable information that can be used for attacking a network. For example, any data sent in clear text, that is, not encrypted, can generally be read directly from the network. In the early days of the Internet, this was a significant amount of the traffic. Reading passwords from data packets was a trivial exercise.

Today, with the widespread use of encryption through secure websites and the use of VPNs for remote access, the risks presented by network sniffing are slightly mitigated, as the attacker can no longer read the data contents of a packet, but they can still get important information about the data packet that can be used in attacks.

It is important to be aware that a network sniffer can only see traffic that crosses the port to which it is connected. So, a sniffer placed on the LAN in a branch office cannot capture traffic from the headquarters network. In a switched environment, leveraging VLANs, the amount of traffic passing any one port can be limited. The ports that offer the most information are the ingress/egress points to the network, where all the traffic from the subnet is concentrated.

This means an attacker cannot directly capture traffic from your network, but that doesn't mean you're safe. A system on your internal network that is infected by a virus can end up running a network sniffer and providing the captured traffic to a remote host.

Another security challenge associated with a network sniffer is that they are passive devices. Unless the attacker has made modifications to the network in order to access more information, it is almost impossible to detect a network sniffer. In fact, there could be a network sniffer on a network node beyond your internal network that could be capturing packets about your Internet access. In that case, there is no access to the network infrastructure to look for changes.

Be aware that wireless networks are particularly susceptible to network sniffing attacks, due to the lack of a port requirement. Once connected to a wireless network, an attacker has access to all the traffic on the network. It's an excellent idea to only use encrypted connections for anything done on a wireless network, beyond general web browsing.

Understanding Common Attack Methods

We have covered the information security challenges associated with computer networking throughout this lesson. The final piece of the network security puzzle relates to the types of attacks that can be expected when working to protect computer networks. While no list of attacks can be complete, if only because attackers are constantly coming up with new attacks, this list covers the major categories of attacks. Common attacks include the following:

Denial-of-Service/Distributed Denial-of-Service (DoS/DDoS) Attacks   The goal of a denial-of-service attack is to flood the network being attacked with overwhelming amounts of traffic, shutting down the network infrastructure like a router or firewall. Because the attacker isn't interested in receiving responses to their attack packets, DoS attacks are ideal opportunities for using spoofed addresses. Spoofed addresses are more difficult to filter, because each spoofed packet appears to come from a different address, and they hide the true source of the attack. This makes backtracking the attack extremely difficult. The new wrinkle to the DoS is the distributed DoS, which leverages botnets to generate DoS attacks from multiple sources. Not only does this make the attack more difficult to defend against, as multiple computers can generate significantly more traffic than a single computer, but it also makes it much more difficult to track down the source of the attack.

A botnet is a distributed network of computers that have been compromised by malicious software and are under the control of an attacker.

IP Spoofing to Bypass Network Security   As we've discussed, IP spoofing is the modification of data packets so the data packets from the attacking computer appear to be from a trusted computer. By appearing as a trusted computer, the attacker is able to bypass network security measures, like a packet filter, or other solutions that rely on IP addresses for authentication. This method of attack on a remote system can be extremely difficult, because the attacker must modify thousands of packets in order to successfully complete the attack. This type of attack generally works best when there are trust relationships between machines. For example, it is not uncommon in some environment to have UNIX hosts on a corporate network that trust each other. Once a user successfully authenticates to one host, they are automatically trusted on the other hosts and do not need a user ID or password to get into the system. If an attacker can successfully spoof a connection from a trusted machine, he may be able to access the target machine without an authentication. Identifying the trusted machine is frequently done using network sniffing.

Man-in-the-middle attacks   A man-in-the-middle attack is a type of attack where the attacker breaks into the communication between the endpoints of a network connection. Once the attacker has broken into the communication stream, they can intercept data being transferred, or even inject false information into the data stream. These types of attacks are frequently used to intercept both HTTP and HTTPS connections. Systems connected to a wireless network are very susceptible to this form of attack.

Back door attack   Back door attacks are attacks against an opening left in a functional piece of software that allows access into a system or software application without the owner's knowledge. Many times, these back doors were left by the application developers, but current code testing has dramatically reduced the number of these found in commercial software. A more common version of this attack occurs when system administrators create system accounts that they can use in the event they are asked to leave the company. As an information security professional, one of your goals should be to validate system accounts belonging to employees at least once a year.

DNS poisoning   A DNS poisoning attack is an attack against the cached information on a DNS server. When a DNS request is made, the result of the request is cached on the DNS server so subsequent DNS requests made for the same server can be returned more quickly, without requiring a lookup by an external DNS server. Unfortunately, these cache files are not particularly secure, and attackers target these files to insert a bogus IP address for a specific server entry into a cache. When this occurs, any host making a request for that site from the poisoned DNS server will be directed to the wrong site. The bogus entry in the cache will remain until the cache expires and is refreshed.

Replay attack   A replay attack occurs when an attacker is able to capture an intact data stream from the network using a network sniffer, modify certain components of the data stream, and then replay the traffic back to the network to complete their attack. For example, an attacker could capture a session where a purchase is being made, modify the delivery address, and replay the traffic to place an order that would be delivered to their address.

Weak Encryption Keys   An attack against weak encryption keys successfully occurs when the keys have a value that permits the breaking of the encryption. Once the encryption is broken, the attacker is able to access the data that is supposed to be encrypted. Probably the highest profile example of this attack was the weakness exploited in the Wired Equivalent Privacy (WEP) security standard used in conjunction with wireless networks. Intended to be used to secure the wireless network, instead WEP keys were found to be weak and could be broken if 5 to 10 MB of wireless traffic could be captured. This traffic could then be run through one of the many tools published by the hacker community, and the result would be the WEP key, which permits the attacker to read the information protected with WEP. This is another example of an attack that relies on a network sniffer to successfully carry out the attack.

Social engineering   Social engineering attacks occur when an attacker will contact an employee of the company and try to extract useful information from them. This information may later be used to help pull off a different attack. Social engineering attacks typically have an attacker trying to appear as harmless or respectful as possible. Generally, the attacker will ask a number of questions in an attempt to identify possible avenues to exploit during an attack. If they do not receive sufficient information from one employee, they may reach out to several others until they have sufficient information for the next phase of an attack.

Password Cracking   Password cracking is an attack that attempts to decrypt stored passwords. A successful password cracking attack requires access to the encrypted password database, and a tool designed to decrypt the database.

Dictionary Attack   A dictionary attack is similar to a password cracking attack, except instead of using a tool to try to decrypt the password, a dictionary attack uses a dictionary of common passwords and repeated logon attempts with those passwords to try to find a logon and password combination that work. A variation on this attack is the password guessing attack, where an attacker will gather information about the victim in an attempt to guess their password. This is why password policies typically prohibit using the names of relatives, pets, and so on for a password.

Brute Force Attack   Brute force attacks are very similar to dictionary attacks, except instead of using a dictionary of common passwords, a brute force attack tries every single key combination known in order to break the password. The longer and more complex the password, the tougher it is for these password type attacks to be successful.

Software Vulnerability Attack   An attack against a software vulnerability exploits a known or unknown vulnerability in an operating system or application to perform malicious activities. This is probably one of the most common avenues for attack, and is used frequently by viruses and worms. A solid patch management practice is the best defense against this type of attack, especially if coupled with a vulnerability management program.

Buffer overflow attack   A buffer overflow attack exploits poorly written code by injecting data into variable fields and leveraging the response to access information in the application. This attack is made possible when the application developer doesn't limit or check the size of the data being entered in an application field. When data that is too long for the field is entered, it creates an error that can be exploited by the attacker to perform malicious actions against the application.

Remote code execution attack   Remote code execution attacks are commonly run against web applications. When an application is improperly coded, an attacker is able to run arbitrary, system level code through the application and use the results to access data or perform other unintended actions against the application or application server.

SQL injection attack   SQL injection attacks are one of the oldest attacks against web applications using the SQL Server database application. In this attack, control characters are entered into the web application and depending on the configuration of the database server, the attack can range from retrieval of information from the web server's database to allowing the execution of code or even full access to the server. This attack relies on database weaknesses as well as coding weaknesses.

Cross-site scripting (XSS) attack   Cross-site scripting attacks are by far the most common and potentially the most dangerous current attack against web users. These attacks allow attackers to bypass the security mechanisms provided by the web browser. By injecting malicious scripts into web pages, and getting users to execute them, an attacker can gain elevated access privileges to sensitive page content, session cookies, and a variety of other information maintained by the browser.

Understanding Denial-of-Service (DoS) Attacks

A *denial-of-service (DoS) attack* is an attack whereby the attacker renders a machine or network resource unavailable. It is usually done by flooding the targeted machine or resources with superfluous requests in an attempt to overload the system. However, a DoS attack can also be caused by disconnecting a power or network cable. Today, most DoS attacks are *distributed denial-of-service (DDoS)* attacks, whereby multiple computers are used to overwhelm the network resource.

Certification Ready

Describe a denial-of-service (DoS) attack. Objective 3.3

When a DoS attack occurs, the usual symptoms include the following:

- Unusually slow network performance, including when opening files or accessing websites
- Unavailability of any or all websites
- Dramatic increase in the number of spam emails received

There are three general types of DDoS attacks:

Volume-Based Attacks   Saturates the bandwidth of an attack site or system by flooding the site or system with UPP packets, ICMP packets, or other spoofed packets.

Protocol Attacks   Consumes resources of server or communication devices, such as firewalls and load balancers. They include SYN floods, fragmented packet attacks, ping of death attacks, and Smurf DDoS.

Application-Layer Attacks   Uses system or device vulnerabilities to crash the server or communication device. They include low-and-slow attacks and GET/POST floods.

Some popular and dangerous types of DDoS attacks include:

UDP flood   Uses *User Datagram Protocol (UDP),* which is a connectionless networking protocol, to flood random ports on a remote host with numerous UDP packets. When the server repeatedly checks for the application listening at that port—to the point at which the system utilizes all its resources responding to it—the system becomes inaccessible.

ICMP (ping) flood   Uses ICMP packets to flood systems. This type of attack can consume both outgoing and incoming bandwidth because the victim's servers often attempt to respond with ICMP Echo Reply packets.

SYN flood   Many TCP protocols use a three-way handshake in which a SYN Request is used to initiate a TCP connection. The host responds with a SYN-ACK response, which is confirmed with an ACK response from the requester. In a SYN flood, the attacker sends multiple SYN requests but does not respond to the SYN-ACK responses; or the attacker sends the SYN request from a spoofed IP address. Too many SYN requests lead to the system not accepting any new connections.

Ping of death   An attack that sends multiple malformed or malicious pings to a computer. The IP package, including the header, is 65,535 bytes in length, and many computer systems were never designed to properly handle ping packets larger than this, because it violates the Internet Protocol. By sending IP fragments with oversized Fragment Offsets, attackers can cause the IP packets, which were split into smaller sizes for travel, to form packets larger than 65,535 bytes after reassembly at the receiver, overflowing the memory buffers. Thus, important memory areas are overwritten, causing denial-of-service for legitimate packets.

HTTP flood   Uses many HTTP GET or POST requests to attack a web server or application. This attack is most effective when it forces the server or application to allocate the maximum resources possible in response to each single request.

Email bomb   Sends so many emails to a user or domain, the server becomes overwhelmed.

Zero-day attacks   These attacks are based on using unknown or recently announced vulnerabilities.

To protect against a DoS attack, use a combination of attack detection, traffic classification, and response tools that can identify and block illegitimate traffic. This includes intruder prevention systems (IPS) and security options available in firewalls, routers, and switches that reduce the impact of flooding. Also, check the documentation for best practices in hardening the server and network equipment. Make sure the servers and network equipment are equipped with the latest security patches.

The final component of network security to be aware of is wireless security.

Securing the Wireless Network

Wireless LANs have become one of the most popular forms of network access, rapidly spreading through homes, to businesses, to public access wireless hotspots like those found in Starbucks or McDonalds. The convenience of wireless networks must be balanced against the security implications of a network that is not contained by the walls of your building. In this section, we will discuss those security implications, and some of the techniques that can be used to secure a wireless network, including encryption keys, SSID, and MAC address filters.

Certification Ready

Which methods can be used to secure a wireless network? Objective 1.4

A wireless LAN (WLAN) allows users to connect to a network while allowing them to remain mobile. While this allows users easy access to the network from areas like conference rooms, offices, lunch rooms, and other such areas that a wired connection wouldn't allow, this also allows potential attackers a similarly easy access to the network. Many corporate wireless networks can be accessed by anyone with a laptop and wireless card. When using a wireless connection in a neighborhood, it is common for your computer to see wireless networks other than your own. Businesses have the same issues as your neighbors. They are broadcasting their network to anyone within range. In fact, with specialized antennas, wireless networks can be accessed from surprisingly long distances, and the access can occur without your knowledge.

In the early days of wireless networking, implementing it was easy, but securing it was not. As a result, there were battles between users, who wanted the ease of access and mobility that wireless promised, and security departments, who were acutely aware of the risks wireless introduced to the environment. As a result, most corporations had strict policies prohibiting the use of wireless to access the internal network directly, frequently requiring users to use VPNs to connect from the production wireless network to the internal network. As a result, users would install wireless access points under their desks, and hope that no one from security would notice. Attackers would drive around office parks looking for these unsecured access points, so they could breach the perimeters of corporate networks and attack the unprotected internal networks. Corporate security organizations would also perform similar exercises, in the hopes of finding rogue wireless connections before the attackers found them. With some of the new security capabilities available with wireless networks, it is now possible to offer reasonably secure wireless access to internal networks, reducing both the frequency of rogue access points and the resources being used to try to find and shut down those access points.

Another capability sometimes discussed when looking at deploying wireless networks is ensuring that wireless access point radio strength is tuned appropriately. While there is the possibility of tuning the wireless signal to reduce the risk of unauthorized users, it is not a good idea to rely on that as a first line of defense when trying to keep a wireless network secure. Frequently, this capability reduces usability far more than it improves security.

Understanding Service Set IDentifier (SSID)

The most basic component of the wireless network is the SSID (Service Set IDentifier). The SSID is defined in the IEEE 802.11 standard as a name for the WLAN. It does not provide any inherent security capabilities, although specifying the SSID name of the WLAN you want to connect to will ensure that you connect to the correct WLAN.

While there aren't any specific security capabilities associated with the SSID, there are some security considerations that should be taken into account:

Choose your own SSID. The first thing to do when setting up a WLAN is to set a unique SSID. Each WLAN access point will come with a default SSID set. If you use the default, there is a risk that one of your neighbors will also use the default, causing confusion and conflicts. So be sure to select a unique yet easy to remember name for your own SSID.

Follow naming conventions. After choosing an SSID name, there are some measures to take to make it a little more challenging for an attacker to identify the owner of a WLAN. It is generally not a good idea for corporations to broadcast the fact that they are the owner of a specific wireless network. Selecting SSIDs based on company name, company product lines, or anything else that might allow an attacker to confirm who owns the WLAN should be avoided. Select an SSID that the employees can remember but that doesn't invite attacks. Choosing things like city names, sports, mythological characters, or other generic SSID names are generally safe choices.

Turn off your SSID. The SSID is used to identify your WLAN and permit computers to connect to it. If this information is broadcasted, then the client systems can search for available wireless networks, and the name of your WLAN will appear in the list. A few clicks and someone can connect to the WLAN. While extremely convenient for an authorized user, broadcasting an SSID makes it equally easy for an attacker to connect in the same way. It is possible to turn off the SSID broadcast for your network, rendering it essentially invisible to casual wireless network browsers. The problem with this idea is two-fold. First, it makes getting authorized users connected to the network more difficult, and second, any attacker trying to get in through your WLAN will most likely have a wireless sniffer, which will show them the SSID of your WLAN whether it's broadcast or not, because that information is in the wireless packets. In this case, it's generally wise to select ease of use over hiding your SSID—in other words, usability over obscurity.

Now let's look at some techniques for securing a WLAN.

Understanding Keys

The best available security mechanism for securing a WLAN is to use authentication and encryption. WLANs provide three key-based security mechanisms to provide that security.

WEP (Wired Equivalent Privacy)

The very first security capability available to WLAN users was *WEP (Wired Equivalent Privacy)*. WEP was included as part of the original IEEE 802.11 standard and was intended to provide privacy. Widely recommended in the early days of WLAN use, WEP rapidly fell out of favor when a flaw with the encryption mechanism was found.

The flaw in WEP makes it relatively easy for an attacker to crack the encryption and access the wireless network, so it is generally only used if no other solution is available (WEP is better than nothing) or the WLAN is being used with older devices, or devices like PDAs or handheld games that require the use of WEP.

One of the other challenges with WEP was the confusing mix of keys vendors used. Some vendors implemented the keys in HEX, some used ASCII characters, and some just used passphrases. Depending on the version of WEP, the length of the keys could also vary. This was particularly problematic for home users who wanted to use equipment from multiple vendors. Consumers ended up with equipment that wouldn't support WEP in the same way.

WPA (Wi-Fi Protected Access)/WPA2 (Wi-Fi Protected Access version 2)

WPA (Wi-Fi Protected Access) was designed as the interim successor to WEP. The WPA protocol implements most of the IEEE 802.11i standard. This was included in the updated WLAN standard. IEEE 802.11i addressed a number of the issues inherent to the original IEEE 802.11 standard. WPA included a new security protocol, Temporal Key Integrity Protocol (TKIP), which, while related to WEP to ensure backwards compatibility, adds new features to help address the issues associated with WEP. Unfortunately, because TKIP uses the same underlying mechanism as WEP, it is also vulnerable to similar attacks. The number of attacks is significantly less than with WEP, but they still exist.

WPA2 (Wi-Fi Protected Access version 2) is the standards-based version of WPA, except WPA2 implements all the IEEE 802.11i standards.

WPA/WPA2 functions in two modes:

Shared-Key WPA   In Shared-key WPA, a passphrase is configured that is entered on both the client and the wireless network. This is similar to how WEP works, but the protection of that passphrase is much more secure due to the use of strong encryption with automatic rekeying. This mode is generally meant to be used by home users.

IEEE 802.1x   In 802.1x mode, WPA/WPA2 uses an external authentication server coupled with the EAP (Extensible Authentication Protocol) standard to enable strong authentication for connection to the WLAN. The typical authentication process includes:

1. **Initialization**

    On detection of a host, the port on the switch is enabled and set to the "unauthorized" state. Only 802.1x traffic is allowed while the port is in this state.

2. **Initiation**

   The host trying to connect to the WLAN transmits EAP-Request Identity frames to a special Layer 2 address on the local network segment. This is known as the authenticator. The authenticator then forwards the packets to a RADIUS authentication server.

3. **Negotiation**

   The authentication server sends a reply to the authenticator. The authenticator then transmits the packets to the connecting host. These packets are used to negotiate the EAP authentication method.

4. **Authentication**

   If the authentication server and connecting host agree on the EAP authentication method, the connecting host is then authenticated. If the authentication is successful, the authenticator sets the port to the "authorized" state and normal traffic is allowed. If it is unsuccessful, the port remains in the "unauthorized" state and the host will not be able to connect.

The use of 802.1x authentication to secure a WLAN is generally reserved for large corporate environments, where there are sufficient resources to support the additional servers and support required by this mode of operation. 802.1x authentication, particularly when used in conjunction with a token-based authentication solution, permits a very secure WLAN implementation.

Understanding MAC Filters

As we discussed earlier in the lesson, a MAC address is the unique hardware address of a network adapter. This information can be used to control what systems are able to connect to a WLAN through the use of MAC filters. By turning MAC filtering on, network access can be limited to only permitted systems by entering the MAC address information into the MAC filters. The table of permitted MAC addresses is maintained by the wireless access points.

Understanding the Advantages and Disadvantages of Specific Security Types

Now that we have discussed the different security mechanisms available when working with WLANs, we will discuss some of the advantages and disadvantages of each type:

WEP   WEP is a solution that, while better than no security at all, is not particularly secure. The vulnerabilities within the WEP protocols encryption scheme make it very easy to crack. WEP will keep neighbors from connecting to a home WLAN, but will not slow a determined attacker very much.

WPA/WPA2   WPA/WPA2 is the best security method for both home and corporate WLAN security. In pre-shared key mode, WPA/WPA2 can secure the WLAN with a passcode that is shared by the clients and the wireless access points. As long as a secure passcode is selected, this is a very secure solution for small networks. For corporate networks, where additional authentication infrastructure can be purchased, the 802.1x security available within WPA/WPA2 permits a highly secure WLAN implementation. The downside with this approach is that it is more expensive, and significantly more complex, than the other solutions. This complexity requires significantly higher support, as user accounts need to be maintained, additional servers will need to be supported, and troubleshooting becomes more challenging. These challenges can be overcome with a well-designed, redundant architecture for the WLAN.

MAC Address Filtering   MAC address filtering is a good solution for a home or small office environment but has significant challenges as the number of permitted devices grows. Manually maintaining a table of MAC addresses becomes a significant challenge when there are more than 10–20 devices, especially in dynamic environments where systems are being purchased and decommissioned regularly. Any changes to the list of permitted devices requires someone updating the MAC address filtering table, which is generally a manual process. Another issue with MAC address filtering is that MAC addresses can be "spoofed" by someone with sufficient knowledge, or with the ability to perform an Internet search for a tool to change a MAC address. If they are able to get the MAC address of an authorized system, they can reset their MAC address to the authorized address, and thus gain access to the WLAN. MAC address filters are a good solution for small, static environments like a home or a small office. While they will not stop a determined attacker, they are one more impediment to ensure that only a truly motivated attacker will try to bypass them.

The good news when reviewing the available security mechanisms for wireless networks is that there are solutions available for just about any situation. In the early days of wireless, WLANs offered great convenience for users, but no security for protecting the company's network. Deploying wireless access was as easy as buying an inexpensive wireless access point and plugging it into the network. As a result, security departments were forced to dedicate resources to track down rogue wireless access points. Fortunately, there are multiple tools available today that can be used to identify rogue access points. While the issue certainly still exists, it is not as prevalent as it was in years past.

Skill Summary

In this lesson, you learned:

- A firewall is a system that is designed to protect a computer or a computer network from network-based attacks. A firewall does this by filtering the data packets traversing the network.

- Firewalls based on packet filtering inspect the data packets as they attempt to traverse the firewall, and based on rudimentary rules, such as permitting all outbound traffic while denying all inbound traffic, or blocking specific protocols from passing through the router, like Telnet or FTP.

- Instead of analyzing each individual packet, a circuit-level firewall monitors TCP/IP sessions by monitoring the TCP handshaking between packets to validate the session.

- Application-level firewalls (also known as proxy servers) work by performing a deep inspection of application data as it traverses the firewall. Rules are set based on analyzing client requests and application responses, then enforcing correct application behavior.

- Stateful multi-level firewalls are designed to provide the best features of both packet-filtering and application-level firewalls.

- Virtual LANs (VLANs) were developed as an alternate solution to deploying multiple routers. VLANs are logical network segments used to create separate broadcast domains, but still allow the devices on the VLANs to communicate at Layer 2, without requiring a router.

- Intrusion detection systems (IDS) are designed to detect unauthorized user activities, attacks, and network compromises.

- An intrusion prevention system (IPS) is very similar to an IDS, except that, in addition to detecting and alerting, an IPS can also take action to prevent a breach from occurring.

- Honeypots, honey nets, and padded cells are complementary technologies to IDS/IPS deployments. A honeypot is a trap for hackers.

- A DMZ is a firewall configuration used to secure hosts on a network segment. In most DMZs, the hosts on the DMZ are connected behind a firewall which is also connected to a public network like the Internet.

- Network Address Translation (NAT) is a technique used to modify the network address information of a host while traffic is traversing a router or firewall. This technique is used to hide the network information of a private network while allowing traffic to be transferred across a public network like the Internet.

- DNS Security Extensions (DNSSEC) adds security provisions to DNS so that computers can verify that they have been directed to proper servers.

- Protocol spoofing is the misuse of a network protocol to perpetrate a hoax on a host or a network device.

- The denial-of-service (DoS) attack floods the network being attacked with overwhelming amounts of traffic, shutting down the network infrastructure like a router or firewall.

- A man-in-the-middle attack is a type of attack where the attacker breaks into the communication between the endpoints of a network connection. Once the attacker has broken into the communication stream, he can intercept data being transferred, or even inject false information into the data stream.

- Back door attacks are attacks against an opening left in a functional piece of software that allows access into a system or software application without the owner's knowledge.

- A DNS poisoning attack is an attack against the cached information on a DNS server.

- A replay attack occurs when an attacker is able to capture an intact data stream from the network using a network sniffer, modify certain components of the data stream, and then replay the traffic back to the network to complete their attack.

- A buffer overflow attack exploits poorly written code by injecting data into variable fields and leveraging the response to access information in the application.

- SQL injection attacks are one of the oldest attacks against web applications using the SQL Server database application.

- A wireless LAN (WLAN) allows users to connect to a network while allowing them to remain mobile.

- The SSID (Service Set IDentifier) is the name for the WLAN. A connecting host must know the SSID to connect.

- WEP (Wired Equivalent Privacy) is an older wireless encryption protocol, which rapidly fell out of favor when a flaw with the encryption mechanism was found.

- WPA (Wi-Fi Protected Access) was designed as the interim successor to WEP.

- WPA2 (Wi-Fi Protected Access version 2) is the standards-based version of WPA, except WPA2 implements all the IEEE 802.11i standards.

- A MAC address is the unique hardware address of a network adapter.

- By turning MAC filtering on, network access can be limited to only permitted systems by entering the MAC address information into the MAC filters.

Knowledge Assessment

Multiple Choice

1. Which of the following should be considered when deciding whether to use a software or hardware firewall? (Choose all that apply.)
   A. Host operating system
   B. Application conflicts
   C. Operating system version
   D. Firewall service efficiency
   E. Stability

2. Which of the following are layers of the OSI model? (Choose all that apply.)
   A. Physical
   B. Control
   C. Application
   D. Network
   E. Encryption

3. Routing occurs at which layer of the OSI model?
   A. Physical
   B. Data-link
   C. Transport
   D. Session
   E. Network

4. Which of the following are valid firewall types? (Choose all that apply.)
   A. Virtual
   B. Network
   C. Packet filtering
   D. IPsec
   E. Application

5. Which of the following are typically examined by a stateful inspection firewall? (Choose all that apply.)
   A. IP address of the sending host
   B. IP address of the receiving host
   C. IP address of the router
   D. Data packet type
   E. Data packet size

6. Which of the following is an attack that relies on having a user execute a malicious script embedded in a web page? (Choose the best answer.)

   A. Man-in-the-middle

   B. Brute force

   C. Cross-site scripting

   D. SQL injection

7. A small business owner has purchased a new wireless access point and wants to ensure that only his systems are able to connect to the wireless. He enables MAC address filtering and puts the MAC addresses for all of his computers in the permitted table.

   This filtering occurs at which layer of the OSI model?

   A. Physical layer

   B. Data-link layer

   C. Network layer

   D. Transport layer

   E. Session layer

8. A sales team for a medium-sized manufacturing company has just deployed a new e-commerce application to allow for the direct sale of products to its customers. To secure that solution, an application firewall is deployed. At which layer of the OSI model does the application firewall occur?

   A. Physical layer

   B. Data-link layer

   C. Network layer

   D. Presentation layer

   E. Application layer

9. Which of the following are password-based attacks? (Choose all that apply.)

   A. Replay

   B. Network sniffer

   C. Brute force

   D. Man-in-the-middle

   E. Dictionary

10. Which of the following is an attack that relies on the attacker being able to trick the sending host into thinking his system is the receiving host, and the receiving host into thinking his system is the sending host? (Choose the best answer.)

    A. Replay

    B. Brute force

    C. Man-in-the-middle

    D. Cross-site scripting

    E. SQL Injection

11. Which of the following are common uses for a VPN? (Choose all that apply.)
    A. Remote access
    B. Server isolation
    C. Intrusion detection
    D. Extranet connections
    E. Domain isolation

12. Which of the following are common types of routing protocols? (Choose all that apply.)
    A. Link vector
    B. Dynamic link
    C. Distance link
    D. Distance vector
    E. Link state

13. Which type of DoS attack uses large ICMP packets to cause an overflow of the memory buffers allocated for packets?
    A. SYN flood
    B. ICMP flood
    C. Ping of death
    D. HTTP flood

Fill in the Blank

1. A network administrator that has been put in charge of registering a company's domain name and setting up the DNS so that people on the Internet can get to the website should use _____ to ensure that DNS entries are not poisoned by an attacker.

2. The two most common protocols that can be used to create the VPN are _____ and _____.

3. The three common types of protocol spoofing are _____, _____, and _____.

4. A type of attack that uses a weakness in an operating system or an application is known as a(n) _____.

5. An attack that relies on access to the physical LAN segment is known as a(n) _____ attack.

6. An attack that records a stream of data, modifies it, and then resends it is known as a(n) _____ attack.

7. The two common types of Network Address Translation are _____ and _____.

8. When setting up a WLAN in a corporate environment, and using 802.1x and a RADIUS server to secure the connections, it is necessary to use _____ or _____ keys.

9. A(n) _____ can be deployed to distract an attacker from the critical systems on a network.

Business Case Scenarios

Scenario 4-1: Using Windows Firewall

You are an administrator for the ABC Corporation and you need to open the Windows Firewall console on a computer running Windows 10 and create a Windows Firewall inbound rule that allows Internet Explorer to communicate over ports 80 and 443. Describe the steps necessary to completing these tasks.

Scenario 4-2: Using a Routing Table

You are administering a computer running Windows 10. Which commands should be used to display the current routes? You want to add a route to the 10.24.57.0 network using the 192.168.50.1 gateway. Display the routes to confirm it has been added. Lastly, delete the new route.

Scenario 4-3: Using Ports

One of your organization's programs needs access to a server that is on the DMZ using the following protocols:

Secure Shell (SSH)

Network News Transfer Protocol

Simple Network Management Protocol

NetBIOS Session Service

Network Time Protocol

Define a port and describe which ports are involved with these protocols.

Scenario 4-4: Accessing and Configuring Wireless Settings

As an administrator at Contoso Corporation, you need to access and configure the D-Link DIR-655 emulator. Describe the steps necessary to performing these tasks.

Real World Scenario

Workplace Ready: Defense in Depth

In Lesson 1, the concept of defense in depth was covered, describing how it provides multiple layers of security to defend your assets. This ensures that if an attacker breaches a layer of your defenses, there are additional layers of defense to keep them out of the critical areas of the environment. To use access control, establish physical security so that no one can gain direct access to the servers without going through the network. Provide firewalls and routers to limit access over the network. Then, use host firewalls, User Account Control, and other components to protect the server itself.

Besides looking at access control, keep in mind the issues of authentication, authorization, and accounting. To protect the network resources, establish a system that will allow access based on authentication and authorization. Also, to ensure that a security breach has not occurred, remember to establish accounting that needs to be monitoring and reviewing regularly.

Lesson

5

Protecting the Server and Client

Lesson Skill Matrix

Technology Skill	Objective Domain Description	Objective Domain Number
Protecting the Client Computer	Understand client protection	4.1
	Understand malware	2.6
Managing Client Security Using Windows Defender	Understand client protection	4.1
Protecting Your Email	Understand email protection	4.2
Securing Internet Explorer	Understand Internet security	1.3
Configuring Microsoft Edge	Understand Internet security	1.3
Protecting Your Server	Understand server protection	4.3
Using Security Baselines	Understand dedicated firewalls	3.1
Locking Down Devices to Run Only Trusted Applications	Understand encryption	2.5
	Understand client protection	4.1
Managing Windows Store Apps	Understand encryption	2.5
	Understand client protection	4.1

Key Terms

adware

antispam

antivirus

AppLocker

backdoor

Bayesian filters

Bring Your Own Device (BYOD)
policies

buffer overflow

content zones

cookie

Line of Business (LOB) apps

malicious software (malware)

Microsoft account

Microsoft Active Protection Service
(MAPS)

Microsoft Edge

offline files

pharming

phishing

polymorphic virus

pop-up windows

PTR record

ransomware

Read-Only Domain Controller (RODC)

rootkit

rule collections

security baseline

Security Compliance Manager 4.0
(SCM 4.0)

security template

Sender Policy Framework (SPF)

spam

spoofing

spyware

Trojan horse

Universal Windows Platform (UWP)
apps

User Account Control (UAC)

virus

virus hoax

Windows Defender

Windows Firewall

Windows Server Update Services
(WSUS)

Windows Store

Windows Store for Business

Windows Update

worm

zero-day attacks

Protecting the Client Computer

The client computer is the computer that a user would use to connect to the servers and network applications. Because the computer is connected to an organization's network, it is important to protect the client computer. You would like to keep your users productive rather than spend time fixing their computers.

Certification Ready

What is needed to secure a client computer? Objective 4.1

After working with computers for a while, you begin to realize that protecting a client computer can become quite complicated when trying to maintain its Windows operating system, its many applications, and the various network applications and services required to make it a productive tool in the face of all the malicious malware to which it's currently exposed.

Protecting Your Computer from Malware

Malicious software, sometimes called *malware*, is software designed to infiltrate and adversely affect a computer system without the owner's informed consent. It is usually associated with viruses, worms, Trojan horses, spyware, rootkits, and dishonest adware. As a network administrator or computer technician, it is important to know how to identify malware, how to remove malware, and how to protect a computer from malware.

Certification Ready

How is a buffer overflow exploited? Objective 2.6

Understanding Types of Malware

Because it is quite common for a computer to be connected to the Internet, there are more opportunities than ever for a computer to be infected by malware. In addition, over the last couple of years, the number of malware attacks perpetrated over the Internet is staggering. Also, it is important to ensure that if a computer gets infected on a network, it does not spread to other computers.

Many early forms of malware were written as experiments or practical jokes (known as pranks). Most of the time, these were intended to be harmless or merely annoying. However, as time goes by, malware has turned more toward vandalism, extortion, and even terrorism, as a tool used to compromise private information, encrypt data for ransom, and generally damage confidence in economic and political systems.

Besides using tools, such as a denial-of-service (DoS) attack, to attack other systems, networks, or websites, causing those systems to have performance problems or otherwise become inaccessible, malware can be identified as one or more of the following:

- Virus
- Worm
- Trojan horse
- Spyware and dishonest adware
- Rootkit
- Backdoor
- Polymorphic virus
- Zero-day attack
- Ransomware

A computer *virus* is a program that can copy itself and infect a computer without the user's consent or knowledge. Early viruses were usually some form of executable code that was hidden in the boot sector of a disk or as an executable file (a file name with an .exe or .com extension).

Later, as macro languages were used in software applications such as word processors and spreadsheets to enhance the programs' power and flexibility, malicious macro programs could be embedded within those documents. These documents can further infect other documents, causing a wide range of problems on computer systems as the macro code is executed (when the document is opened).

Today's websites can be written in various programming and scripting languages and can include many executable programs. Therefore, when accessing the Internet, a system is placed under constant threat.

A *worm* is a self-replicating program that copies itself to other computers over the network without the need for any user intervention. Different from a virus, a worm does not corrupt or modify files on a target computer. Instead, it consumes bandwidth and ties up processor and memory resources, slowing the system down, and causing the system to become unusable. Worms usually spread by using security holes found within the operating system or TCP/IP software implementations.

A *Trojan horse* is a program named after the Trojan horse story in Greek mythology. A Trojan horse is an executable program that appears as a desirable or useful program. Because it appears to be a desirable or useful program, users are tricked into loading and executing the program on their system. After the program is loaded, it can cause a computer to become unusable, or it can bypass a system's security, allowing private information such as passwords, credit card numbers, and Social Security numbers to be read and copied, as well as executing adware.

Spyware is a type of malware that is installed on computers and collects personal information and browsing habits, often without the user's knowledge. Spyware can also install additional software, which can redirect your web browser to other sites or change your home page.

One type of spyware is the keylogger, which records every key a user presses. Therefore, when typing credit card numbers, Social Security numbers, and passwords, that information gets recorded and is eventually sent to and read by someone without the user's knowledge. It should be noted that not all keyloggers are bad, because some corporations use them to monitor their corporate users.

Adware is any software package that automatically plays, displays, or downloads advertisements to a computer after the software is installed on it or while the application is being used. While adware may not necessarily be bad, it is often used with ill intent.

A *rootkit* is a software or hardware device designed to gain administrator-level control over a computer system without being detected. Rootkits can target the BIOS, hypervisor, boot loader, kernel, or, less commonly, libraries or applications.

A *backdoor* is a program that gives some remote user unauthorized control of a system or automatically initiates an unauthorized task. Some backdoors have been installed by viruses or other forms of malware. Other backdoors may be created by programmers within commercial applications or inside a customized application made for an organization.

Certification Ready

Which type of malware constantly changes in an effort to hide itself? Objective 2.6

A *polymorphic virus* mutates, or changes its code, so that it cannot be as easily detected. Stealth viruses try to hide themselves by monitoring and intercepting a system's call. For example, when the system seeks to open an infected file, the stealth virus disinfects the file and allows the operating system to open it. When the operating system closes the file, the virus re-infects the file.

Certification Ready

How can a system be protected against zero-day attacks? Objective 2.6

Viruses and worms often exploit a buffer overflow. In all application programs including Windows itself, there are buffers that hold data. These buffers have a fixed size. If too much data is sent to these buffers, a buffer overflow occurs. Depending on the data sent to the overflow, a hacker uses the overflow to obtain passwords, alter system files, install backdoors, and/or cause errors on the computer. When patches are released to fix a potential buffer overflow, the patch adds code to check the length of data sent to the buffer to make sure that it does not overflow.

Zero-day attacks are attacks based on using unknown or recently announced vulnerabilities. To help prevent these types of attacks, operating systems, network devices, and antivirus software should use the latest security updates and definitions.

Certification Ready

Which type of malware encrypts data so that the data cannot be accessed? Objective 2.6

Ransomware is one of the fastest growing forms of malware; it encrypts data files and then demands a ransom to decrypt the files. As the user tries to access the files, the files are unreadable until they are decrypted. Ransomware, also considered a denial-of-service attack, prevents the user from accessing the files. Ransomware attacks are typically carried out using a Trojan horse from a website or through email.

To protect against ransomware, keep in mind the following recommendations:

- Install and use an up-to-date antivirus solution.

- Make sure the operating system and software is up-to-date with the newest security patches.

- Avoid clicking links or opening attachments or emails from people you don't know or from companies you don't do business with.

- Ensure that SmartScreen Filter (in Microsoft Internet Explorer and Microsoft Edge) is turned on.

- Ensure that a pop-up blocker is enabled in your web browser.

- Back up important files on a regular basis. If your files get encrypted, it may be necessary to pay a ransom to get the files decrypted if you're unable to restore the files from backup.

Identifying Malware

The first step in removing malware is detecting the existence of malware. Sometimes it is easy to see that a system is infected with malware. Other times, you may never know that malware exists on your computer.

Some of the symptoms of malware include the following:

- System performs poorly

- System has less available memory than it should have

- System performs poorly while connected to the Internet
- Computer stops responding frequently
- Computer takes longer to start up
- Browser closes unexpectedly or stops responding
- Browser default home or search pages change
- Advertising windows unexpectedly pop up
- Additional toolbars are unexpectedly added to the browser
- Programs start unexpectedly
- Programs cannot start
- Components of Windows or other programs no longer work
- Programs or files are suddenly missing
- Messages or displays on a monitor are unusual
- Sounds or music that are unusual play at random times
- Programs or files that are unknown have been created or installed
- Browser has unknown add-ins
- Files have become corrupted
- File size unexpectedly changes

Of course, to see these symptoms, you may need to actively look for them.

First, to make the most of determining which processes and services are rogue, create a baseline of what processes and services are running on the system under normal conditions so that you have a basis for comparison. Then, when your machine begins running slow, start Task Manager to view processor and memory utilization. Look at the processes to see which process is using the most processor and/or memory resources. Also, review the processes and services in memory (using Task Manager). In addition, use System Configuration to look for changes in the system. Finally, to detect malware, use an up-to-date antivirus program and an up-to-date antispyware package, which can scan an entire system and look for malware in real time when opening files and accessing websites.

With today's computers generally connecting to the Internet and/or other type of network on a continual basis, it's clear that a computer needs to be protected from all types of malware threats. And, as usual, a little common sense can go a long way in protecting a computer and network.

Understanding Security Updates and Antivirus Software for Clients

Some viruses, worms, rootkits, spyware, and adware are made possible because they exploit a security hole within Windows, Internet Explorer, Microsoft Office, and/or other software packages. Therefore, the first step that should be taken to protect yourself against malware is to keep your system up-to-date with the latest service packs, security patches, and other critical fixes.

The second step to protect your computer from malware is to use an up-to-date antivirus software package. In addition, if your antivirus software does not include an antispyware component, install an antispyware software package. Perform a full system scan with your antivirus software at least once a week and do a quick scan whenever you see any of the symptoms listed in the "Identifying Malware" section of this lesson.

Windows Defender is a software product from Microsoft that prevents, removes, and quarantines spyware in Microsoft Windows. It will help protect a computer against pop-ups, slow performance, and security threats caused by spyware and other unwanted software by detecting and removing known spyware from a computer. Windows Defender features real-time protection, a monitoring system that recommends actions against spyware when it's detected, minimizes interruptions, and helps users stay productive. Like an antivirus package, it is necessary to keep Windows Defender up-to-date.

Using Common Sense with Malware

To avoid malware, be sure to use common sense by following these suggestions:

- Don't install unknown software or software from an unknown source.

- Don't open strange email attachments.

- Don't click hyperlinks from strangers or if it's unclear what the link is supposed to do. This also applies to sources like Yahoo!, AOL, and MSN.

- If your email client supports auto launch, turn it off. Otherwise, you might automatically activate a computer virus just by opening the email.

- Don't visit questionable websites, especially sites that allow downloading software from music and video piracy sites and porn sites.

- If your web browser alerts you that a site is known for hosting malware, pay attention to these warnings.

- If you surf the Internet and browser pop-ups indicate that you need to download the newest driver or check your system for viruses, use caution.

- Don't forget to perform regular backups. So, if a computer does get a virus and data is lost, you can restore from a backup.

 While this list may be common knowledge for IT personnel, frequent reminders and awareness training for network users are always a good idea.

Removing Malware

If some of the malware symptoms listed earlier in this lesson begin to make an appearance, try to detect and remove any malware that is found. The first step in removing malware is to run an antivirus software package and perform a full scan. If an antivirus software package isn't installed, it's time to purchase one. If the package cannot be downloaded directly to the computer, try downloading it from another machine or to an optical disk such as a CD or DVD, or use a thumb drive to transfer it to your system. If it finds malware and removes the malware, reboot your computer and run it again to be sure your system is clean. If it keeps finding different malware, keep running it until your machine is clean.

> Be sure that your antivirus is up-to-date. If it is not up-to-date, it will not know about newer viruses.

If your antivirus software package keeps finding the same malware, make sure you are not accessing a disk or other device that continues infecting the system. Also, it may be necessary to reboot Windows into Safe mode and try another scan. If the option is available, try to boot from a CD or DVD and run the scan.

If a virus cannot be removed, do some research on the Internet. Often, step-by-step instructions can be found for removing specific malware, including deleting files and keys in the registry. Of course, be sure that the instructions are from a reliable source and follow the instructions precisely.

> If an antivirus software package has trouble removing malware, don't be afraid to contact the company to get assistance.

Remember, that if your antivirus package does not have an antispyware component, install an antispyware package to check for spyware. Also, consider using Windows Defender.

> Because some malware includes keylogging capabilities, consider updating logon information for your online accounts using a different computer—if you suspect such malware on your computer.

Microsoft also includes a Microsoft Windows Malicious Software Removal Tool, which checks computers running Windows for infections by specific, prevalent malicious software. Microsoft releases an updated version of this tool on the second Tuesday of each month and as needed to respond to security incidents. The tool is available from Microsoft Update, Windows Update, and the Microsoft Download Center.

As a reminder, remember to use the following tools when trying to locate and remove possible malware:

- Use Task Manager to view and stop unknown processes and to stop unknown or questionable services.

- Use the Services MMC to stop unknown or questionable services.

- Use System Configuration to disable unknown or questionable services and startup programs.

- Disable unknown or questionable Internet Explorer add-ins.

Understanding Virus Hoaxes

A *virus hoax* is a message warning the recipient of a non-existent computer virus threat, usually sent as a chain email that tells the recipient to forward it to everyone they know. This is a form of social engineering that plays on people's ignorance and fear. Some hoaxes may tell people to delete key system files to make the system work properly or they tell people to download software from the Internet to clean the virus. But instead, these hoaxes install some form of malware. Antivirus specialists agree that recipients should delete virus hoaxes when they receive them, instead of forwarding them.

Configuring Windows Updates

Windows Update provides Windows 10 users with a way to keep their computers current by checking a designated server. The server provides software that patches security issues, installs updates that make Windows and your applications more stable, fixes issues with existing Windows programs, and provides new features. The server can be hosted by Microsoft, or it can be set up and managed in your organization by running the Windows Server Update Services (WSUS) or System Center 2012 R2/2016 Configuration Manager.

Microsoft routinely releases security updates on the second Tuesday of each month on what is known as "Patch Tuesday." Most other updates are released as needed, which are known as "out-of-band" updates. Before immediately installing updates on production systems, test updates to make sure they will not cause problems. While Microsoft does intensive testing, occasionally problems do occur, either as a bug or a compatibility issue with third-party software. Therefore, always have a good backup of your system and data files before installing patches and have a backout plan, if needed.

Updates are classified as Important, Recommended, or Optional:

Important Updates   Offer significant benefits, such as improved security, privacy, and reliability. They should be installed as they become available, and can be installed automatically with Windows Update.

Recommended Updates   Address noncritical problems or help enhance your computing experience. While these updates do not address fundamental issues with your computer or Windows software, they can offer meaningful improvements.

Optional Updates   Can include updates, drivers, or new software from Microsoft to enhance your computing experience. These optional updates need to be installed manually.

Depending on the type of update, Windows Update can deliver the following:

Security Updates   Broadly released fixes for a product-specific security-related vulnerability. Security vulnerabilities are rated based on their severity, which is indicated in the Microsoft security bulletin as critical, important, moderate, or low.

Critical Updates   Broadly released fixes for a specific problem, addressing a critical, non-security-related bug.

Service Packs   A tested, cumulative set of hotfixes, security updates, critical updates, and updates, as well as additional fixes for problems found internally since the release of the product. Service packs might also contain a limited number of customer-requested design changes or features. When an operating system is released, many corporations consider the first service pack as a time when the operating system matures enough to be used throughout the organization.

Not all updates can be retrieved through Windows Update. Sometimes, when researching a specific problem, Microsoft may have a fix for the problem by installing a hotfix, or cumulative patch. A hotfix is a single, cumulative package that includes one or more files that are used to address a problem in a software product, such as a software bug. Typically, hotfixes are made to address a specific customer situation and often have not gone through extensive testing as have other patches retrieved through Windows Update.

For small environments, configure your system to perform automatic updates to ensure that critical, security, and compatibility updates are made available for installation automatically without significantly affecting your regular use of the Internet. Automatic updates work in the background when a computer is connected to the Internet, to identify when new updates are available, and to download them to your computer. When a download is completed, you will be notified and prompted to install the update. Either install the update then, get more details about what is included in the update, or let Windows send a reminder later. Some updates may require a reboot, but others do not.

When first installing Windows 10, choose how Windows Update should function. On a Windows 10 computer, click the Start button, click Settings, and click Update & security to open the Windows Update page (see Figure 5.1).

FIGURE 5.1   The Windows Update page

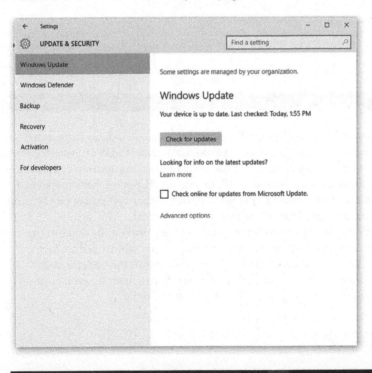

Click Advanced options to configure for automatic updates, get updates for other Microsoft products when Windows is updated, defer upgrades, and view the update history (as shown in Figure 5.2).

FIGURE 5.2   The Windows Update Advanced Options page

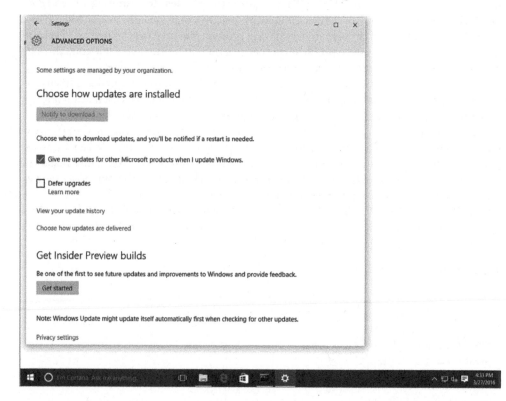

Click the "Choose how updates are delivered" option to see the "Updates from more than one place" page (see Figure 5.3). Unless your corporation uses WSUS or System Center 2012 R2/2016 Configuration Manager, you must use your Internet connection to retrieve updates from Microsoft. Starting with Windows 10, enable the "Updates from more than one place" option, which also can be used to get updates from other computers on the same network as your local computer and from computers on the Internet.

On the Advanced Options page, customize how updates are installed. By default, the "Choose how updates are installed" option is set to Automatic (recommended), which means Windows selects a time when a computer is inactive to install the updates and reboot the system. Most organizations would prefer the Notify to schedule restart option so that Windows does not reboot a computer when it is least expected.

FIGURE 5.3   The "Updates from more than one place" page

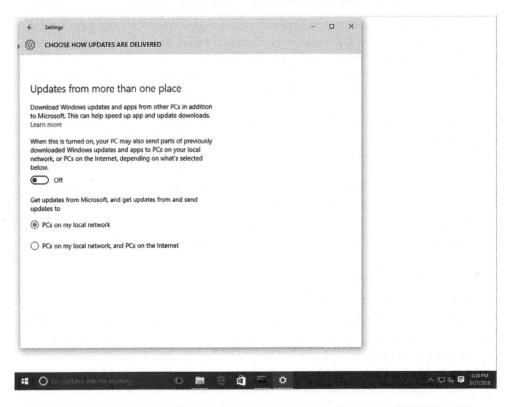

Some Windows 10 editions can defer upgrades to your PC. By selecting the "Defer upgrades" option, new Windows features won't be downloaded or installed for several months. This option is usually used to help avoid problems with an update that might cause problems within your organization.

Deferring upgrades does not affect security updates, but it does prevent you from getting the latest Windows features as soon as they are available.

For corporations, consider using *Windows Server Update Services (WSUS)* or System Center Configuration Manager (SCCM) to keep your systems updated. The advantage of using one of these two systems is that it can be used to test the patch, schedule the updates, and prioritize client updates. After determining that the patch is safe to deploy, the patch can be enabled for deployment.

Understanding User Account Control (UAC)

User Account Control (UAC) is a feature that was introduced in Windows Vista and is included with Windows 10. UAC helps prevent unauthorized changes to your computer, thereby helping to protect your system from malware.

If logged on as an administrator, UAC prompts you for permission; and if logged on as a standard user, UAC will prompt for an administrator password before performing actions that could potentially affect your computer's operation or other users' computers. UAC is designed to make sure that unauthorized changes are not made by potentially malicious software that you may not know is running. Be sure to read the warnings carefully and then ensure that the name of the action or program that's about to start is the one you intended to start.

As a standard user in Windows 10, the following actions can be performed without requiring administrative permissions or rights:

- Install updates from Windows Update
- Install drivers from Windows Update or those that are included with the operating system
- View Windows settings
- Pair Bluetooth devices with the computer
- Reset the network adapter and perform other network diagnostic and repair tasks

When an application requests elevation or is run as an administrator, UAC will prompt for confirmation and, if consent is given, allow access as an administrator. See Figure 5.4.

FIGURE 5.4   UAC confirmation with secure desktop

UAC can be enabled or disabled for any individual user account. Of course, if UAC is disabled for a user account, the computer will be at higher risk. However, if you perform a lot of administrative tasks on a computer, the UAC prompts can be annoying and can stop you from doing certain activities, including saving to the root directory of a drive, or using an application that is not compatible with UAC.

Enable or Disable UAC

To enable or disable UAC, perform the following steps:

1. Open Control Panel and click User Accounts.
2. On the User Accounts page, click User Accounts.
3. Click Change User Account Control settings.
4. Drag the slider to the appropriate option, as shown in Table 5.1. See Figure 5.5. Click OK.

FIGURE 5.5   UAC Settings

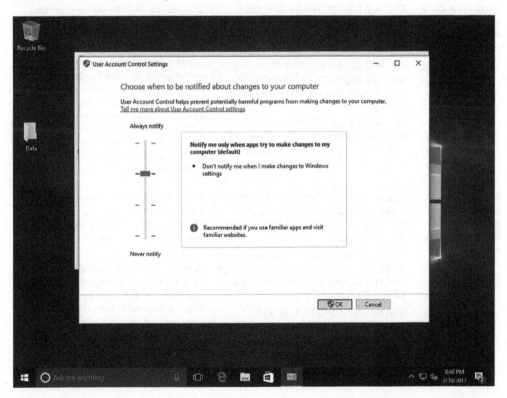

5. When prompted to restart the computer, click Restart Now or Restart Later as appropriate for the changes to take effect.

TABLE 5.1   UAC Settings

Setting	Description	Security Impact
Always notify	You will be notified before apps make changes to your computer or to Windows settings that require the permissions of an administrator. When you're notified, your desktop will be dimmed, and you must either approve or deny the request in the UAC dialog box before you can do anything else on your computer. The dimming of your desktop is referred to as the secure desktop because other apps can't run while it's dimmed.	This is the most secure setting. When notified, carefully read the contents of each dialog box before allowing changes to be made to your computer.
Notify me only when apps try to make changes to my computer	You will be notified before apps make changes to your computer that require the permissions of an administrator. You will not be notified if you try to make changes to Windows settings that require the permissions of an administrator. You will be notified if an app outside of Windows tries to make changes to a Windows setting.	It's usually safe to allow changes to be made to Windows settings without you being notified. However, certain apps that come with Windows can have commands or data passed to them, and malicious software can take advantage of this by using these apps to install files or change settings on your computer. You should always be careful about which apps you allow to run on your computer.
Notify me only when apps try to make changes to my computer (do not dim my desktop)	You will be notified before apps make changes to your computer that require the permissions of an administrator. You will not be notified if you try to make changes to Windows settings that require the permissions of an administrator. You will be notified if an app outside of Windows tries to make changes to a Windows setting.	This setting is the same as "Notify me only when apps try to make changes to my computer," but you are not notified on the secure desktop. Because the UAC dialog box isn't on the secure desktop with this setting, other apps might be able to interfere with the visual appearance of the dialog box. This is a small security risk if you already have a malicious app running on your computer.

Setting	Description	Security Impact
Never notify	You will not be notified before any changes are made to your computer. If you are logged on as an administrator, apps can make changes to your computer without you knowing about it. If you are logged on as a standard user, any changes that require the permissions of an administrator will automatically be denied. If you select this setting, you will need to restart the computer to complete the process of turning off UAC. Once UAC is off, people that log on as administrator will always have the permissions of an administrator.	This is the least secure setting. When you set UAC to never notify, you open up your computer to potential security risks. If you set UAC to never notify, you should be careful about which apps you run, because they will have the same access to the computer as you do. This includes reading and making changes to protected system areas, your personal data, saved files, and anything else stored on the computer. Apps will also be able to communicate and transfer information to and from anything your computer connects with, including the Internet.

Using Windows Firewall

Another important client tool is a firewall. As discussed in Lesson 4, a firewall is software or hardware that checks information coming from the Internet or a network and then either blocks it or allows it to pass through to a computer, depending on the firewall settings. A firewall can help prevent hackers or malicious software (such as worms) from gaining access to a computer through a network or the Internet. A firewall can also help prevent a computer from sending malicious software to other computers.

Microsoft recommends always using the *Windows Firewall*. However, because some security packages and antivirus packages include their own firewall, only one firewall should be in use.

 While your network may have a firewall to help protect you from unwanted network traffic from the Internet, it is still recommended to have a host firewall on your computer for an extra level of protection. It is especially recommended when the client computer is a mobile computer that may be moved outside of your organization's network.

In addition to the Windows Firewall found in Control Panel, newer versions of Windows include Windows Firewall with Advanced Security. Windows Firewall with Advanced Security combines a host firewall and Internet Protocol security (IPsec). Windows Firewall and Windows Firewall with Advanced Security are tightly coupled together, allowing better control of a firewall. In addition, Windows Firewall with Advanced Security provides computer-to-computer connection security, because it can be used to require authentication and data protection for communications via IPsec.

Enable or Disable Windows Firewall

To enable or disable Windows Firewall, perform the following steps:

1. Open Control Panel.

2. If you are in Category view, click System And Security ➤ Windows Firewall. If you are in icons view, double-click Windows Firewall.

3. In the left pane, click Turn Windows Firewall On Or Off. If prompted for an administrator password or confirmation, type the password or provide confirmation.

4. Click Turn On Windows Firewall under the appropriate network location to enable Windows Firewall or click Turn Off Windows Firewall (not recommended) under the appropriate network location to disable Windows Firewall. See Figure 5.6. Typically, users should want to block all incoming traffic when connecting to a public network in a hotel or airport or when a computer worm is spreading over the Internet. When blocking all incoming connections, you can still view most web pages, send and receive email, and send and receive instant messages.

FIGURE 5.6 Customizing settings for Windows Firewall

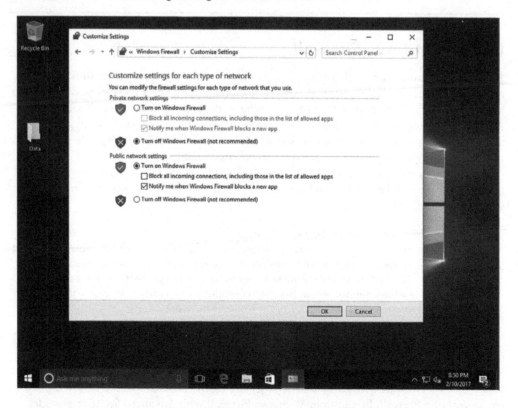

5. If desired, select the "Block all incoming connections, including those in the list of allowed apps" check box and the "Notify me when Windows Firewall blocks a new app" check box.

6. Click OK.

By default, most programs are blocked by Windows Firewall to help make a computer more secure. To work properly, some programs might require you to allow them to communicate through the firewall.

Allow a Program through Windows Firewall

To allow a program to communicate through Windows Firewall, perform the following steps:

1. Open Control Panel and click Windows Firewall.

2. In the left pane, click "Allow a program or feature through Windows Firewall."

3. Click Change Settings. If prompted for an administrator password or confirmation, type the password or provide confirmation.

4. Select the check box next to the program you want to allow, select the network locations on which you want to allow communication, and then click OK.

Open a Port on Windows Firewall

If the program isn't listed, you might need to open a port. To open a port on Windows Firewall, perform the following steps:

1. Open Control Panel and click Windows Firewall.

2. In the left pane, click Advanced Settings. If prompted for an administrator password or confirmation, type the password or provide confirmation.

3. In the Windows Firewall with Advanced Security window, in the left pane, click Inbound Rules, and then, in the right pane, click New Rule. See Figure 5.7.

4. Click Port and click Next. See Figure 5.8.

5. Click TCP or UDP and specify the port numbers. Click Next.

6. Click "Allow the connection," "Allow the connection if it is secure," or "Block the connection." Click Next.

7. By default, the rule will apply to all domains. If you don't want the rule to apply to a domain, deselect the domain. Click Next.

8. Specify a name for the rule and a description, if desired. Click Finish.

FIGURE 5.7   Inbound Rules options

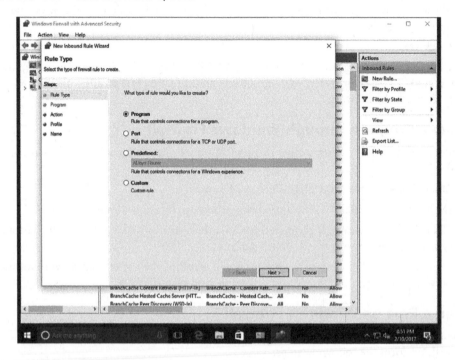

FIGURE 5.8   Specify a port to open in the firewall.

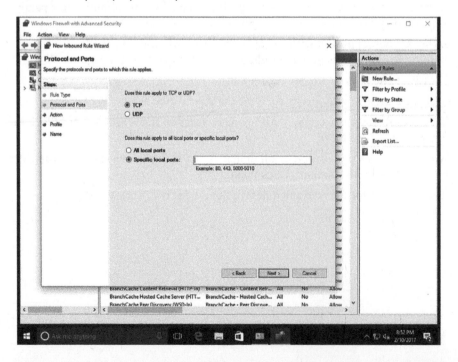

Using Offline Files

Offline files are copies of network files that are stored on your computer so that they can be accessed when not connected to the network or when the network folder with the files is not connected.

Offline files are not encrypted unless you choose to encrypt them. It might be a good idea to encrypt offline files if they contain sensitive or confidential information and you want to make them more secure by restricting access to them. Encrypting your offline files provides an additional level of access protection that works independently of NTFS file system permissions. This can help safeguard your files in case your computer is ever lost or stolen.

Enable Offline Files

To enable offline files, perform the following steps:

1. Right-click the Start button and choose Control Panel.
2. In the Search Control Panel text box, type **offline,** and click Manage Offline Files in the search results.
3. Click Enable Offline Files and click OK.
4. If prompted, reboot the computer.

Encrypt Offline Files

To encrypt offline files, perform the following steps:

1. Right-click the Start button and choose Control Panel.
2. In the Search Control Panel text box, type **offline,** and click Manage Offline Files in the search results.
3. Click the Encryption tab.
4. Click Encrypt to encrypt your offline files and click OK.

When encrypting your offline files, you encrypt only the offline files stored on your computer, and not the network versions of the files. An encrypted file or folder stored on your computer does not need to be decrypted before using it. This is done for you automatically.

Locking Down a Client Computer

When working with end users for an extended period of time, you will soon learn that some users can be their own worst enemy. Therefore, you should consider locking down a computer when necessary, so that users cannot do harm to the computer.

For example, unless a user has a need to be an administrator on their own computer, they should just be a standard user. Therefore, if they are affected by malware, malware will have minimum access to the system. When needed, they could use the runas command options as discussed in Lesson 2.

When working within an organization, it is often advantageous to standardize each company computer. Therefore, when moving from one computer to another, they will be similar. To keep computers standardized, an organization may choose to use group policies so that users cannot access certain features, such as Control Panel, to make changes to the system that may be detrimental.

Allowing users to install software may:

▪ Introduce malware to a system.

▪ Bypass safeguards already put in place to protect against malicious viruses and Trojan horse programs.

▪ Cause conflicts with software already on a baseline computer within an organization.

Limiting your users to standard accounts can limit what software users can install. Group policies can also be used to restrict what software can be executed on a client computer.

Windows 10 supports two mechanisms for restricting applications, both of which are based on group policies:

▪ Software restriction policies

▪ AppLocker

Managing Client Security Using Windows Defender

Windows Defender is designed to protect a computer against viruses, spyware, and other types of malware. It protects against these threats by providing real-time protection and notifying you of malware attempts or when an application tries to change critical settings.

Certification Ready

Which software is intended to damage, disable, or degrade a computer or computer systems? Objective 4.1

Windows Defender can also be configured to scan a computer on a regular basis and remove or quarantine any malware it finds.

 Windows Defender automatically disables itself when installing another antivirus product.

At the heart of Windows Defender are its definition files, which are downloaded from Windows Update. The definition files, which contain information about potential threats, are used by Windows Defender to notify you of potential threats to your system.

To access Windows Defender from the Windows 10 menu, click Start, type **Windows Defender,** and click it in the results. Figure 5.9 shows the Windows Defender Home tab.

FIGURE 5.9   Viewing the Windows Defender Home tab

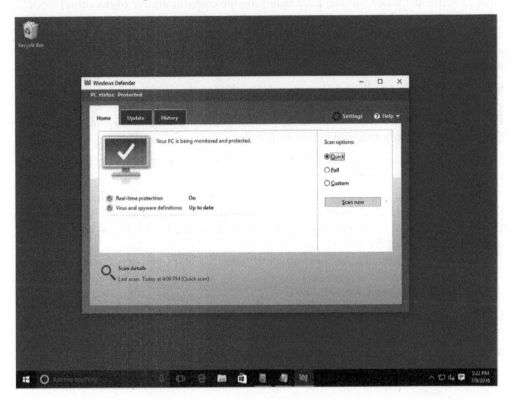

The Home tab can be used to check the status of Windows Defender, including whether Windows Defender is up-to-date and whether Windows Defender is protecting your system. It also provides the option to initiate a scan.

When looking at the Home tab, always look for a green message indicating *Your PC is being monitored and protected* and also make sure your system is up-to-date. Other components include:

Real-Time Protection   Real-time protection uses signature detection methodology and heuristics to monitor and catch malware behavior. Signature detection uses a vendor's definition files to detect malicious programs. If the program contains code that matches the signature, the program most likely contains the virus. This works well when the threat has already been identified, but what happens between the time the virus is released and the time the definition file is made available? That's where heuristics can help. It is used to monitor for suspicious activity by a program. Suspicious activity includes a program trying to copy itself into another program, a program trying to write to the disk directly, or a program trying to manipulate critical system files required by the operating system. These are indicators of possible malware activity that heuristics can detect.

Virus and Spyware Definitions   When a new virus is discovered, Microsoft creates a new virus signature/definition update. Each definition file contains a piece of the actual virus code that is used to detect a specific virus or malware. During scans, the content on the computer is compared with information in the definition files. Because new viruses are created every day and existing viruses are modified regularly, it's important to keep your definitions updated.

Scan Options (Quick, Full, and Custom)   A Quick scan checks the areas that malicious software (including viruses, spyware, and unwanted software) are most likely to infect. A Full scan checks all the files on your disk, including running programs. A Custom scan is designed to check only specified locations and files.

Scan Details   This area of the Home tab provides information on when the last scan was performed on the computer.

The Update tab provides information about your virus and spyware definitions. It is important to keep these current to ensure your computer is protected at all times. Windows Defender updates the definition files automatically. Click Update definitions on this tab to manually check for updates.

The History tab provides information about items that have been detected in the past and the actions that were taken with them.

The categories of items are as follows:

Quarantined Items   These items were not allowed to run and were not removed from your computer.

Allowed Items   These items were allowed to run on your computer.

All Detected Items   These items provide a list of all items detected on your computer.

Remove a Quarantined Item

To remove a quarantined item, perform the following steps:

1. Open Windows Defender.
2. Click the History tab.
3. Click Quarantined Items.
4. Click View Details.
5. Select the detected item and then read the description.
6. Click Remove.

Click Windows Defender Settings to open the Windows 10 Settings ➤ Update & Security ➤ Windows Defender page, as shown in Figure 5.10. Use the Settings page to fine-tune how Windows Defender works.

FIGURE 5.10   The Windows Defender Settings page

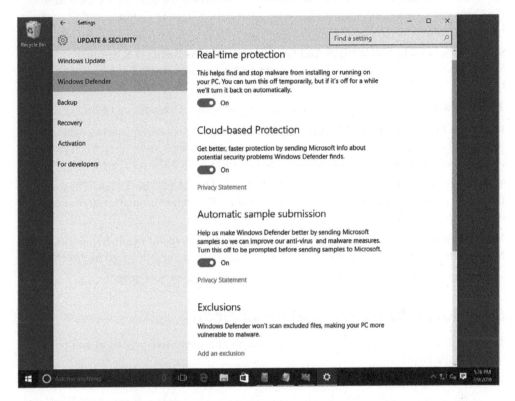

On the Settings page, the following options are available:

- Enable or disable real-time protection
- Select whether you want to use cloud-based protection
- Select the files and locations to be excluded from the scanning process
- Select the file types to exclude from the scan
- Select the processes to exclude
- Display the Windows 10 version information
- Open Windows Defender

Microsoft Active Protection Service (MAPS) is an online community that can help you decide how to respond to certain threat types and it serves as a resource to help stop the spread of new viruses and malware. The information sent helps Microsoft create new definition files. It can be enabled or disabled via the Windows Defender settings. When enabled, information is sent to Microsoft regarding where the software came from, the actions taken, and whether the actions taken were successful.

Windows Defender can also be configured via the Local Group Policy Editor or Group Policy Management Editor (AD domains). The following policies are located in the Computer Configuration\Administrative Templates\Windows Components\Windows Defender node:

Scan/Check For The Latest Virus And Spyware Definitions Before A Scheduled Scan   When enabled, Windows Defender checks for new signatures before running the scan.

Turn Off Windows Defender   This setting turns Windows Defender on or off.

Real-Time Protection/Turn Off Real-Time Monitoring   This setting controls whether Windows Defender monitors your system in real time and displays an alert when malware or potentially unwanted software attempts to install or run on the computer.

Threats/Specify Threats Upon Which Default Action Should Not Be Taken When Detected   This setting determines whether Windows Defender automatically takes action on malware that it identifies.

MAPS/Join Microsoft MAPS   This setting determines the type of membership used with MAPS. Options include No Membership, Basic Membership, or Advanced Membership.

To keep your system more secure, schedule a Windows Defender scan.

Schedule a Windows Defender Scan

To schedule a Windows Defender scan, log on with administrative privileges and perform the following steps:

1. Click Start and type **taskschd.msc**. From the results, click Task Scheduler.

2. In the left pane, expand Task Scheduler Library ➤ Microsoft ➤ Windows ➤ Windows Defender.

3. Double-click Windows Defender Scheduled Scan.

4. In the Windows Defender Scheduled Scan Properties (Local Computer) dialog box (see Figure 5.11), click the Triggers tab and click New.

5. In the Begin the task field, click On A Schedule.

6. Under Settings, select One Time. In the Start field, change the time to 5 minutes from your current time.

7. Make sure the Enabled check box is selected and click OK.

8. To close the Windows Defender Scheduled Scan Properties (Local Computer) dialog box, click OK.

9. Open Windows Defender to see the status of the scan on the Home tab.

FIGURE 5.11 Scheduling a Windows Defender scan

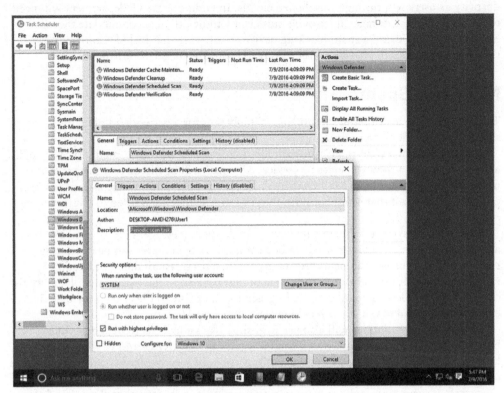

Protecting Your Email

Email has become an essential service for virtually every corporation. Unfortunately, most email received will be unsolicited emails called *spam* or junk email, some of which can carry malware and may lead to fraud or scams.

Certification Ready

How can users protect their system from viruses sent through email? Objective 4.2

The idea behind spam is that it sends lots of unsolicited bulk messages indiscriminately, hoping that a few people will open the email and open a website, purchase a product, or fall for a scam. For spammers, spam has minimal operating costs. Over the last few years, spam grew exponentially, and today composes at least 90% of all the email in the world.

For email recipients, besides the risk of malware and fraud, there is also a loss of productivity as users sort through unsolicited emails. In addition, the IT department will need to install additional storage and provide sufficient bandwidth to accommodate the extra email. Therefore, install a spam blocking device or software that includes antivirus protection. The antivirus will provide another layer to protect your network from viruses.

Managing Spam

To keep your systems running smoothly, it is important for a network administrator put some effort into blocking spam.

The best place to establish an antispam filtering system is on a dedicated server or appliance or as part of a firewall device or service. All email will be directed to the antispam filter by changing your DNS Mail Exchanger (MX) record to point to the antispam server or device. Any email that is not considered to be spam will be forwarded to your internal email servers.

Spam filtering systems will not catch every single spam message. Like an antivirus package, the spam filtering solution needs to be kept up-to-date and needs to be constantly tweaked. Also, consider adding a threatening email address, email domain, IP address range, or keywords into a black list. Any email that is listed in the black list will automatically be blocked. Be sure to take care when using a black list, so the criteria for blocking email isn't so broad that it starts blocking legitimate email.

Many antispam solutions will also use Real-time Blackhole Lists (RBLs) or a DNS-based Blackhole List (DNSBL), which can be accessed freely. RBLs and DNSBL are lists of known spammers that are updated frequently. Most mail server software can be configured to reject or flag messages that have been sent from a site listed on one or more such lists. Of course, as spammers look for ways to get around this, it is just one tool that can help reduce the amount of spam that gets through.

Any email identified as spam is usually quarantined or stored temporarily, in case a legitimate email is identified as spam. While this number should be relatively low, train your help desk personnel and possibly your users to access the quarantined email to release legitimate email to its destination. In addition, add the sender's email address or domain to a white list so that it will not be identified as spam in the future.

Detecting spam can be a daunting task when it must be done manually. Besides the obvious advertisement and keywords, antispam systems will also look at the email header to analyze information about the email and its origin. For example, in Outlook 2003, open the email and choose View ➢ Options. Under Internet Headers, the history for an email delivery path is shown. In Outlook 2010, select the message, click the File menu, and then under Info, click Properties.

Sometimes, spammers will try to spoof a legitimate email address or IP address when the message actually comes from one with an email address or IP address that would likely be identified as spam. One way to detect this is via a reverse lookup. For example, if email claims to be sent from a yahoo.com domain, an antispam system could do a reverse lookup using the DNS PTR record to find the actual IP address of the yahoo.com domain. If it does not match where the email said it came from, it is considered spam and will be blocked.

DNS Pointer (PTR) records are probably the most practical component of the DNS database because Internet users depend on them to turn fully qualified domain names (FQDNs) like www.microsoft.com into the IP addresses that browsers and other components use to find Internet resources.

However, the host record has a lesser-known but still important twin: the pointer (PTR) record. The format of a PTR record appears as follows:

```
reversed_address.in-addr.arpa. optional_TTL IN PTR targeted_domain_name
```

A records correspond to IPv4 and AAAA records corresponds to IPv6. These records (A and AAAA) map a hostname to an IP address. The PTR record does the opposite, it maps an IP address to a hostname through the use of the in-addr.arpa zone. *Sender Policy Framework (SPF)* is an email validation system designed to prevent email spam that uses source address spoofing.

SPF allows administrators to specify only those hosts that are allowed to send email from a given domain, as specified in a specific DNS SPF record in the public DNS. If email for a domain is sent from a host not listed in the DNS SPF, it will be considered spam and blocked.

Today, antispam packages use special algorithms, such as *Bayesian filters*, to determine if email is considered spam. These algorithms usually analyze previously received emails and create a database on several attributes based on those previously analyzed emails. When it receives an email, it will compare that email with the attributes it has collected to determine whether it is spam.

Email Spoofing

Email spoofing is the creation of a false email header where an attacker is tricking the recipient into thinking that the email came from a trusted source. The attacker alters parts of the email of it to look as though it were written by someone else. Because email protocols do not have an internal method of authentication, it is common for spam and phishing emails to be used to try to trick the recipient into believing the origin of the message.

The ultimate goal of email spoofing is to get the recipient to open and potentially respond to a solicitation. Maybe even click a link to a fake website that is intended to collect personal information (a process known as phishing).

The reason attackers change email information is to get people to trust them. Email is usually insecure and prone to a variety of address spoofing techniques. Make sure to never reveal your personal or financial information in an email. Never respond to email requests that ask for sensitive information and be extremely cautious when providing information after following web links embedded in an email.

A popular method is to include a survey link in an email that may be offering a prize and then asking questions. Some of the questions may be regarding their computing environment such as, "How many firewalls do you have?" or "What firewall vendor do you utilize?" Sometimes employees are so used to seeing these type of email surveys in their inbox that they hardly think twice about responding to them.

Relaying Email

One of the primary email protocols is SMTP. Simple Mail Transfer Protocol (SMTP) is used to transfer email from one server to another, and it is responsible for outgoing mail transport. SMTP uses TCP port 25.

Email servers are not only used for your users to send and retrieve email: they are also used to relay email. For example, web and application servers may relay email through their email servers when you order something over the Internet and a confirmation email is sent to you.

Usually, only your internal servers should relay email through your mail servers. Unfortunately, spammers look for unprotected SMTP servers to relay their email. As a result, other organizations may flag your server or domain as a spammer, and you may be placed on one of the RBLs or DNSBLs. To get off this list, close up your security hole so that other people cannot relay emails through your server, and then contact the organizations that host the RBLs or DNSBLs to remove your server or domain from their list.

Securing Internet Explorer

Because browsing a website can expose users to a wide range of hazards, it is important to rely on the browser to help protect systems. Today's browsers include pop-up blockers, security zones, and other built-in security features.

Certification Ready

What is the source of most malware? Objective 2.6

Understanding Cookies and Privacy Settings

When using a browser to access the Internet, much can be revealed about a user's personality and personal information. Therefore, it is important to take steps to ensure that this information cannot be read or used without your knowledge.

A *cookie* is a piece of text stored by a user's web browser. It can be used for a wide range of items including user identification, authentication, storing site preferences, and shopping cart contents. While cookies can give a website a lot of capabilities, they can also be used by spyware programs and websites to track people. Unfortunately, some websites will not operate without cookies.

Delete Cookies in Internet Explorer 11

To delete cookies in Internet Explorer 11, perform the following steps:

1. Open Internet Explorer.
2. Click the Tools button and click Internet Options. See Figure 5.12.

FIGURE 5.12   Deleting cookies and temporary files

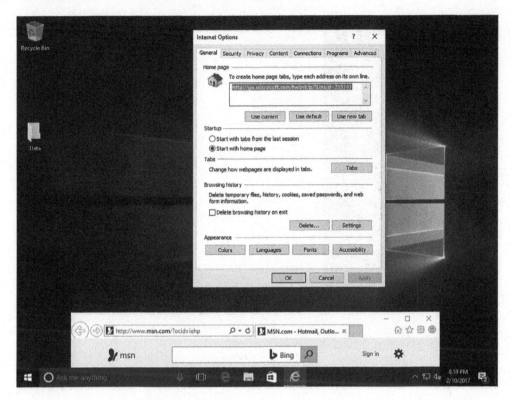

3. On the General tab, under Browsing History, click Delete.

4. Select the Cookies And Website Data check box if it isn't already selected. Clear or select check boxes for any other options you also want to delete. If you want to keep cookies for your saved favorites, select the Preserve Favorites Website Data check box. Click Delete.

Being aware of how your private information is used when browsing the web is important to help prevent targeted advertising, fraud, and identity theft.

Change Privacy Settings

To access Internet Explorer privacy settings, perform the following steps:

1. Open Internet Explorer.

2. Click the Tools button and click Internet Options.

3. In the Internet Options dialog box, click the Privacy tab. See Figure 5.13.

FIGURE 5.13 The Internet Options Privacy tab

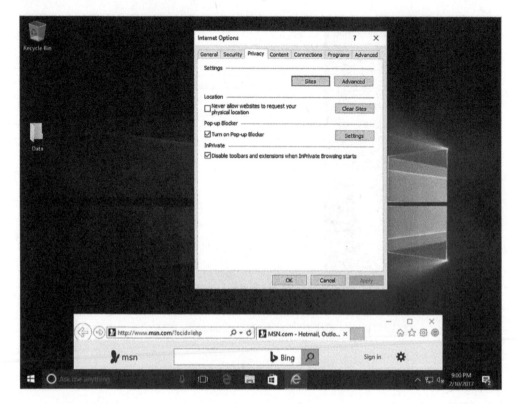

4. To block websites from requesting your physical location, select "Never allow websites to request your physical location."

5. To choose how cookies are handled, click the Advanced button. In the Advanced Privacy Settings dialog box, select "Accept, Block, or Prompt for first-party and third-party cookies." Click OK.

6. Close the Internet Options dialog box by clicking OK.

    The rest of this section will discuss the various options available on the Privacy tab. Use the Advanced button to access and override certain settings.

    Pop-up windows are very common. While some pop-up windows are useful website controls, most are simply annoying advertisements, with a few attempting to load spyware or other malicious programs. To help protect your computer, Internet Explorer has the capability to suppress some or all pop-ups. To configure the pop-up blocker, use the following procedure.

Configure the Pop-Up Blocker

To configure the Pop-up Blocker settings, perform the following steps:

1. After logging on to a computer running Windows 10, right-click the Start button and choose Control Panel. The Control Panel window opens.

2. Click Network And Internet ➤ Internet Options. The Internet Properties dialog box opens.

3. Click the Privacy tab. Make sure the Turn On Pop-up Blocker check box is selected.

4. Click Settings. The Pop-up Blocker Settings dialog box opens.

5. To allow pop-ups from a specific website, type the URL of the site in the Address of website to allow text box and click Add. Repeat the process to add additional sites to the Allowed sites list.

6. In the Blocking level drop-down list, select one of the following settings:

   - High: Block all pop-ups

   - Medium: Block most automatic pop-ups

   - Low: Allow pop-ups from secure sites

7. Click Close to close the Pop-up Blocker Settings dialog box.

8. Click OK to close the Internet Properties dialog box.

Using Content Zones

To help manage Internet Explorer security when visiting websites, Internet Explorer divides your network connection into four *content zones* or types. These content zones can be viewed on the Security tab of the Internet Options dialog box. For each of these zones, a security level is assigned.

The security for each content zone is assigned based on dangers associated with the zone. For example, it is assumed that connecting to a server within your own corporation would be safer than connecting to a server on the Internet.

The four default content types are:

Internet Zone   This zone includes anything that is not assigned to any other zone and anything that is not on your computer, or your organization's network (intranet). The default security level of the Internet zone is Medium.

Local Intranet Zone   This zone includes computers that are part of the organization's network (intranet) that do not require a proxy server, as defined by the system administrator. These include sites specified on the Connections tab as network paths, such as \\computername\foldername, and local intranet sites, such as http://internal. Sites can be added to this zone. The default security level for the Local intranet zone is Medium-Low, which means Internet Explorer will allow all cookies from websites in this zone to be saved on your computer and read by the website that created them. Lastly, if the website requires NTLM or integrated authentication, it will automatically use your user name and password.

Trusted Sites Zone   This zone contains sites from which you believe you can download or run files without damaging your system. Sites can be assigned to this zone. The default security level for the Trusted sites zone is Low, which means Internet Explorer will allow all cookies from websites in this zone to be saved on your computer and read by the website that created them.

Restricted Sites Zone This zone contains sites that are not trusted and from which downloading or running files may damage your computer or data, or sites that are considered a security risk. Sites can be assigned to this zone. The default security level for the Restricted sites zone is High, which means Internet Explorer will block all cookies from websites in this zone.

To tell which zones the current web page falls into, open the File menu and click Properties. The Properties dialog box also displays the connection, such as DLS 1.2, AES with 128-bit encryption, and the status of Protected Mode. Click the Certificates button to see the SSL digital certificate.

Modify the Security Level for a Web Content Zone

To modify the security level for a web content zone, perform the following steps:

1. Open Internet Explorer.

2. Click the Tools button and click "Internet options."

3. In the Internet Options dialog box, click the Security tab and click the zone on which you want to set the security level. See Figure 5.14.

FIGURE 5.14 Configuring the security content zones

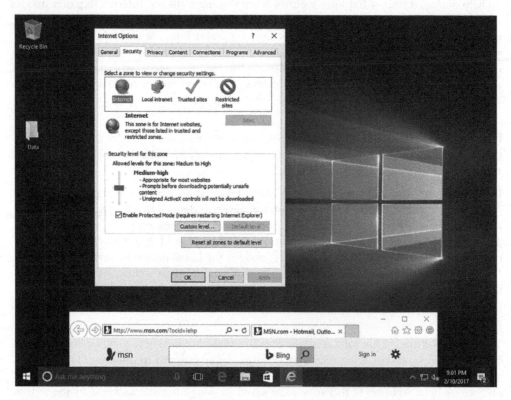

4. Drag the slider to set the security level to High, Medium, or Low. Internet Explorer describes each option to help you decide which level to choose. You are prompted to confirm any reduction in security level. Click the "Custom level" button for more detailed control.

5. Click OK to close the Internet Options dialog box.

For each of the web content zones, there is a default security level. The security levels available in Internet Explorer are:

High   Excludes any content that can damage your computer by maximizing safeguards and disabling less secure features.

Medium-High   Appropriate for most websites; prompts before downloading potential unsafe content.

Medium   Warns you before running potentially damaging content.

Medium-Low   Appropriate for local network\intranet websites; allows most content to be run without prompting.

Low   Does not warn you before running potentially damaging content.

Custom   Creates a security setting of your own design.

The easiest way to modify the security settings that Internet Explorer imposes on a specific website is to manually add the site to a security zone. The typical procedure is to add a site to the Trusted sites zone, to increase its privileges, or add it to the Restricted sites zone, to reduce its privileges. To do this, use the following procedure.

Add a Site to a Security Zone

Log on to Windows 10. To add a site to a security zone, perform the following steps:

1. Right-click Start and choose Control Panel.
2. Click Network And Internet ➤ Internet Options. The Internet Properties dialog box opens.
3. Click the Security tab.
4. Click either the Trusted Sites or Restricted Sites zone to which you want to add a site.
5. Click Sites. The Trusted sites dialog box or Restricted sites dialog box opens.
6. Type the URL of the website you want to add to the zone into the "Add this website to the zone" text box and click Add. The URL appears in the Websites list.
7. Click Close to close the Trusted sites or Restricted sites dialog box.
8. Click OK to close the Internet Properties dialog box.

To modify the security properties of a zone, use the following procedure.

Modify Security Zone Settings

Log on to Windows 10. To modify security zone settings, perform the following steps:

1. Right-click Start and choose Control Panel.
2. Click Network And Internet ➤ Internet Options. The Internet Properties dialog box opens.

3. Click the Security tab.

4. Select the zone for which you want to modify the security settings.

5. In the "Security level for this zone" box, drag the slider to increase or decrease the security level for the zone. Moving the slider up increases the protection for the zone and moving the slider down decreases the protection.

6. Select or clear the Enable Protected Mode check box, if desired.

7. To exercise more precise control over the zone's security settings, click Custom Level. The Security Settings dialog box for the zone opens.

8. Select radio buttons for the individual settings in each of the security categories. The radio buttons typically make it possible to enable a setting, disable it, or prompt the user before enabling it.

9. Click OK to close the Security Settings dialog box.

10. Click OK to close the Internet Properties dialog box.

Understanding Phishing and Pharming

Phishing and pharming are forms of attacks to get users to access a bogus website so the phisher or pharmer can spread malware and/or collect personal information.

Phishing is a technique based on social engineering. With phishing, users are requested (usually through email or other websites) to supply personal information by:

- Receiving an email that requests your user name, password, and other personal information such as account numbers, PINs, and Social Security numbers.

- Redirecting a user to a convincing-looking website that requires users to supply personal information, such as passwords and account numbers.

For example, an email states that your account has just expired or that you may need to validate your information. Within the email, there is a link to click. When you click the link, the fake website appears. However, just by logging on, you provide the user name and password to the hacker, which can then be used to access your account.

To help protect against phishing, Internet Explorer 8 introduced SmartScreen Filter that examines traffic for evidence of phishing activity and displays a warning to the user if it finds any. It also sends the address back to the Microsoft SmartScreen service to be compared against lists of known phishing and malware sites. If SmartScreen Filter discovers that a website you're visiting is on the list of known malware or phishing sites, Internet Explorer will display a blocking webpage and the address bar will appear in red. From the blocking page, choose to bypass the blocked website and go to your home page instead, or continue to the blocked website (this is not recommended). If you decide to continue to the blocked website, the address bar will continue to appear in red.

One of the best ways to avoid such ploys is to know that they exist. When an email requests personal information, look for signs that the email is fake and that the actual links may go to bogus websites (for example, instead of going to ebay.com, it goes to ebay.com.com or ebay_ws.com). Don't trust hyperlinks. Never supply a password or any other confidential information to a website unless you type the URL yourself and are sure that it is correct.

Pharming is an attack aimed at redirecting a website's traffic to a bogus website. This is usually accomplished by changing the hosts file (text that provides name resolution for host or domain names to IP addresses) on a computer or by exploiting a vulnerability on a DNS server.

Understanding Secure Sockets Layer (SSL) and Certificates

When surfing the Internet, there are times when it is necessary to transmit private data over the Internet such as credit card numbers, Social Security numbers, and so on. During these times, it is important to use HTTP over SSL (HTTPS) to encrypt the data sent over the Internet. By convention, URLs that require an SSL connection start with https: instead of http:.

SSL is short for Secure Sockets Layer. It's a cryptographic system that uses two keys to encrypt data—a public key known to everyone and a private or secret key known only to the recipient of the message. The public key is published in a digital certificate, which also confirms the identity of the web server.

When connecting to a site that is secured using SSL, a lock appears in the address bar, along with the name of the organization to which the CA issued the certificate. Clicking the lock icon displays more information about the site, including the identity of the CA that issued the certificate. For even more information, click the View Certificate link to open the Certificate dialog box.

When visiting certain websites, Internet Explorer may find problems with the digital certificate such as that the certificate has expired, it is corrupted, it has been revoked, or it does not match the name of the website. When this happens, IE will block access to the site and display a warning stating that there is a problem with the certificate. At this point, close the browser window or ignore the warning and continue on to the site. Of course, the warning should be ignored only if you trust the website and believe that you are communicating with the correct server.

Configuring Microsoft Edge

Microsoft Edge is the new Microsoft lightweight web browser with a layout engine built around web standards designed to replace Internet Explorer as the default web browser. It integrates with Cortana, annotation tools, Adobe Flash Player, a PDF reader, and a reading mode. Extension support was developed and added to the Windows 10 Anniversary Update in July 2016.

Certification Ready

Which security settings are available in Microsoft Edge that are also available in Microsoft Explorer? Objective 1.3

The following buttons display at the top of the Microsoft Edge window:

- Reading view
- Add to Favorites or Reading List
- Hub (Favorites, reading lists, history, and downloads)
- Make a web note
- Feedback
- Settings

To open Edge settings (as shown in Figure 5.15), click the Settings (...) button and click the Settings option.

FIGURE 5.15   Configuring Microsoft Edge

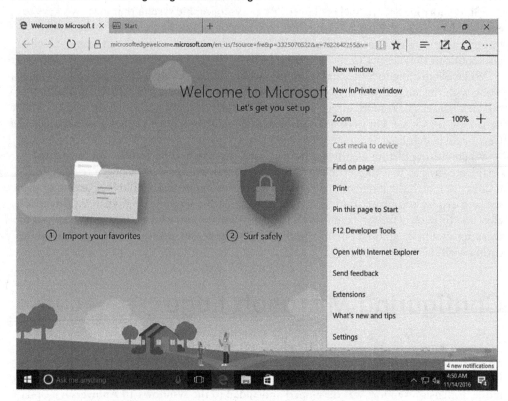

Under Settings, the following tasks can be performed:

- Enable or disable the favorites bar
- Set Edge to start with a New tab page, My previous tabs, or a specified web page
- Set whether new tabs will be top sites and suggested content or a blank page
- Set the search engine to Bing, Google, or any search engine of your choice

- Clear browsing history and delete media licenses, pop-up exceptions, and location permissions
- Set the Reading style to Default, Light, Medium, or Dark, and specify the Reading font size

Clicking the Advanced Settings option provides access to these additional tasks:

- Enable or disable Flash Player
- Opt to use caret browsing
- Set privacy options
- Manage saved passwords
- Opt to save form entries
- Choose to block pop-ups and cookies
- Manage protected media licenses
- Send Do Not Track requests
- Enable or disable page prediction
- Enable or disable SmartScreen Filter
- Turn on or off Cortana integration

Protecting Your Server

When looking at security, it is important to consider securing everything—the network, the clients, and the servers. Securing all three forms a layered approach that makes it more difficult for hackers and malware to breach your organization. Previous lessons discussed how to keep your network secure, and earlier in this lesson, you learned how to keep your clients secure. This section covers how to secure the server.

Certification Ready

How can servers be protected so that they are always up and running? Objective 4.3

Servers are computers that are meant to provide network services and applications for your organization. Different from workstations, if a server fails, it will affect multiple users. Therefore, it is more important to keep a server secure than a workstation.

Separating Services

The first step in securing a server is deciding where to physically place the server. Of course, the server should be kept in a secure location. In addition, the servers should be in their own subnet to reduce the amount of traffic to the servers, especially broadcasts.

To minimize one service or application from interfering with and affecting another service or network application, it is recommended that services or network applications should be run on their own server. This allows you to customize access to the individual service or network application. With today's virtual machine technology, it is easy to allow a separation between services while keeping costs to a minimum.

Using a Read-Only Domain Controller (RODC)

Windows Server 2008 introduced the *Read-Only Domain Controller (RODC)*, which contains a full replication of the domain database. It was created to be used in places where a domain controller is needed but where the physical security of the domain controller could not be guaranteed. For example, it might be placed in a remote site that is not very secure and that provides a slower WAN link. Also, because a site may have a slow WAN link, a local domain controller would benefit the users at that site.

An RODC does not perform any outbound replication and accepts only inbound replication connections from writable domain controllers. Because the RODC has only a read-only copy of the Active Directory database, the administrator needs to connect to a separate, writable, domain controller to make changes to Active Directory.

To deploy an RODC, do the following:

- Ensure that the forest functional level is Windows Server 2003 or higher.

- Deploy at least one writable domain controller running Windows Server 2008 or higher.

Hardening Servers

The next step in securing a server is to harden the server by reducing its surface of attack and thereby reducing the server's vulnerabilities. To harden a server, look for security guides/guidelines and best practices for Windows servers and for the specific network services that are being installed, such as Microsoft Exchange or Microsoft SQL Server.

One of the most important steps in securing a server is to make sure that Windows, Microsoft applications, and other network applications are kept up-to-date with the newest security patches. As with clients, you use Windows updates, WSUS, and SCCM to provide updates to servers. Of course, before applying patches to a production system, be sure to test the security updates.

To reduce the surface of attack, disable any service that is not necessary so that those services cannot be exploited in the future. In addition, consider using the host firewalls (such as Windows firewalls) that will block all ports that are not being used.

To reduce the effect of losing a server, it's a good idea to separate the services—do not install all your services on one server. Also, plan for the rest and hope for the best. In other words, anticipate that a server will eventually fail. Therefore, consider using redundant power supplies, RAID disks, redundant network cards, and clusters.

Also, disable or delete any unnecessary accounts. For example, although the administrator account cannot be deleted, it can be renamed to something else so that it would be more difficult for a hacker to guess what it is. And, of course, the guest account should be disabled. In addition, you should not use the administrator account for everything. For example, if a service is required, create a service account for that service and give the account the minimum rights and permissions needed to run the service.

Besides disabling or deleting any unnecessary accounts and assigning only the minimum rights and permissions for users to do their jobs, you should also restrict who can log on locally to the server.

In addition, disable any unsecure authentication protocols. For example, you should not use Password Authentication Protocol (PAP) when using remote access protocols. You should not use FTP with passwords. Instead, use anonymous, which does not require passwords (assuming it uses only content that does not need to be secure), or use secure FTP, which will encrypt the password and content when being transmitted over the network. For similar reasons, use SSH instead of telnet.

Lastly, enable a strong audit and logging policy and review these logs on a regular basis. Then, if someone tries to hack a server or do something they should not be doing, there will be a record of his or her activities. This should include being alerted to both successful and failed account logons.

Understanding Secure Dynamic DNS

Since Windows Server 2003, Windows servers have provided support for the dynamic DNS update functionality. Dynamic DNS lets client computers dynamically update their resource records in DNS. When using this functionality, DNS administration is improved by reducing the time that it takes to manually manage DNS zone records. Use the DNS update functionality with DHCP to update resource records when a computer's IP address is changed.

With typical unsecured dynamic updates, any computer can create records on your DNS server which leaves your system open to malicious activity. To keep your DNS server secure, secure DNS makes it so that only members of an Active Directory domain can create records on the DNS server.

Using Security Baselines

As has been made very clear, one of the biggest concerns of any organization is security. To secure systems, it is necessary to configure a wide range of settings. Windows 10 includes more than 3,000 Group Policy settings and more than 1,800 settings for Internet Explorer. Many of these settings are security-related settings that must be managed within an organization.

Certification Ready

How can the current security settings in Windows be collected to determine which settings are not compliant? Objective 3.1

A *security baseline* is a collection of security settings. Security baselines should include Microsoft's recommendations for configuring those settings. To help with faster deployments, and to ease the managing of Windows, Microsoft provides customers with security baselines that can be used with Group Policy Objects (GPOs).

Using Security Templates

Group policies are often used to make a computer more secure. Use security templates to implement security settings quickly and efficiently, copy and apply security settings from one computer to another, and check the security settings based on a security template.

A *security template* is a collection of configuration settings stored in a text file with the .inf extension. They can be used for the following tasks:

- Save the security configuration to a file
- Deploy the security settings to a computer or group policy
- Analyze compliance of a computer's current configuration against the desired configuration

Use a security template to configure the following policies and settings:

Account Policies   Configure password restrictions, account lockout policies, and Kerberos policies

Local Policies   Configure audit policies, user rights assignments, and security options policies

Event Log Policies   Configure maximum event log sizes and rollover policies

Restricted Groups   Specify users who are allowed to be added to a specific group such as domain administrators

System Services   Specify the startup types and permissions for system services

Registry Permissions   Set access control permissions for specific registry keys

File System Permissions   Specify access control permissions for NTFS files and folders

Security templates can be deployed using the following:

- Active Directory group policy objects
- Security Configuration and Analysis snap-in

To manage security templates, use the Security Templates snap-in. This snap-in is not included in Administrative Tools—you need to open Microsoft Management Console (MMC) to manually add the snap-in.

Open the Security Templates Snap-In

To open the Security Templates snap-in, perform the following steps:

1. Right-click Start and choose Command Prompt (Admin).
2. At the command prompt, execute the mmc command. An empty console opens.

3. Click File ➤ Add/Remove Snap-in.

4. In the Add or Remove Snap-ins dialog box, scroll down to and click Security Templates. Click Add. Click OK. The Security Templates snap-in is available (see Figure 5.16).

FIGURE 5.16   Adding the Security Templates snap-in to MMC

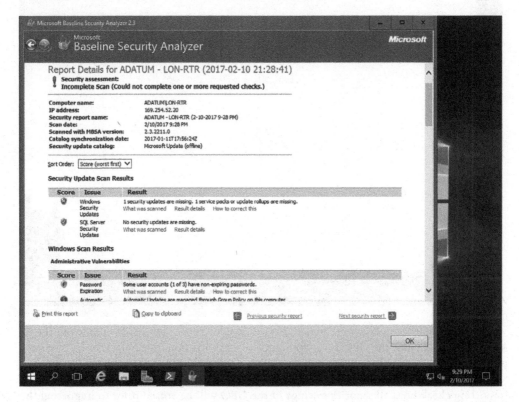

5. To create a new security template, right-click the node where you want to store the security template and choose New Template.

6. In the dialog box, in the "Template name text box," type a descriptive name. Click OK. The security template is added in the console. Figure 5.17 shows the security templates.

Settings are configured the same way a GPO is configured. The only exception is when adding registry settings that are not already listed in the Local Policies\Security Options portion of the template. After making your changes, right-click the template and choose Save. For an updated security baseline for Windows 10 and Server 2016 computers, search the www.microsoft.com website and download the Windows 10 RS2 and Server 2016 Security Baseline.

FIGURE 5.17 Viewing a security template

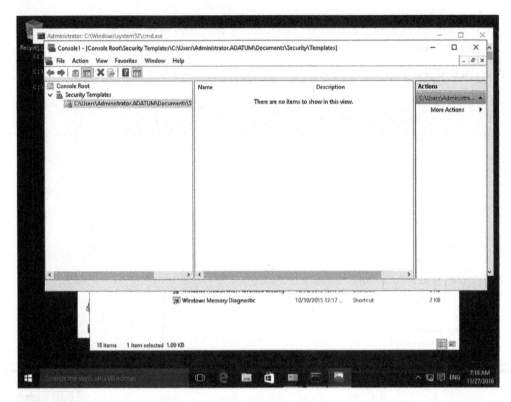

After a security template is created and saved, deploy those settings by importing the security template into the GPO for a domain, site, organization unit object, or local computer. To import a security template into a GPO, open the GPO, right-click the Security Settings node, and choose Import Policy. If you select the Clear This Database Before Importing check box, all security settings in the GPO will be erased prior to importing the template settings, so the GPO's security settings will match the template's settings.

Compare Settings with a Security Template

To compare settings with a security template, perform the following steps:

1. Right-click the Start menu and choose Command Prompt (Admin).

2. At the command prompt, execute the mmc command. An empty console opens.

3. Click File ➤ Add/Remove Snap-in.

4. In the Add Or Remove Snap-ins dialog box, scroll down and then click Security Configuration And Analysis. Click Add. Click OK. The Security Configuration And Analysis console is available (see Figure 5.18).

FIGURE 5.18   Viewing the Security Configuration and Analysis console

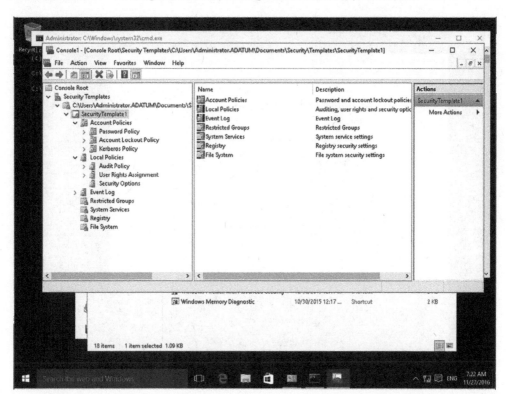

5. Right-click Security Configuration And Analysis and choose Open Database.

6. In the Open database dialog box, in the File name text box, type **SecDB** and click Open.

7. In the Import Template dialog box, click SecurityTemplate1.inf and click Open.

8. To analyze a computer based on the security template, click Analyze Computer Now.

9. In the Perform Analysis dialog box, click OK.

10. When the analysis is done, look for settings that are not compliant. For example, Figure 5.19 shows that the Minimum Password Age and Minimum Password Length settings are not compliant.

FIGURE 5.19 Comparing a security template with actual settings

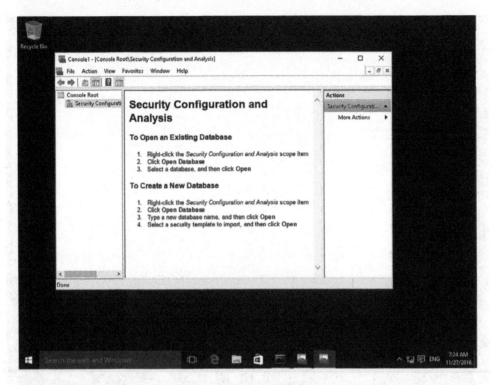

11. Close the Security Configuration And Analysis console.

Using Security Compliance Manager

Security Compliance Manager 4.0 (SCM 4.0) is a free tool from Microsoft that can be used to quickly configure and manage your desktops, traditional data center, and private cloud using Group Policy and System Center Configuration Manager. It includes creating new baselines for Windows Server 2016, Windows 10, and Internet Explorer 11. To install Security Compliance Manager, .NET Framework 3.5 must be installed.

Certification Ready

Which free tool can help to quickly configure and manage your desktops? Objective 3.1

SCM provides ready-to-deploy policies and configuration packages that are based on Microsoft Security guide recommendations and industry best practices. When deployed as a GPO, you can manage configuration drift, address compliance requirements, and reduce security threats.

Install Security Compliance Manager

To install Security Compliance Manager 4.0, perform the following steps:

1. Double-click the Security_Compliance_Manager_Setup.exe file. When you are prompted to confirm that you want to run the executable program, click Run.

2. In the Microsoft Visual C++ 2010 x86 Redistributable Setup dialog box, click the "I have read and accept the license terms" option and click Install.

3. After the Visual C++ 2010 x86 Redistributable is installed, click Finish.

4. In the Microsoft Security Compliance Manager Setup window, on the Welcome screen, click Next.

5. On the License Agreement page, click the "I accept the terms of the license agreement" option and click Next.

6. On the Installation Folder page, click Next.

7. On the Microsoft SQL Server 2008 Express page, click Next.

8. On the SQL Server 2008 Express License Agreement page, click the "I accept the terms in the license agreement" option and click Next.

9. On the Ready To Install page, click Install.

10. When the SQL Server Express And Microsoft Security Compliance Manager is installed, click Finish. Microsoft Security Compliance Manager (SCM) 4.0 opens.

11. Click File ➤ Check For Updates.

12. In the Downloads Updates dialog box, click Download.

13. When you are prompted to confirm that you want to run this software, click More Options. Then click the Always Run Software From "Microsoft Corporation" option and click Run. Repeat the process until all there are no more security warnings.

14. In the Import Baselines Wizard, on the Select Packages File page, click Next.

15. On the Baseline Details page, click Import.

16. On the Results page, click Finish.

Expand the Windows Server 2016 category in the left pane to see a list of baseline templates for several different server roles, such as Domain Controller Security Compliance 1.0, Domain Security Compliance 1.0, and Member Server Security Compliance. Microsoft recommends that organizations only apply Domain Controller, Domain Security, and Member Server security templates to servers.

Figure 5.20 shows the Windows 10 Computer Security Compliance Manager. As shown in the figure, there are 765 unique settings, and the Authentication Types group has 43 settings. However, when you click a setting—because this is a baseline template that's provided by Microsoft—you need to duplicate it before you can make changes. The settings can then be modified, as shown in Figure 5.21.

FIGURE 5.20   Viewing Windows 10 settings with Computer Security Compliance Manager

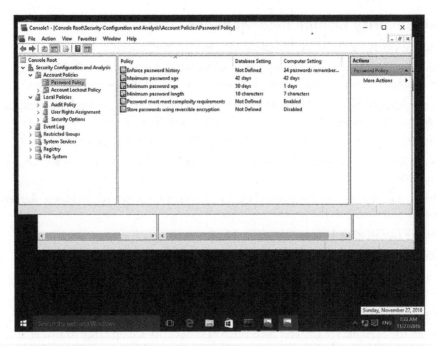

FIGURE 5.21   Changing a Windows 10 setting with Computer Security Compliance Manager

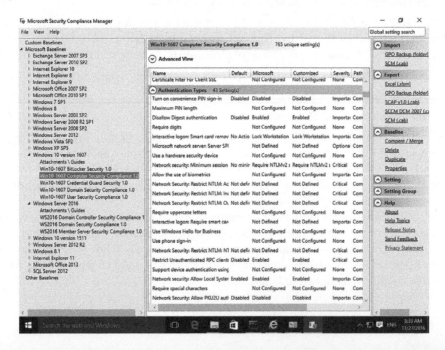

After configuring the desired settings, export the SCM Template Settings as a GPO Backup. Then, use the backup to create a new GPO and link it to an organizational unit or domain.

In 2017, Microsoft announced that it was ending support for the Security Compliance Manager (SCM) tool. However, it can still be downloaded from the Microsoft website at: `https://www.microsoft.com/en-us/download/details.aspx?id=53353`.

Microsoft has provided some alternative tools since it has ended support for the SCM tool. These include:

Security Compliance Toolkit 1.0   This is the tool replacing the Microsoft Security Compliance Manager (SCM). This tool can be downloaded from the Microsoft website at `https://www.microsoft.com/en-us/download/details.aspx?id=55319`.

PowerShell Desired State Configuration   This also has an Environment Analyzer module for producing compliance reports.

The Security Compliance Toolkit (SCT)   A set of tools that allows enterprise security administrators to download, analyze, test, edit, and store Microsoft-recommended security configuration baselines for Windows and other Microsoft products.

Using the toolkit, administrators can compare their current GPOs with Microsoft-recommended GPO baselines or other baselines, edit them, store them in GPO backup file format, and apply them via a Domain Controller or inject them directly into a test host to test their effects.

The toolkit contains a Policy Analyzer tool, which compares Group Policy objects (GPOs), and a Local Group Policy Object (LGPO) tool. The LGPO tool is used to transfer a Group Policy between a host's registry and a GPO backup file, bypassing the Domain Controller.

Windows PowerShell Desired State Configuration (DSC)   DSC enables the deployment and management of configuration information for software services and helps manage the environment where the services run. DSC allows administrators to use Windows PowerShell language extensions along with Windows PowerShell cmdlets and resources. DSC allows an administrator to specify how an organization would like their software environment to be configured and maintained. The benefits and the reason that Desired State Configuration exists is to:

- Decrease the complexity of scripting in Windows
- Increase the speed of iteration

Locking Down Devices to Run Only Trusted Applications

Removing users from the administrative role on computers can reduce the number of applications they can install, but it does not prevent them from loading apps that do not require administrative privileges to run. Use AppLocker to establish rules that determine which programs your users are allowed to run.

Certification Ready

How can you ensure that only authorized applications run on your company computers? Objective 2.5

Certification Ready

How can you ensure that users do not install software that they download from the Internet? Objective 4.1

Use *AppLocker* to control how users access and use programs and files and extend the functionality originally provided by the Software Restriction policy found in earlier versions of Windows operating systems. In Windows 10, AppLocker is located in the Local Group Policy Editor.

Access AppLocker

To access AppLocker using the Local Group Policy editor (gpedit.msc), perform the following steps:

1. Press Windows logo key+r.
2. In the Run box, type **gpedit.msc** and click OK. The Local Group Policy Editor displays.
3. Click Computer Configuration ➤ Windows Settings ➤ Security Settings ➤ Application Control Policies ➤ AppLocker.

AppLocker uses rules and file properties to determine which programs and files are allowed to run on the computer. As shown in Figure 5.22, AppLocker includes four *rule collections*:

- Executable Rules
- Windows Installer Rules
- Script Rules
- Packaged app Rules

These rule collections can be used to differentiate the rules for different types of applications. AppLocker uses rules and a file's properties to determine which applications are allowed to run.

FIGURE 5.22   The AppLocker rule collections

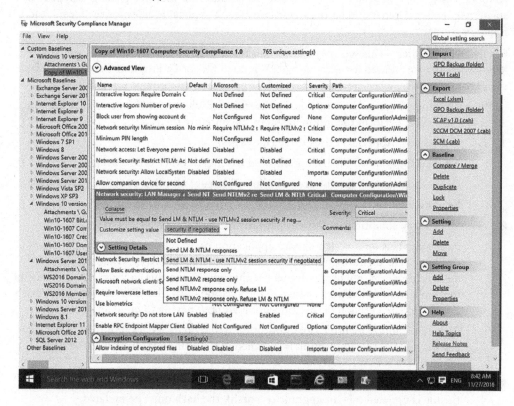

A traditional app consists of several components (.exe files, scripts, and so on). These components might not share the same publisher, product, or product version attribute. In order to manage traditional apps, AppLocker needs to control them using different rule collections. On the other hand, a Windows app (packaged app) shares the same attributes; therefore, a single rule can be created to control the entire application.

Rule collections include the following:

- Executable files (.exe, .com)
- Scripts (.ps2, .bat, .js, .cmd, vbs)
- Windows Installer files (.msi, .mst, .msp)
- Packaged apps and Packaged app installers (.appx)

By default, there are no rules in any of the rule collections; therefore, AppLocker will allow every file covered in each collection to run.

When creating rules with AppLocker, the following options are available:

Create New Rule   Use this wizard to walk through the process of creating one AppLocker rule at a time—setting permissions, publishers, exceptions, and providing a name for the rule.

Automatically Generate Rules This wizard creates rules for multiple packaged apps in a single step. Select a folder and let the wizard create the applicable rules for the files in the folder or for packaged apps.

Create Default Rules This wizard creates rules that are meant to ensure that some key Windows paths are allowed for execution (C:\Windows files or C:\Program files). If the default rules are not in place, when creating a new rule, AppLocker will prompt you to create them.

Prior to configuring a rule, install the application for which you want to create the rule. After it is installed, perform the following steps to configure the rule:

1. Set permissions. AppLocker uses three rule types:

   Allow: Programs on the list are allowed to run; all other programs are blocked.

   Deny: Programs on the list are not allowed to run; all other programs are allowed.

   Exceptions: Used for both allow and deny rules to provide exceptions to the rule.

2. Set the primary condition (publisher, path, or file hash):

   Publisher: This option identifies an application based on the manufacturer's digital signature. The digital signature contains information about the company that created the program (publisher). If you use this option, the rule can survive an update of the application as well as a change in the location of its files. This allows you to push out the updated version of the application without having to build another rule.

   Path: This option identifies an application based on its location in the file system. For example, if the application is installed in the Windows directory, the App-Locker path is %WINDIR%.

   File hash: This option causes the system to compute a hash on the file. Each time the file is updated (via an upgrade or patch), the hash must be updated.

3. Add an exception (optional). In this step, you can add an exception to the rule (if applicable). For example, you might have enabled access for a suite (such as Microsoft Office) but do not want selected users to be able to use Microsoft Access because there are a limited number of licenses.

4. Type a name for the rule. In this step, give the rule a name and add an optional description.

Rules created for a packaged app can use only the Publisher condition. Windows does not support unsigned packaged apps or installers.

Create and Test an AppLocker Rule

To create and test an AppLocker rule that blocks the use of the Remote Desktop Connection client (mstsc.exe), log on to a Windows 10 computer as an administrator, and then perform the following steps:

1. Press Windows logo key+r and in the Run box, type **services.msc** and click OK. The Services console displays.

2. Right-click the Application Identity service and choose Start. Close the Services console after confirming that the service is running.

3. Press Windows logo key+r and in the Run box, type **gpedit.msc** and click OK. The Local Group Policy Editor displays.

4. Click Computer Configuration ➤ Windows Settings ➤ Security Settings ➤ Application Control Policies ➤ AppLocker.

5. Right-click Executable Rules and choose Create New Rule.

6. Read the Before You Begin screen and click Next.

7. Select Deny.

8. Click Select and in the "Enter the object name to select" box, type **Users** and click OK.

9. Click Next to continue.

10. Select Publisher and click Next.

11. Click Browse and navigate to the C:\Windows\System32 directory. Click the mstsc.exe file and click Open.

12. Drag the slider to File Name (see Figure 5.23) and click Next.

    This setting ensures the rule will block all instances of the Remote Desktop Connection client (mstsc.exe), regardless of the version.

FIGURE 5.23   Viewing the executable rules/publisher information for the AppLocker rule

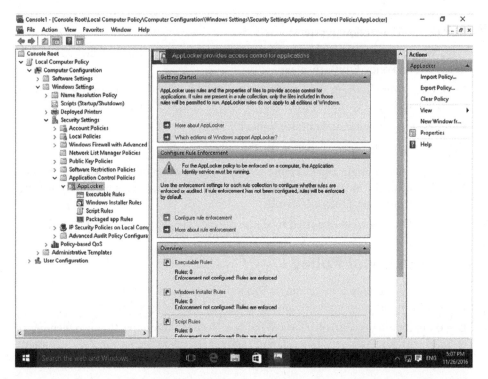

13. Click Next. You do not set an exception to this rule.

14. Type a name for the rule and a description (optional). For example, you might type **Disallow Remote Desktop Connection client on Company Systems.**

15. Click Create.

16. When you are prompted to create the default rules, click Yes. This ensures important rules are allowed to run.

17. Close the Local Group Policy Editor.

18. To force Group Policy to update, press Windows logo key+r and in the Run box, type **Gpupdate /force** and then click OK.

19. Log on with any non-administrative account and test the policy.

20. Press Windows logo key+r and in the Run box, type **mstsc.exe** and click OK. The user will see the "Your system administrator has blocked this program" message.

When creating a policy using the Local Group Policy Editor, you are applying the policy to the local computer and the users who log on to it. If you decide later that you want to use the same policy but apply it to multiple computers across your Active Directory domain, export the policy and then import it into a Group Policy Object linked to a container in the Active Directory hierarchy (site, domain, or organizational unit). This eliminates the need to re-create the policy settings.

Export the Local Policy

To export the local policy, log on to the Windows 10 client computer as an administrator, and then perform the following steps:

1. Press Windows logo key+r and in the Run box, type **gpedit.msc** and click OK. The Local Group Policy Editor displays.

2. Click Computer Configuration ➤ Windows Settings ➤ Security Settings ➤ Application Control Policies.

3. Right-click AppLocker and choose Export Policy.

4. In the File name field, type a name for the policy and click Save.

For example, you might type **Remote Desktop Connection client on Company Systems.** Make a note of the location where you are saving the policy. This location must be accessible from your domain controller.

5. When the "4 rules were exported from the policy" message displays, click OK.

Import the Local Policy

To import the local policy settings into a Group Policy Object in Active Directory and apply it to all computers in your domain, perform the following steps:

1. Log on to a domain controller or a Windows 10 client computer that is a member of a domain with an administrative account that has access to the Group Policy Management console.

2. Press Windows logo key+r and in the Run box, type **gpmc.msc** and click OK. The Group Policy Management Editor window opens.

3. Right-click the Group Policy Objects folder and choose New.

4. Type a name for the new GPO and click OK.

    For example, you might type **Disallow Remote Desktop Connection client on Company Systems**.

5. Right-click the GPO and choose Edit.

6. Click Computer Configuration ➤ Policies ➤ Windows Settings ➤ Security Settings ➤ Application Control Policies.

7. Right-click AppLocker and choose Import Policy.

8. Browse to the local policy file you exported earlier, select the policy file, and then click Open.

9. When prompted to import the policy now, click Yes.

10. When the "4 rules were imported from the policy" message displays, click OK.

11. Close the Group Policy Management Editor.

12. In the Group Policy Management console, right-click the domain name (contoso) and choose Link an Existing GPO.

13. In the Group Policy objects section, click "Disallow Remote Desktop Connection client on Company Systems" and click OK.

    Now, no computer in your domain will be allowed to use the Remote Desktop Connection program.

Managing Windows Store Apps

Windows Store apps are a class of applications for Windows devices, including PCs, tablets, phones, Xbox One, Microsoft Hololens, and the Internet of Things. They are typically distributed and updated through the Windows Store.

Certification Ready

How can users find and install only applications that an administrator approves from the Windows Store? Objective 2.5

Certification Ready

How can access to the Windows Store be disabled? Objective 4.1

Universal Windows Platform (UWP) apps are a special type of Windows Store app that can be installed on multiple hardware platforms, such as an Intel tablet that is running Windows 10 Pro, an Xbox One, or a Windows 10 Phone. Windows Store apps differ from traditional applications in that they are designed to run in a single, full window display across multiple form factor devices (for example, desktops, laptops, or tablets). These devices can be touch-based or they can use a standard mouse and keyboard.

Configuring the Windows Store

The *Windows Store* provides a central location for purchasing and downloading Windows apps that run on Windows 8 and higher operating systems. Windows Store apps are special types of apps that work on computers that are running Windows 8 and higher operating systems. Windows Store apps do not run on Windows 7 or earlier versions of Windows. Windows Store apps tend to be smaller and faster than desktop apps.

Windows 10 includes the Windows Store app, which can be accessed directly from the taskbar. In Windows 10, the Windows Store enables users to deploy both Windows Store apps and desktop apps. To browse the Windows Store, it is not necessary to sign in with a Microsoft account. However, to download and install apps from the Windows Store, you do have to sign in with a Microsoft account.

A *Microsoft account*, previously called Windows Live ID, is a unique account that is the combination of an email address and a password that you use to sign in to services like Outlook.com, MSN.com, Hotmail.com, OneDrive, Windows Phone, or Xbox Live. When setting up a computer running Windows 10 for the first time, create a Microsoft account using an email address that you provide. The email address can come from any provider. After the account is set up, Microsoft will use it, along with your password, to help manage your settings across all your PCs that run Windows 10. Microsoft accounts can be used to synchronize your desktop across multiple Windows 10 devices and provide a consistent experience when working with Windows Store apps. Purchased apps will be available from each device, feeds will be synced across all devices, and state information will be maintained, so you can start a game or read a book and pick it up later on another device. You can create a Microsoft account during the initial installation of the operating system or after the system is running.

When you open the Windows Store, click the Sign in icon (the icon next to the Search text box). If you click the Sign up button, you can also configure the following:

Downloads and Updates   View the current downloads and check for updates for the Windows Store apps.

Settings   Enable automatic updates, show products on the Live Tile, streamline purchases, and manage your devices that are connected to the Microsoft account. Figure 5.24 shows the Windows Store Settings page.

FIGURE 5.24   Managing Windows Store settings

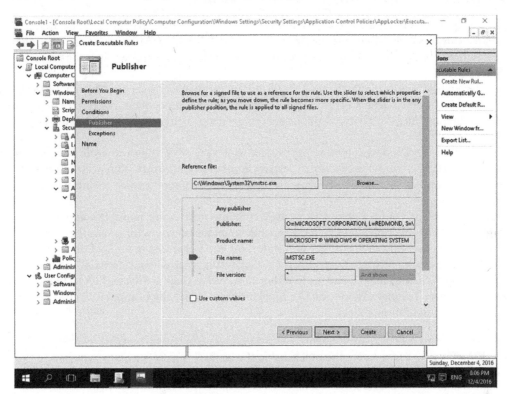

Configure the Windows Store

To configure the Windows Store, perform the following steps:

1. On the taskbar, click the Windows Store button.

2. To sign in to the Windows Store, click the Sign In button and click Sign In.

3. When you are prompted to choose an account, click Microsoft Account.

4. Specify the proper credentials in the Email or phone dialog box and click Sign In.

5. Click the user icon and click Settings.

6. To update apps automatically, ensure that the "Update apps automatically" option is set to On.

7. To streamline your purchases so that you will not be prompted for a password, ensure that the "Streamline my purchase experience" option is set to On.

8. To view your downloads and updates, click the user icon again and click Downloads And Updates.

Implementing Windows Store Apps

Searching for a Windows Store app is quite easy. Type the search term (a specific name or a desired category) and Microsoft provides a list of available apps. After you select apps, they install in the background. When the installation is done, the app appears in a tile on the Start menu.

The applications available through the Windows Store must be certified by Microsoft for compatibility and content. Certified apps cannot contain adult content and cannot advocate discrimination, illegal activity, alcohol, tobacco products, drugs, weapons, profanity, or extreme violence.

Although the Windows Store can provide a wide variety of apps and tools to enhance Windows 10, it might be necessary to restrict access for your users. This restriction would ensure that users are working with only authorized applications within your organization.

To deny access, set up a policy for a single computer/user or for multiple computers and users. The tool that should be used depends upon where you want to use the policy. For example, to configure the policy and test it, use the Local Group Policy Editor on a Windows 10 client machine. To deploy the policy settings across your domain, use the Group Policy Management Console. In either case, the settings are located under the Administrative Templates\Windows Components\Store under the Computer Configuration and User Configuration nodes.

 If you create the policy using the Local Group Policy Editor, you can export and import it into a GPO at the domain level. It does not have to be re-created.

When configuring the policy using the Local Group Policy Editor for a user (User Configuration\Administrative Templates\Windows Components\Store), there is only one option to set within the policy:

- Turn off the Store application:

    Not Configured (default): Access to the Store is allowed.

    Enabled: Access to the Store is denied.

    Disabled: Access to the Store application is allowed.

When setting the policy for a computer (Computer Configuration\Administrative Templates\Windows Components\Store), the following options are available:

- Turn off Automatic Download of updates:

    Not Configured (default): Download of updates is allowed.

    Enabled: Automatic downloads are turned off.

    Disabled: Automatic downloads of updates are allowed.

- Allow Store to install apps on Windows To Go workspaces:

  Not Configured (default): Access to the Store is not allowed.

  Enabled: Access to the Store is allowed on the Windows To Go Workspace. Use this option only when the device is used with a single PC.

  Disabled: Access to the Store is denied.

- Turn off the Store application:

  Not Configured (default): Access to the Store is allowed.

  Enabled: Access to the Store is denied.

  Disabled: Access to the Store application is allowed.

Restrict Access to the Windows Store Using a Local Group Policy

To restrict access to the Windows Store using a Local Group Policy, log on to a Windows 10 computer with administrative credentials, and then perform the following steps:

1. Click the Start button, type **gpedit.msc,** and press Enter. The Local Group Policy Editor opens.

2. Expand Computer Configuration ➤ Administrative Templates ➤ Windows Components and click Store.

3. Double-click the "Turn off the Store application" setting. In the Turn Off The Store Application dialog box, click Enabled.

4. Attempt to access the Windows Store. Click the Store tile located on the Windows 10 Start menu. The Windows Store isn't available on this PC message appears.

5. Return to the group policy setting you enabled in Step 3 and click Not Configured to regain access to the Windows Store.

In some situations, you might administer a computer in a public area (such as a library or kiosk) that needs to run just a single Windows app. In these situations, configure Windows 10 settings to restrict access to a single application.

When you assign access to a single Windows Store app, you restrict the application to a user account. When the user logs on to the computer, that user can only access the assigned app.

Restrict a User Account to Run a Single Windows Store App

To restrict a user account to run a single Windows Store app, perform the following steps:

1. Click the Start button and click Settings.

2. Click Accounts and click Family & Other Users.

3. In the right pane, click Set Up Assigned Access.

4. Click Choose An Account and select the account that you want to restrict.

5. Click Choose An App and select the installed app to which you want to restrict the account.

6. Sign out of the computer to make the changes effective.

Implementing Windows Store for Business

To support larger organizations that need to control which apps are installed on the organization's computers, Microsoft developed the Windows Store for Business. The *Windows Store for Business* supports volume purchases of Windows apps, flexible distribution options, and the ability to reclaim or reuse licenses. You can also create a private store for your employees that includes apps from the Windows Store as well as the organization's private apps.

Many organizations enforce policies that are designed to standardize the apps used on company-supplied computers. They do not want their users installing just any application they find, even if those apps are certified to work with Windows 10. *Bring Your Own Device (BYOD) policies* might also be in place, requiring you to control access to the Windows Store. A BYOD policy defines the standards, restrictions, and procedures for end users who have authorized access to company data from their personal devices (tablets, laptops, or smartphones). The policy also includes hardware and related software that is not approved, owned, or supplied by the company. In either case, as the administrator, ensure that your strategy for accessing the Windows Store aligns with your company's policies.

In addition to determining your strategy for controlling access to Windows apps and the Windows Store, consider the deployment of *Line of Business (LOB) apps.* LOB apps include apps that are critical to running the company business as well as apps that are unique to the company's main business. To use the new Windows Apps format for your LOB apps, deploy them via the Windows Store or a process called sideloading. To deploy your LOB apps via the Windows Store, they must go through a certification process with Microsoft to ensure they are compatible with Windows 10 and meet the criteria for apps being deployed from the Windows Store. The apps will also be available to the public, which may not be desirable. To bypass the Windows Store requirements and make the apps available to your internal users only, consider sideloading them as part of the overall design strategy.

The general steps for using the Windows Store for Business include:

1. Sign up for Windows Store for Business.
2. Assign roles.
3. Get apps and content.
4. Distribute apps and content.

Sign Up for Windows Store for Business

To sign up for Windows Store for Business, perform the following steps:

1. Open Internet Explorer and go to https://www.microsoft.com/en-us/business-store.
2. Click the SIGN UP NOW link.
3. In the Sign Up dialog box, in the Enter an email address text box, type the desired Microsoft Azure Active Directory (AD) account email address and click Next.

4. If the account is not a Microsoft Azure Active Directory (AD) account, you are prompted to create the Azure AD account by clicking Sign Up.

5. On the Welcome page, enter all of the following information and then click Next:

    Country: Specify the appropriate country

    First name: *<Your first name>*

    Last name: *<Your last name>*

    Business email address: Same email address that you used in Step 3.

    Business phone number: *<Your cell phone number>*

    Company name: *<Your Last Name>* Corporation

    Size of organization: **25-49 people**

6. On the Create Your User ID page, enter the following information and then click Next:

    Enter a user name: *<FirstInitial><LastName>*

    Your company: *<Your Last Name>* Corporation

7. On the Prove. You're. Not. A. Robot. page, in the Phone number text box, type your cell phone number and click Text Me.

8. In the Enter Your Verification Code text box, type the code that you received on your cell phone. Click Create My Account.

9. Click "You're ready to go."

10. When the Terms Of Use are displayed, scroll down to the bottom. Select "I accept this agreement and certify that I have the authority to bind my organization to its terms" and click Accept.

11. In the Welcome To The Windows Store For Business dialog box, click OK.

After signing up for Windows Store for Business, you can assign roles to other employees in your organization. To add more people, click Settings ➤ Permissions, and click "Add people." You will be prompted to type the names or email addresses and to choose one of the following roles:

Admin Can configure account settings, acquire apps, distribute apps, and sign policies and catalogs

Purchaser Can acquire apps and distribute apps

Device Guard signer Can sign policies and catalogs

To manage your applications:

- To see your inventory, click Manage ➤ Inventory, as shown in Figure 5.25.
- To add your own LOB apps, click Manage ➤ New LOB Apps.
- To show your order history, click Manage ➤ Order History.

FIGURE 5.25   Managing inventory settings

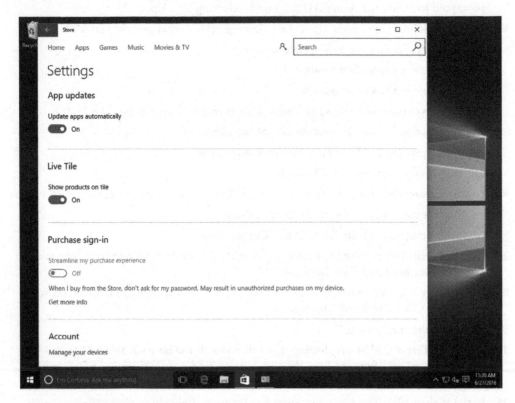

To distribute apps and content, use the following distribution options:

- After purchasing an app, email employees a link they can click to install the app.

- Curate a private store for all employees. Add the app to the private store and users can install the app when needed.

- Distribute the app with a mobile device management (MDM) tool that can synchronize your Store for Business inventory; this tool is installed and configured in Azure Active Directory (AD).

- Organizations that use an MDM to manage apps can use a policy to show only the private store.

Skill Summary

In this lesson, you learned:

- Because a client computer is connected to an organization's network, which may have direct and indirect access to servers and the network resources, it is important to protect the client computer.

- A computer virus is a program that can copy itself and infect a computer without the user's consent or knowledge.

- A backdoor is a program that gives some remote, unauthorized control of a system or initiates an unauthorized task.

- Some viruses, worms, rootkits, spyware, and adware are made possible because they exploit some security hole within Windows, Internet Explorer, or Microsoft Office.

- The first step that should be taken to protect yourself against malware is to keep your system up-to-date with the latest service packs, security patches, and other critical fixes for Windows (as well as other Microsoft products, such as Internet Explorer and Microsoft Office).

- A virus hoax is a message warning the recipient of a non-existent computer virus threat, usually sent as a chain email that tells the recipient to forward it to everyone they know. It is a form of social engineering that plays on people's ignorance and fear and may include emotive language and encouragement to forward the message to other people.

- User Account Control (UAC) is a feature that was introduced in Windows Vista and is included with Windows 10 that helps guard against malware.

- Microsoft recommends always using the Windows Firewall.

- Offline files are copies of network files that are stored on your computer so that they can be accessed when not connected to the network or when the network folder with the files is not connected.

- Offline files are not encrypted unless you choose to encrypt them. Consider encrypting your offline files if they contain sensitive or confidential information, and you want to make them more secure by restricting access to them.

- By restricting users to standard user accounts, you can limit what software those users can install.

- Use group policies to restrict what software can be executed on a client computer.

- Most of the email will be unsolicited emails called spam or junk email.

- The best place to establish an antispam filtering system is on your email relay, on a dedicated server or appliance, or as part of a firewall device or service.

- Many antispam solutions will also use Real-time Blackhole Lists (RBLs) or a DNS-based Blackhole List (DNSBL), which can be accessed freely. RBLs and DNSBL are lists of known spammers that are updated frequently.

- Sometimes, spammers will try to spoof a legitimate email address or IP address when the message actually comes from one with an email address or IP address that would likely be identified as spam.

- Simple Mail Transfer Protocol (SMTP) is used to transfer email from one server to another and it is also responsible for outgoing mail transport.

- Spammers look for unprotected SMTP servers through which they can relay their email.

- A cookie is a piece of text stored by a user's web browser. It can be used for a wide range of items, including user identification, authentication, storing site preferences, and shopping cart contents.

- While some pop-up windows are useful website controls, most are simply annoying advertisements, with some attempting to load spyware or other malicious programs.

- To help manage Internet Explorer security when visiting sites, Internet Explorer divides a network connection into four content zones or types. For each of these zones, a security level is assigned.

- Phishing and pharming are forms of attacks to get users to a bogus website in an attempt to spread malware or collect personal information.

- When surfing the Internet, there are times when it is necessary to transmit private data such as credit card numbers, Social Security numbers, and so on. During these times, it is important to use HTTP over SSL (HTTPS) to encrypt the data sent over the Internet.

- The server should be kept in a secure location. In addition, the servers should be in their own subnet to reduce the amount of traffic to the servers, especially broadcasts.

- To secure a server is to harden the server by reducing its surface of attack and thereby reducing the server's vulnerabilities. To harden a server, look for security guides and best practices for Windows servers and for the specific network services that you are installing.

- Windows servers provide support for the dynamic update functionality. Dynamic DNS lets client computers dynamically update their resource records in DNS.

- To keep your DNS server secure, secure DNS makes it so that only members of an Active Directory domain can create records on the DNS server.

Knowledge Assessment

Multiple Choice

1. Which type of malware copies itself onto other computers without the owner's consent and will often delete or corrupt files?

   A. Virus

   B. Worm

   C. Trojan horse

   D. Spyware

2. Which type of malware collects personal information or browsing history, often without the user's knowledge?

   A. Virus

   B. Worm

   C. Trojan horse

   D. Spyware

3. Which of the following is most likely the problem when a computer seems to be slow and a different default web page displays?

   A. The ISP has slowed the network connection.

   B. The computer has been infected with malware.

   C. The computer has not been updated.

   D. The user accidentally clicked the turbo button.

4. Which of the following is the best thing to do to protect a computer against malware, besides installing an antivirus software package? (Choose the best answer.)

   A. Keep the computer up-to-date with the latest security patches.

   B. Reboot the computer on a regular basis.

   C. Change the password on a regular basis.

   D. Spoof the IP address.

5. Which of the following refers to a thoroughly tested, cumulative set of hotfixes and other patches?

   A. Recommended update

   B. Hotfix pack

   C. Service pack

   D. Critical update

6. Which technology is used by Windows to prevent unauthorized changes to your system?

   A. UAC

   B. Protected mode

   C. Windows Defender

   D. ProtectGuard

7. When using UAC, which of the following tasks requires administrative permissions or rights?

   A. Install updates from Windows Update.

   B. Change the date and time.

   C. Reset the network adapter.

   D. Install drivers from Windows Update.

8. When attempting to change the display settings, which of the following causes a pop-up that prompts if a user wants to continue?

   A. Windows Firewall

   B. Protected Mode

   C. Windows Update

   D. UAC

9. Which host-based firewall software comes with today's version of Windows?

   A. Windows Firewall

   B. Windows Protected Mode

   C. UAC

   D. Windows GuardIt

10. Which program can be used to configure IPsec on a computer running Windows Server 2016?

    A. Windows Firewall with IPsec Plugin

    B. IPsec Monitor

    C. Windows Firewall with Advanced Security

    D. IPsec Configuration console

11. Which of the following tasks is recommended if sensitive or confidential information is stored in offline files?

    A. Clear the cache.

    B. Encrypt the offline files.

    C. Clear the cookies.

    D. Execute `ipconfig /renewip`.

12. Which of the following tasks should be performed if legitimate emails are being blocked at a spam-blocking device?

   A. Flush out the quarantined items.

   B. Reboot the spam-blocking device.

   C. Add the email address or domain to the white list.

   D. Add the email address or domain to the black list.

13. SMTP uses which of the following TCP ports?

   A. 43

   B. 25

   C. 80

   D. 443

14. When using IE, how many content zones are there?

   A. 1

   B. 2

   C. 4

   D. 8

15. Which of the following refers to a social engineering technique in which a user receives an email stating that his account has just expired and he should log on to a legitimate-looking website to fix the problem?

   A. Phishing

   B. Pharming

   C. Phaking

   D. Spoofing the IP address

16. Which of the following is used to stop a program from running on a Windows 10 system?

   A. AppLocker

   B. Windows Defender

   C. Microsoft Passport

   D. Smart card

17. Which type of account is used with outlook.com and OneDrive and can be used to synchronize a desktop across multiple computers?

   A. Domain account

   B. Microsoft account

   C. Local account

   D. Virtual account

18. Which of the following is a collection of security settings that can be used to configure client settings?

   A. Biometrics

   B. Windows Defender

   C. Security baseline

   D. Windows Store

19. Which of the following is a free tool that allows administrators to quickly configure and manage desktops and users using Group Policy?

   A. STRIDE

   B. DREAD

   C. Trusted Platform Module

   D. Security Compliance Manager

Fill in the Blank

1. _____ is software that is designed to infiltrate or infect a computer usually with ill intent.

2. A(n) _____ is a self-replicating program that copies itself to other computers while consuming network resources.

3. Microsoft's built-in antivirus and antispyware program is _____.

4. For antivirus software to be effective, it must be _____.

5. An example of a(n) _____ is a message that states you should delete the win.com file, because it is a virus.

6. To control which updates get pushed to clients within an organization, an administrator would use _____ or _____.

7. When a user is notified of an attempt by programs to make changes to their computer, the desktop will be dimmed. This dimming indicates the computer is in _____ mode, because other programs can't run until the changes are approved or disapproved.

8. _____ are copies of network files that are stored on a computer so that a user can access them when they are not connected to the network.

9. _____ is another name for junk email.

10. _____ is an email validation system that is designed to verify if an email is coming from the proper email server.

Business Case Scenarios

Scenario 5-1: Enforcing Physical Security

You were just hired as an IT administrator for the ABC Company. Across from your desk, there is a table with seven physical servers. You ask your supervisor why the servers aren't locked up. He replies that they can be easily monitored and watched. Describe a more effective way to enforce security of these servers.

Scenario 5-2: Programming Backdoors

You are hired as a security consultant for the Contoso Corporation and are working with the CIO on a new comprehensive security policy for the company. Because the CIO is not a programmer, he asks how he can prevent a programmer from creating a backdoor on programs they write. Describe your recommended solution.

Scenario 5-3: Configuring a Windows Defender Quarantine

After working on a Windows 10 computer running Windows Defender, the computer maintains quarantined files from the past several months. Is it possible to configure the computer to remove quarantined files on a weekly basis? If so, explain the steps involved.

Scenario 5-4: Protecting Your Resources

Recently, your organization has detected several instances of malware that accessed confidential information and opened backdoors to your network. You need to defend against these malware attacks, detecting and stopping the malware as soon as it is detected. Describe your recommended course of action.

Scenario 5-5: Reviewing Windows Updates

As an administrator for the Contoso Corporation, you need to review Windows Updates on a Windows 10 computer by launching Internet Explorer, and going to https://blogs .technet.microsoft.com/msrc/. Read the most recent advance notification or most recent security bulletin summary and review the executive summary. Determine how many security bulletins apply to the most recent month. Describe how to run Windows Update to update your Windows system with the newest patches in Windows.

Real World Scenario

Workplace Ready: Keeping Up with Security

Maintaining security for an organization is often a full-time job that usually requires more than one person to maintain. For example, one person may be responsible for the routers and firewalls, another person may be responsible for the servers, and yet another person may be responsible for the client computers. There might also be a security manager who oversees all items related to security, including physical security. Of course, the people who are ultimately responsible for security would be the CEO, CIOs, and other executives of a company.

However, for security to be effective, remember that it requires everyone to participate. This includes the executives, who need to support the IT department and help enforce and support security-related decisions, and the IT staff to establish and monitor the security. Also, because the weakest link could well be the end users, ensuring that they receive training in best practices and are constantly reminded to use them, is key.

Appendix

Answer Key

Lesson 1: Understanding Security Layers

Answers to Knowledge Assessment
Multiple Choice

1. a, b, d
2. a, c, d
3. b, d
4. a
5. c
6. a, d
7. c
8. b
9. d
10. a
11. a

Fill in the Blank Answers

1. Confidentiality
2. access control
3. defense in depth
4. threat
5. risk register
6. Social engineering
7. integrity
8. keylogger
9. Residual risk
10. cost

Matching and Identification

S Spoofing
T Tampering
R Repudiation
I Information Disclosure

D Denial-of-Service

E Elevation of Privilege

Build List

____2____ Create an architecture overview.

____1____ Identify assets.

____6____ Rate the threats.

____3____ Decompose the security components and applications.

____4____ Identify the threats.

____5____ Document the threats.

Answers to Business Case Scenarios

Scenario 1-1: Designing a Physical Security Solution

The following are some of the technologies that could be used in each of the areas:

- **External perimeter:** Security cameras, parking lot lights, perimeter fence, gate with guard, gate with access badge reader, guard patrols

- **Internal perimeter:** Locks (exterior doors, internal doors, office doors, desks, filing cabinets, and so on), keypads, security cameras, badge readers (on doors and elevators), guard desk, guard patrols, smoke detectors, turnstiles, mantraps

- **Secure area:** Badge readers, keypads, biometric technology (fingerprint scanner, retinal scanner, voice recognition, and so on), security doors, x-ray scanners, metal detectors, cameras, intrusion detection systems (light beam, infrared, microwave, and ultrasonic)

Scenario 1-2: Securing a Mobile Device

Some of the technologies that might be used include the following:

- **Docking station:** Virtually all laptop docking stations are equipped with security features to secure a laptop. This can be with a key, a padlock, or both, depending on the vendor and model.

- **Laptop security cables:** Used in conjunction with the USS (Universal Security Slot), these cables attach to the laptop and can be wrapped around a secure object like a piece of furniture.

- **Laptop safe:** A steel safe specifically designed to hold a laptop and be secured to a wall or piece of furniture.

- **Theft recovery software:** An application run on the computer that enables the tracking of a stolen computer so it can be recovered.

- **Laptop alarms:** A motion-sensitive alarm that sounds in the event that a laptop is moved. Some are also designed in conjunction with a security cable system, so the alarm sounds when the cable is cut.

Employees should be trained on the following best practices:

- Keep your equipment with you: Mobile devices should be kept with you whenever possible. This means keeping mobile devices on your person or in your hand luggage when traveling. Keep mobile devices in sight when going through airport checkpoints.

- Use the trunk: When traveling by car, lock the mobile device in the trunk after parking, if you are unable to take the mobile device with you. Do not leave a mobile device in view in an unattended vehicle, even for a short period of time, or in a vehicle overnight.

- Use the safe: When staying in a hotel, lock the mobile device in a safe, if available.

Scenario 1-3: Understanding Confidentiality, Integrity, and Availability

CIA stands for Confidentiality, Integrity, and Availability. Because John was able to see other user's paychecks, confidentiality was not followed. Because he was able to change other people's paycheck amounts, integrity was not followed. Also, because he was able to delete people's paychecks, he caused the paychecks not to be available to some of the users (availability).

Scenario 1-4: Managing Social Engineering

Answers will vary. Some of the more common social engineering attacks would include:

- A telephone or ISP repair person shows up to fix your telephone lines and asks for access to your wiring closet.

- A person who poses as an auditor from the corporate office asks to set up in a conference room with a computer and network connection.

A person walks up to someone who works at the company and says that he left his keys or badge at home and he cannot get into a secure room. He asks the employee if she can give him access to the secure room

Lesson 2: Understanding Authentication, Authorization, and Accounting

Answers to Knowledge Assessment

Multiple Choice Answers

1. c
2. a
3. c
4. b

5. a

6. c

7. d

8. c

9. a

10. a

11. b

12. a, b, c

13. b

14. c

15. d

16. a

17. d

Fill in the Blank Answers

1. personal identification number (PIN)

2. smart card

3. security token

4. domain controller

5. 5

6. permission

7. inherited

8. ownership

9. registry

10. auditing

Answers to Business Case Scenarios

Scenario 2-1: Understanding Biometrics

While biometrics offers enhanced security, it is not ideal for every situation. First, the biometric solution will cost more money and will have to be installed and placed at all doors that should be protected. Second, it would be necessary to set up each user who will use biometrics, in addition to setting up at least a workstation and an administrator to add users to the biometric system. You will also need a place to store the database. Then, as every new employee starts with your organization, you will need to add the user. In addition, when a person leaves the organization, it will be necessary to disable or remove their account.

Scenario 2-2: Limiting Auditing

For auditing to be effective, determine what needs to be audited and then enable the auditing for the activity, task, or resource. In addition, auditing does take up some system resources. Therefore, if you enable too many items to audit, it will slow down a system. In addition, if you enable auditing for everything, the logs will quickly fill up, the system will slow significantly, and when you need to find a specific event, you might be overwhelmed by the amount of information.

Scenario 2-3: Assigning NTFS Permissions

1. Log on as an administrator.
2. Click the Start button and click Windows Administrative Tools ➤ Computer Management.
3. In Computer Management, navigate to Local Users and Groups ➤ Users.
4. Right-click Users and choose New Users.
5. Type the User Name as JSmith and assign a Password of Pa$$w0rd. Deselect the "User must change password at next logon" check box. Click Create.
6. Type the User Name as JHamid and assign a Password of Pa$$w0rd. Deselect the "User must change password at next logon" check box. Click Create.
7. Click Groups.
8. Right-click Groups and choose New Group. For the Group name, type **Managers**. Click Add. Type **JSmith** and click OK. Click Create.
9. Click the Close button to close the New Group dialog box.
10. Close Computer Management.
11. Right-click the desktop and choose New ➤ Folder. Type **SharedTest** and press Enter.
12. Right-click the SharedTest folder and choose Properties.
13. Click the Sharing tab.
14. Click the Advanced Sharing button.
15. Select the "Share this folder" check box.
16. Click the Permissions button.
17. With Everyone selected, click Allow Full Control and click OK.
18. Click OK one more time to get to the Properties dialog box.
19. Click the Security tab.
20. Click the Edit button.
21. Click the Add button. Type **Managers** and click OK.
22. Click OK to close the Permissions dialog box.
23. Click OK to close the Properties dialog box.
24. Double-click the SharedTest folder to open it.

25. Right-click the empty space of the SharedTest folder and choose New ➤ Text File. Type **test** and press Enter.

26. Double-click the test.txt file and type your name.

27. Log out as administrator and log on as JHamid. Try to access \\localhost\SharedTest and open the test.txt file.

28. Log out as JHamid and log on as JSmith. Try to access \\localhost\SharedTest and open the test.txt file.

Scenario 2-4: Using EFS

1. Log on as an administrator.

2. Click the Start button and click Windows Administrative Tools ➤ Computer Management.

3. In Computer Management, navigate to Local Users and Groups ➤ Groups.

4. Double-click the Managers group.

5. Click the Add button. Type **JHamid** and click OK.

6. Click OK to close the Properties dialog box.

7. Close Computer Management.

8. Double-click the ShareTest folder.

9. Right-click the test.txt file and choose Properties.

10. Click the Advanced button.

11. Select the "Encrypt contents to secure data" check box. Click OK.

12. Click OK to close the Properties dialog box.

13. When warned as to what to encrypt, click OK.

14. Log out as the administrator and log on as JSmith.

15. Open \\localhost\SharedTest and try to open the test.txt file.

Lesson 3: Understanding Security Policies

Answers to Knowledge Assessment

Multiple Choice Answers

1. c, d

2. a, c, e

3. c

4. c

5. a, d, e

6. d

7. b

8. d

9. b, c

10. c

11. c

12. d

Fill in the Blank Answers

1. Group Policy Object

2. account lockout threshold

3. password history

4. dictionary attack

5. sniffing

6. reset account lockout counter after

7. 99,999

8. Default Domain Policy

9. account lockout duration, account lockout threshold, reset account lockout counter after

10. service account

Answers to Business Case Scenarios

Scenario 3-1: Understanding Long Passwords

a. $10 \times 10 \times 10 \times 10 = 10,000$ different possible combinations

b. $26 \times 26 \times 26 \times 26 = 456,976$ combinations

c. $26 \times 26 \times 26 \times 26 \times 26 \times 26 = 308,915,776$ combinations

d. $26 \times 26 \times 26 \times 26 \times 26 \times 26 \times 26 \times 26 = 208,827,064,576$

e. $52 \times 52 \times 52 \times 52 \times 52 \times 52 \times 52 \times 52 = 53,459,728,531,456$ combinations

f. $94 \times 94 \times 94 \times 94 \times 94 \times 94 \times 94 \times 94 = 6,095,689,385,410,820$

Scenario 3-2: Using Keys and Passwords

One hacking technique when trying to figure out a password is to try every combination of characters until you figure out the password. The longer the password, the more combinations the hacker would have to try. In addition, if using a strong password that requires uppercase letters, lowercase letters, digits, and special characters, the hacker would also have more combinations to try than if you were only using digits or lowercase letters.

A computer can be programmed to try these different combinations. Computers can go through a list of combinations much faster than humans. As computers get faster and faster, a computer can check for password combinations more rapidly than in the past. Therefore, besides keeping the password long, passwords should be changed often so that the person would have to start all over in trying all of the different combinations with every new password.

Scenario 3-3: Managing User Accounts

1. Right-click Start and choose Control Panel. The Control Panel window opens.
2. Click User Accounts and click User Accounts again. The User Accounts window opens.
3. Click Manage User Accounts. The User Accounts dialog box opens.
4. To create a new account, click the Add a new user in PC settings option.
5. Click the Add someone else to this PC option.
6. On the How will this person sign in page, click the I don't have the person's sign in information option.
7. On the Let's create your account page, click the Add a user without a Microsoft account page.
8. On the Create an account for this PC page, in the User name text box, type **JAdams**. In the Enter password text box and the Re-enter password text box, type **Pa$$w0rd**. In the Password hint text box, type **default**. Click Next.
9. Click the JAdams account and click Change account type.
10. In the Change account type dialog box, for the Account type, select Administrator. Click OK.

Scenario 3-4: Configuring a Local Security Policy

1. Log on to a computer running Windows 10.
2. Click Start and click Windows Administrative Tools ➤ Local Security Policy.
3. Expand Local Computer Policy.
4. Expand Account Policies and click Password Policy.

5. The Password Policy settings are:

   0 passwords remembered

   Maximum password age: 42 days

   Minimum password age: 0 days

   Password must meet complexity requirements: Disabled

6. Click Account Lockout Policy.

7. The Account Lockout Policy settings are:

   Account lockout duration: Not applicable

   Account lockout threshold: 0 invalid logon attempts

   Reset account lockout counter after: Not applicable

8. Close the Local Security window.

Lesson 4: Understanding Network Security

Answers to Knowledge Assessment

Multiple Choice Answers

1. a, b, e
2. a, c, d
3. e
4. c, e
5. a, b, d
6. c
7. b
8. e
9. c, e
10. c
11. a, d
12. d, e
13. c

Fill in the Blank Answers

1. DNSSEC
2. IPsec, SSL/TLS
3. ARP spoofing, DNS spoofing, IP address spoofing
4. software vulnerability attack
5. network sniffing
6. replay
7. static, dynamic
8. WPA, WPA2
9. honeypot

Answers to Business Case Scenarios

Scenario 4-1: Using Windows Firewall

1. Right-click the Start button and choose Control Panel.
2. In the Control Panel, click System and Security ➤ Windows Firewall.
3. Click the Turn Windows Firewall on or off option.
4. Click the Back button.
5. Click the Allow a program or feature through Windows Firewall option.
6. Click the Allow Another app button.
7. Browse to and select iexplore.exe and click the Add button.
8. Click the OK button.
9. Click the Advanced settings option.
10. Right-click the Inbound Rules.
11. Choose the New Rule option.
12. Select the Port option and click the Next button.
13. Click the TCP option, specify port 80 and 443 in the "Specific local ports" field, and then click the Next button.
14. With the "Allow the connection" option selected, click the Next button.
15. When prompted to specify which profiles to enable this rule for, keep all profiles selected and click the Next button.
16. For the name, type **Web Interface** and click the Finish button.
17. Close the Windows Firewall.

Scenario 4-2: Using a Routing Table

Windows includes routing functionality including hosting a routing table. Therefore, to look at the routing table, perform the following steps:

1. Click the Start button and execute the following command:

   cmd

2. At the command prompt, enter the following command:

   route print

3. To add a route to the 10.24.57.0 network that is sent to the 192.168.50.1 pathway, execute the following command:

   route add 10.24.57.0 mask 255.255.255.0 192.168.50.1

4. Use the route print command to verify that the new route is added.

5. To remove this route, execute the following command:

   route delete 10.24.57.0

6. View the routing table once more to verify that the route has been removed.

Scenario 4-3: Using Ports

Ports are used to describe a network service or program that allows network packets to pass through. This way, when a packet is received, the packet can be routed to the correct software component. The programs listed use the following ports:

Secure Shell (SSH)	TCP/UDP 22
Network News Transfer Protocol	TCP 119
Simple Network Management Protocol	TCP/UDP 161
NetBIOS Session Service	TCP/UDP 139
Network Time Protocol	TCP/UDP 123

Scenario 4-4: Accessing and Configuring Wireless Settings

1. Open your favorite browser and browse to the http://support.dlink.com/ emulators/dir655/ web page.

2. Modify the SSID:

   a. Click the Setup link on the top banner. If you are asked to login, click the Log In button.

   b. Click the Wireless Settings link on the left side.

   c. Click the Manual Wireless Network Setup button. This should display the Wireless page.

   d. Look for the Wireless Network Name. This is the SSID. The default for D-Link devices is none other than dlink. It is highly recommended that you modify the default SSID on any WAP. Change it now to something a bit more complex.

3. Modify the wireless configuration:

   a. Examine the 802.11 Mode drop-down menu. Note the variety of settings. Modify this so that it says 802.11n only.

   b. Deselect the Enable Auto Channel Scan check box. This should enable the Wireless Channel drop-down menu. Select channel 11, which is centered at 2.462 GHz. Subsequent WAPs should be set to channel 6 and channel 1 in order to avoid channel overlapping.

   c. Modify the Channel Width setting to 40 MHz. This incorporates channel bonding.

4. Enable encryption:

   a. At the Security Mode drop-down menu, select WPA-Personal. This should display additional WPA information. You would only select WPA-Enterprise if you have an available RADIUS server.

   b. Scroll down and in the WPA Mode drop-down menu, select WPA2 Only.

   c. In the Cipher Type drop-down menu, select AES.

   d. Finally, type in a complex pre-shared key. This is the passphrase that clients will need to enter in order to connect to the WLAN.

   This is the highest level of security this device offers (aside from WPA-Enterprise).

5. Disable the SSID:

   a. When all clients are connected to the WAP, the SSID should be disabled. This does not allow new connections to the WAP unless the person knows the SSID name, but computers that have already connected may continue to do so.

   b. To do so, in the Visibility Status field, click the Invisible radio button.

6. Save the settings:

   a. At this point, you would save the settings. The emulator doesn't allow anything to be saved. It reverts to defaults when you log off or disconnect from the website, so clicking Save Settings doesn't do anything. But on an actual DIR-655, the settings would save, and a reboot would be necessary.

   b. It's also important to back up the configuration. This can be done by clicking Tools on the top banner, then System on the left side, and then Save Configuration—a real time-saver, in the case that you have to reset the unit. It is also wise to update the device to the latest firmware. Save your settings before doing so because they will be lost when the upgrade is complete; then, they can be loaded back in.

Lesson 5: Protecting the Server and Client

Answers to Knowledge Assessment

Multiple Choice Answers

1. a
2. d
3. b
4. a
5. c
6. a
7. b
8. d
9. a
10. c
11. b
12. c
13. b
14. c
15. a
16. a
17. b
18. c
19. d

Fill in the Blank Answers

1. Malicious software (malware)
2. worm
3. Windows Defender
4. up-to-date
5. virus hoax
6. Windows Server Update Services (WSUS), System Center Configuration Manager

7. Secure Desktop
8. Offline files
9. Spam
10. Sender Policy Framework (SPF)

Answers to Business Case Scenarios

Scenario 5-1: Enforcing Physical Security

If someone can get physical access to a server, they could yank or cut cables or shut down a server, causing a denial-of-service. In addition, if they remove the hard drives from a server, they could connect them to another computer in which the thief is an administrator. They could then access all files on the hard drive.

Scenario 5-2: Programming Backdoors

When programmers are writing applications for your organization, be sure to establish a review and auditing process that will check the work of the programmers. This would include reviewing all source code.

Scenario 5-3: Configuring a Windows Defender Quarantine

Yes. Open Windows Defender and click the Settings tab. From the menu, click Advanced, select the drop-down box next to the option Remove quarantined files, and then select 1 week.

Scenario 5-4: Protecting Your Resources

First, ensure you have an up-to-date antivirus solution. Then ensure that your systems and software are properly updated. Next, review your network logs, looking for suspicious traffic. Thus, when a backdoor is opened, you will be able to find it quickly and close it.

Scenario 5-5: Scanning with Microsoft Baseline Security Analyzer

1. Download and install the newest Microsoft Baseline Security Analyzer.
2. Double-click the executable file that you downloaded.
3. If prompted to install the file, click Run.
4. On the Welcome screen, click Next.
5. Click the I accept the license agreement option and click Next.
6. Enter the location of the destination folder and click Next.
7. Click the Install button.
8. After the program is successfully installed, click OK.
9. Click Start and click Microsoft Baseline Security Analyzer.

10. Click Scan a computer.

11. Click the Start Scan button.

12. View the Results.

Scenario 5-6: Reviewing Windows Update

1. Click the Start button and click Settings.

2. In the Settings window, click Update & security.

3. If necessary, reboot the computer.

Index

Note to the Reader: Throughout this index boldfaced page numbers indicate primary discussions of a topic. *Italicized* page numbers indicate illustrations.

9781119650744: Networking Fundamentals

- Understand wired and wireless networks
- Work with fiber optic and twisted pair cables
- Learn Internet protocol (IP) and categorize IPv4 Addresses
- Validate your skills and knowledge with MTA Certification

9781119650669: Security Fundamentals

- Gain knowledge of essential IT security concepts
- Learn physical, Internet, and wireless security
- Identify different types of hardware firewalls
- Validate your skills and knowledge with MTA Certification

9781119650515: Windows Operating System Fundamentals

- Install and upgrade Windows 10 client
- Setup user accounts and account controls
- Customize user profiles
- Configure LAN settings and remote assistance and management
- Validate your skills and knowledge with MTA Certification

9781119650652: Windows Server Administration Fundamentals

- Install and manage Windows Server
- Use Disk Management Tools
- Manage devices and drivers
- Optimize server performance
- Configure Windows Network Services
- Administer remote and virtual servers
- Validate your skills and knowledge with MTA Certification